# Conversations with Walter Mosley

Literary Conversations Series
*Peggy Whitman Prenshaw*
*General Editor*

# Conversations
# with Walter Mosley

Edited by Owen E. Brady

University Press of Mississippi    Jackson

www.upress.state.ms.us

The University Press of Mississippi is a member of the Association
of American University Presses.

Copyright © 2011 by University Press of Mississippi
All rights reserved
Manufactured in the United States of America

First printing 2011

∞

Library of Congress Cataloging-in-Publication Data

Mosley, Walter.
    Conversations with Walter Mosley / edited by Owen E. Brady.
        p. cm. — (Literary conversations series)
    Includes index.
ISBN 978-1-60473-942-8 (cloth : alk. paper)—ISBN 978-1-60473-943-5 (pbk. : alk. paper) —
ISBN 978-1-60473-944-2 (ebook) 1. Mosley, Walter—Interviews. 2. Novelists, American—
20th century—Interviews. 3. African Americans in literature. I. Brady, Owen Edward, 1946–
II. Title.
    PS3563.O88456Z595 2011
    813'.54—dc22
    [B]                              2010034990

British Library Cataloging-in-Publication Data available

# Books by Walter Mosley

**Easy Rawlins Series**
*Devil in a Blue Dress*. New York: W. W. Norton, 1990.
*A Red Death*. New York: W. W. Norton, 1991.
*White Butterfly*. New York: W. W. Norton, 1992.
*Black Betty*. New York: W. W. Norton, 1994.
*A Little Yellow Dog*. New York: W. W. Norton, 1996.
*Gone Fishin'*. Baltimore: Black Classic Press, 1997.
*Bad Boy Brawly Brown*. New York: Little, Brown and Company, 2002.
*Six Easy Pieces*. New York: Atria, 2003.
*Little Scarlet*. New York: Little, Brown and Company, 2004.
*Cinnamon Kiss*. New York: Little, Brown and Company, 2005.
*Blonde Faith*. New York: Little, Brown and Company, 2007.

**Socrates Fortlow Series**
*Always Outnumbered, Always Outgunned*. New York: W. W. Norton, 1998.
*Walkin' the Dog*. New York: Little, Brown and Company, 1999.
*The Right Mistake: The Further Philosophical Investigations of Socrates Fortlow*. New York: Basic Civitas Books, 2008.

**Fearless Jones Series**
*Fearless Jones*. New York: Little, Brown and Company, 2001.
*Fear Itself*. New York: Little, Brown and Company, 2003.
*Fear of the Dark*. New York: Little, Brown and Company, 2006.

**Leonid McGill Series**
*The Long Fall*. New York: Riverhead Books, 2009.
*Known to Evil*. New York: Riverhead Books, 2010.

**Speculative Fiction**
*Blue Light*. New York: Little, Brown and Company, 1998.

*Futureland: Nine Stories of an Imminent Future*. New York: Warner Books, 2001.

*47*. New York: Little, Brown and Company, 2005.

*The Wave*. New York: Warner Books, 2006.

## Other Fiction

*RL's Dream*. New York: W. W. Norton, 1995.

*The Man in My Basement*. New York: Little, Brown and Company, 2004.

*Fortunate Son*. New York: Little, Brown and Company, 2006.

*Killing Johnny Fry: A Sexistential Novel*. New York: Bloomsbury USA, 2007.

*Diablerie*. New York: Bloomsbury USA, 2008.

*Tempest Tales*. Baltimore: Black Classic Press, 2008.

## Nonfiction

*Workin' on the Chain Gang: Shaking Off the Dead Hand of History*. New York: Ballantine, 2000.

*What Next: A Memoir Toward World Peace*. Baltimore: Black Classic Press, 2003.

*Life Out of Context, Which Includes a Proposal for the Non-violent Take-over of the House of Representatives*. New York: Nation Books, 2006.

*This Year You Write Your Novel*. New York: Little, Brown and Company, 2007.

## Books Edited by Walter Mosley

*Black Genius: African American Solutions to African American Problems*. New York: W. W. Norton, 1999. With Manthia Diawara, Clyde Taylor, and Regina Austin.

*The Best American Short Stories 2003*. With Katrina Kenison. Boston: Mariner Books, 2003.

*Maximum Fantastic Four*. By Stan Lee and Jack Kirby. New York: Marvel Comics, 2005.

## Film, Television, and Plays by Walter Mosley

*Devil in a Blue Dress*. (TriStar) 1995.

*Fallen Angels*: "Fearless, Episode 15." (Showtime TV) 1995.

*Always Outnumbered, Always Outgunned*. (HBO TV) 1998.

*The Fall of Heaven*. (The Playhouse in the Park, Cincinnati, OH) 2010.

# Contents

# Introduction

Walter Mosley is a prolific and protean writer, critically acclaimed and commercially successful. Starting relatively late on a writing career has spurred Mosley's astounding output and virtuosity in the twenty years from 1990 to 2010: thirty-three books, several screenplays, a theatrical adaptation of one of his novels, and numerous essays and stories in newspapers and magazines. While many novels are in the popular mystery and science fiction genres, he has also penned a variety of literary novels and an experimental young adult novel. In addition to fiction, he has published three nonfiction monographs raising sociopolitical questions and arguing for political engagement with domestic and international issues. Mosley's writing in all literary modes has garnered critical praise and a number of literary prizes: the O. Henry Award for short fiction; the Edgar, Shamus, and John Creasy awards for detective fiction; and a Parallax Award for speculative fiction. He has also received awards for his literary novels. The Black Caucus of the American Library Association's Literary Award went to *RL's Dream* (1995) and the Anisfield-Wolf Award to *Always Outnumbered, Always Outgunned* (1998) for its contribution to racial understanding. For his lifetime achievement, he received the TransAfrica International Literary Prize and the PEN USA Lifetime Achievement Award; the Sundance Institute honored him with its Risktaker Award for activism and creative achievement. Popular success has accompanied critical praise and literary accolades: his books have regularly appeared on best seller lists.

The interviews in this collection range widely across Mosley's oeuvre, but recurring themes provide a unifying vision of his career. The overarching theme emerging from the interviews is Mosley's belief in the transformative power of reading and writing. His comments testify to literature as a dialogue, a process of self-discovery and self-recreation for both writer and reader. For Mosley writing is an existential activity which discovers not only characters and plots but also creates new knowledge and, with this knowledge, the power to change self and society. Viewing Mosley over time through the interviews, one sees a growing social and political commitment to liberate people from the social and economic chains that constrain human potential.

Within this overarching theme, Mosley sounds the subthemes that characterize his work. The interviews reveal the tension inherent in being perceived as a popular writer of genre fiction and Mosley's own seriousness of purpose and experimental bent. They often focus on issues of race, community, and identity. In these conversations, one sees Mosley's attempt to merge what W. E. B. Du Bois called the African American double consciousness. Mosley speaks of his pride in a cultural identity rooted in African American experience but also his deeply felt identity as an American, a citizen of the United States and the world. Another recurring theme related to identity and community is Mosley's self-proclaimed discovery that his real genre is black male heroes. He describes his exploration of black male identity as a redemptive process, a literary undermining of longstanding social stereotypes in American culture. In several interviews, Mosley espouses the ancient concept that literature should be useful as well as entertaining: *utile et dulce.* Read chronologically the interviews reveal that Mosley's understanding of what is entertaining remains constant—compelling plots and sympathetic characters—while he expands his understanding of what is useful. In terms of usefulness, Mosley sees literature, especially mystery fiction, as providing moral dilemmas that readers can sympathetically identify with and perhaps find comforting. Social responsibility resounds as another subtheme. After 1997, Mosley adopts a more politically active stance in his writing and in action. Initially he focused on domestic and national issues, but after September 11, 2001, the issues become global. The final subtheme in the interviews is Mosley's sense of himself as a man of letters, a self-conscious artist, highly aware of literary technique and literary tradition.

The tension between the perception of genre writers as mere entertainers and Mosley's own serious literary aspirations becomes clear in several interviews, notably the one with Paula Woods. He defends the cultural importance and literary merit of genre fiction, in particular the hard-boiled detective novel, but he also feels compelled to rebel against any attempts at pigeonholing him exclusively as a mystery writer by critics or literary agents. His rebellions have resulted in numerous experiments in literary form. These rebellious literary forays outside the confines of mystery fiction also reveal Mosley's virtuosity and interest in experimentation. Using diverse literary forms allows him to explore his central topic, black male heroes, from multiple perspectives: a blues novel like *RL's Dream*, a novel of ideas like *The Man in My Basement* (2004), a science fiction collection like *Futureland* (2001), and an erotic novel like *Killing Johnny Fry: A Sexistential Novel* (2007).

Discussing his periodic escapes from mystery novels, what Tavis Smiley in his interview calls his "bread and butter," Mosley reveals an artistic integrity that puts personal growth and social conscience ahead of economic gain. His penchant for experimentation with new forms is also seen in his fascination with dramatic form. He speaks several times about writing a screenplay or adapting one of his novels for a film or television deal. Yet there is only modest evidence that he has been successful; and in the Paula Woods interview he humorously satirizes the commercial limitations on turning books into films or television scripts. Recently, however, he had success in dramatic form. In February 2010, the Playhouse in the Park in Cincinnati staged *The Fall of Heaven*, Mosley's dramatic adaptation of *The Tempest Tales* (2008), to positive reviews. His interview with Rick Pender reveals Mosley's characteristic enthusiasm for new projects and his excitement in learning more about drama from working with theater director Marion McClinton.

Throughout the interviews, questions about racial identity and community recur, often in an attempt to find autobiographical influences in Mosley's writing. The child of Leroy Mosley, an African American originally from the Deep South, and Ella Mosley, a Jewish American whose family lived in the East, Mosley frequently fields questions about race and his parents' influence on his fiction. He talks extensively about his father's influence. Leroy Mosley was a product of the Jim Crow South and a World War II combat veteran who moved to Los Angeles for the promise it offered. According to his son, Leroy's experiences provided a rich resource for the construction of Easy Rawlins, his murderous alter ego Raymond "Mouse" Alexander, and their post–World War II Los Angeles milieu. Mosley also attributes his gift as a compelling storyteller to his father who had a rich imagination as well as graphic stories from his southern youth and the war. Moreover, Mosley notes in interviews that touch on his nonfiction essay *What Next: A Memoir Toward World Peace* (2003) that his father's discovery of his American identity when under fire in World War II parallels his own deeper understanding of his American identity after the September 11, 2001, terrorist attacks. What is most important to Mosley is his father's perspective on the world. As Mosley told Kerri Miller of Minnesota Public Radio, his father gave him "a way of seeing the world, which opened me up to be able to think in other ways, to be able to question, in creative ways, who and what I am."

While Mosley comments less on his mother's influence, he acknowledges her by pointing to sympathetic Jewish characters like Chaim Wenzler in *A Red Death* (1991) and Saul Lynx in *Black Betty* (1994) and *Cinnamon Kiss* (2005). Perhaps his mother's family, which Mosley tells interviewers had intellectuals, socialists, and communists, presaged his increasingly critical appraisal of unfettered capitalism and an American democracy dominated by big money's interests. As time progresses, in the interviews, Mosley adopts a somewhat passive-aggressive stance to any claims that he is "part white." Rather, Mosley claims that Jews are not really whites because like African Americans they are marginalized in American society and historically oppressed globally. Thus, he claims a double minority heritage rather than a biracial one.

Mosley's understanding of race and racial identity is complex because he sees the place of African Americans in America in historical flux. This sense of flux is apparent in discussions of the Easy Rawlins series. Like August Wilson's plays, the Easy Rawlins novels chart the Great Migration of African Americans out of the rural, Jim Crow South, revealing the human details in one of the epic movements in American history. In these novels, Mosley planned to embody the transformation of an African American everyman's race consciousness as well as the transformation of American society's views of race over an extended period. In his original vision for the series, Mosley had projected taking Easy through a "fifty-year arc of black Los Angeles history," according to the *Los Angeles Times'* David Streitfeld in his 1992 interview. That would have made Easy almost eighty around the end of the twentieth century. But Mosley altered his original design, taking Easy from 1948 to only 1967. With the publication of *Blonde Faith* (2007), which concludes with Easy's seeming death in 1967, Mosley owed avid Easy Rawlins readers an explanation for the hero's early demise. In the interviews, he explains that he ended the series because he recognized that the Watts riots in 1965 had complicated the racial context of America so much that Easy, with his background and racial experience, could no longer adapt. And to explore the more complicated contemporary racial context of America, Mosley needed new characters. To do this, he launched a new mystery series with the publications of *The Long Fall* (2009) and *Known to Evil* (2010) featuring Leonid McGill, another flawed character in search of redemption, who operates in contemporary New York City.

While Mosley takes pride in his African American roots, he often makes statements in the interviews that point out communal bonds between African Americans and Euro-Americans. In interviews about *Workin' on the*

*Chain Gang: Shaking Off the Dead Hand of History* (2000), he notes the African American historical experience of slavery as a metaphor for contemporary Americans of all races subject to the chains of capitalism and moneyed interests. Progressing chronologically through the interviews, the reader finds Mosley increasingly asserting his American identity as a political agent, a critical member of a free democracy that he believes has been failing the common citizen. Though he identifies himself as a black male, he quickly notes that this identity is socially constructed, imposed on him and other African American men by the larger American society. When C-SPAN's Brian Lamb asked him about racial identity—what he sees when he looks in the mirror—Mosley asserts his unique individuality; he sees "a person . . . somebody who reflects . . . family . . . history," stripped of society's imposed racial and gendered view of him but informed by personal and historical experience.

Although asserting his individuality, Mosley identifies with and "loves the black community." This statement operates on several levels. He loves the black community as a rich literary resource full of fascinating stories and characters but also as a sort of home, full of caring and hard-working people trying their best to survive and thrive in America. He fills his fictional streets with African American characters drawn from memory and daily observation and sometimes overlaid with folklore, as in the case of characters like Mouse and Mama Jo. Mosley's fiction paints a caring but realistic and complex picture of the African American community infused with an intuitive sense of history.

Another aspect of Mosley's love for the African American community may be found in an artistic agenda that aims at redeeming the image of black males from negative stereotypes. In several interviews, such as the ones with William Mills, Woods, and Smiley, Mosley asserts that his work centers on black male heroes, a demeaned and underappreciated group. To redeem the black male from negative, socially constructed stereotypes, Mosley uses realistic fictional characters that portray their daily heroic struggle to lead good lives in an imperfect world that constantly threatens their human dignity and survival. While admittedly flawed, Easy Rawlins is loyal to friends, loves his adopted children deeply, and resists racial oppression with a variety of strategies. Socrates Fortlow, an ex-con guilty of murder and rape, works assiduously toward virtue and self-redemption as he represses his violent tendencies and pursues practical philosophical musings aimed at improving life for an ever-widening social circle: from friends, to neighbors, to other American citizens. The intended effects of this focus on black male heroes are to build a wider readership of black males and to open a white audience's eyes to the full humanity of his black male heroes.

Mosley's concern for the African American community also has an altruistic dimension, a sense of responsibility to return something tangible to the source of his own fame and wealth. By 1997 Mosley had established himself as a successful writer. Recalling the failure he had finding a publisher for *Gone Fishin'*, written in the 1980s but unpublished until 1997, Mosley relishes echoing the publishers' words of rejection throughout the interviews: "White people don't read about black people. Black women don't like black men. And black men don't read." Part of the problem in the rejection of *Gone Fishin'* as Mosley saw it was not that black people don't read but that the publishing industry had few editors of color who could identify minority audiences and interests. To combat this inequity, Mosley initiated discussions with Yolanda Moses, president of the City College of New York (CCNY), about starting a publishing certificate program to prepare minority students to work in the white-dominated publishing industry. To spur the effort, Mosley partially funded an endowment; and CCNY inaugurated a program that continues to attract and place students in publishing firms. As he comments in the interviews, the integration of people of color into a "closed" industry provides professional employment and, importantly, opens doors for minority writers. A second supportive gesture occurred in the same year when he gave W. Paul Coates, head of Black Classic Press, the opportunity to publish *Gone Fishin'*. Mosley had hoped that this action would prompt other African American writers to do the same; he notes in the interviews, that didn't happen. With satisfaction, he tells Woods that *Gone Fishin'* proved modestly successful, earning money for him as well as a black-owned business. He collaborated with Coates again in 2008 when Black Classic Press published *The Tempest Tales*, Mosley's homage to Langston Hughes's Simple stories.

While Mosley has a deep commitment to the African American community, as a writer he also has a sharply defined sense of and commitment to his broad, popular audience. When speaking about writing fiction, he tells his interviewers frankly that readers need to be entertained, that plot must keep them turning pages to find out what happens next. But Mosley also conceives of the relationship between a book and its readers as a dialectic, a dialogue to stimulate aggressive and critical thought about self and society as he tells Hugo Perez and others. Consequently, he intends to help readers improve their lives by providing them with sympathetic characters facing moral challenges in his fiction and by articulating commonly perceived problems in society in his nonfiction.

Beyond helping individuals, Mosley aims at social transformation. In works like *Black Genius: African American Solutions to African American Problems* (1999) and *Workin' on the Chain Gang: Shaking Off the Dead Hand of History,* he focuses primarily on American problems. After the September 11, 2001, destruction of the World Trade Towers, which he witnessed from his West Greenwich Village apartment, Mosley's social and political concerns expanded to a global scope. In the interviews discussing *What Next: A Memoir Toward World Peace* and *The Man in My Basement,* Mosley talks of these expanded social and moral concerns. In his conversation with Maria Louisa Tucker centering on *Life Out of Context* (2006), Mosley stresses the relationship between writing and social action and encourages his readers to put their interests and ideals into action in order to transform self and others.

The synergistic relationship among Mosley's fiction, sociopolitical works, and activism becomes clear in interviews with Elizabeth Farnsworth and Libero Della Piana that reveal Mosley's thinking about the American individual's responsibility within the system of global capitalism. *The Man in My Basement* mirrors this discovery of individual responsibility. Its African American hero, Charles Blakey, is a disengaged Long Islander. Confronting a white man voluntarily imprisoned in his basement, Blakey discovers his own and America's connection with evil worldwide. Through Blakey's self-discovery, Mosley merges the African American's double consciousness in a painful way. In an interview with Kerri Miller, Mosley underscores the point that a black man can't shirk moral responsibility by hiding in his marginalized social position. Mosley tells Miller, no African American can say, "I'm just a black man. . . . [Y]ou're an American too. . . . We have to take responsibility." The same interaction between fiction and political thinking appears in interviews touching on Socrates Fortlow. Mosley tells Farnsworth that writing the Socrates Fortlow stories led him to discover the central ideas for his nonfiction *Workin' on the Chain Gang.* Socrates' progress through three books moves him from an isolated, marginalized "invisible man" in *Always Outnumbered, Always Outgunned* to an engaged social activist who leads grassroots discussions of American and international social problems in *The Right Mistake: The Further Philosophical Investigations of Socrates Fortlow* (2008). Socrates' developing social vision mirrors Mosley's own thinking about citizen action, providing a sort of fictive model of democracy that

Mosley espouses in *Life Out of Context* (2006), subtitled *Which Includes a Proposal for the Non-violent Takeover of the House of Representatives*.

The interviews also provide snapshots of Mosley as a conscious literary craftsman. Reading them, one is repeatedly struck by the catholicity and range of his reading. He frequently discusses literary favorites and influences ranging from classics like Camus's *The Stranger*, Shakespeare's plays, and Dickens's novels to popular literature like *Treasure Island*, Stan Lee's *Fantastic Four* comics, and Brian Aldiss's science fiction novel *Hothouse*. His knowledge of the *noir*, hard-boiled detective genre is deep. Conscious of his literary forebears like Hammett, Chandler, and Macdonald, he recognizes how his detectives both fit into and modify the conventions of the genre. Easy Rawlins, for example, is hard-boiled; but unlike the existential loners, the Continental Op and Philip Marlowe, he changes in response to changing times and situates his existential choices within the realm of the domestic—friends and family. Mosley's interviews with Charles Brown and Perez as well as his free-ranging discussion with Colson Whitehead reveal his recognition of the pleasures and uses of speculative and science fiction to re-imagine what is possible. His affection for and knowledge of the African American cultural tradition, both oral and written, also inform his comments. In interviews with Mills and Thulani Davis, Mosley explores the blues as a sensibility, the African American appreciation of loss and tragedy. He spices his conversations and books with language demonstrating a sharp ear for speech, especially African American speech. Often in the interviews, he "does voices," using dialect to make a point or skewer an object of criticism. With Colson Whitehead, he notes the importance of African American folklore, in particular heroic figures like John Henry; and his novels are filled with folk archetypes like the bad man and the conjure woman. In *47*, his prize-winning excursion into young adult fiction, Mosley innovatively combines slave history, African American folklore, and science fiction.

When asked about literary technique, he often emphasizes the importance of plot, especially in mysteries where it is essential to keep the reader turning pages. But he also focuses on the sentence as a lyric and generative tool. He notes that he begins all his novels with one sentence; character and plot flow from it. In discussing his lean yet lyric prose style, he tells Christopher Farley that prose should be like a clear pane of glass; it should never obscure the story, never call attention to the lens itself. His admiration for French writers like Camus has undoubtedly influenced his spare yet evocative style. While favoring an unadorned, plain style, he also discusses the importance of poetic techniques for the prose fiction writer. He cites his work at the City University of New York with poet William Matthews as significantly influencing his prose, noting the importance of imagery and metaphor and the linguistic discipline that poetry imposes. When asked by Susan Stamberg to talk about his favorite book, Mosley chooses to read from and discuss the allusive and evocative language of T. S. Eliot's *Four Quartets*.

In responding to questions about his composing process, Mosley describes it as an intuitive, one might say existential, approach to writing. He tells interview audiences that he doesn't know what will happen next because he writes from the point of view of his characters and is surprised along with them as events unfold. And he also emphasizes adhering to a strict regimen of writing several hours every day and the importance of rewriting. To encourage others to explore their selves and their world, Mosley collected much of his common-sense knowledge of writing in a sort of do-it-yourself manual, *This Year You Write Your Novel* (2007). This book testifies to Mosley's strongly held belief that the act of writing is self-discovery, and transformative, personally and potentially politically.

When C-SPAN's Lamb asks what would make him happy, Mosley replies writing and living in a great nation. This statement brings together two of Mosley's great passions, literary art and politics in the arena of morality. A great nation for Mosley does not involve military or economic power only; it must involve national commitment to doing what is morally right, domestically and globally. As the interviews demonstrate, Mosley sees his writing, both fiction and nonfiction, in the service of critiquing America and exploring its potential for greatness, often by revealing the gap between social realities and American ideals. In this way, Mosley, the literary artist, puts his own greatest strength in the service of his country, playing the role of an American gadfly, goading citizens toward the goal of making America a great nation. Clearly, for Mosley art must entertain, but it must also serve higher ends: *utile et dulce*.

Reading the interviews also creates an impression of the man. Some describe him in brief profiles as affable, informal, colloquial, humorous, serious, and wryly witty. His thoughts often race ahead of his words, resulting sometimes in fragmented sentences. He switches voices, often dramatizing dialogues between himself and characters who embody a position he questions. He uses dialect or tells anecdotes that sometimes seem only tangentially related to whatever question prompted his reply. Such spontaneity often challenged me as editor and may occasionally challenge a reader. I encourage readers to locate and listen to some of the interviews or the many others online for a more immediate sense of Mosley.

Editing *Conversations with Walter Mosley* presented me with the formidable task of finding and selecting from a huge number of interviews in a variety of media: newspapers, magazines, websites, audio recordings of conference proceedings, YouTube videos, and national and local radio and television shows, most often affiliates of NPR and PBS, as well as C-SPAN. The geographic distribution of the interviews—Portland, Los Angeles, Las Vegas, Minneapolis, Chicago, New York, Miami, Canada, and the United Kingdom to name only a few—reflects Mosley's national and international prominence as artist and cultural commentator—and also, his unflagging energy. In a volume like this one, space limits required me to select only a few interviews to cover Mosley's twenty-year career as well as the breadth of his literary production and political positions. Inevitably, some excellent interviews were left out. Using excerpts in this introduction from a few of those not selected is my attempt to suggest the rich possibilities beyond this collection for literary scholars and the many readers who have a more general interest in Mosley.

The process of finding, selecting, acquiring permission to reprint, and preparing interviews for publication entails a kind of literary sleuthing that requires working with a team of investigators, questioning likely suspects, and doing hardnosed editing. So, concluding any highly collaborative project like this one must include sincere thanks to the many people who made it happen. I must thank the numerous interviewers and editors who were both generous and enthusiastic in support of *Conversations with Walter Mosley.* Closer to home, I would like to thank my colleagues at Clarkson University, in particular my department chair William Vitek for his moral and material support, John Serio for his encouragement and sage editorial advice, Barbara Osgood for her speedy help with interlibrary loans, and Robin Bunstone for her secretarial skill and good humor. But chiefly, I am indebted to Barbara Schofield Brady who has been involved in every phase of this work. Her encouragement, internet sleuthing, record-keeping, and critical editorial eye helped make this book a reality.

OEB

**Works Cited**

Lamb, Brian. "Workin' on the Chain Gang: Shaking Off the Dead Hand of History." *Booknotes*. C-SPAN. April 23, 2000.

Miller, Kerri. "A legend of the crime novel." *Talking Volumes*, Minnesota Public Radio. November 26, 2007.

Stamberg, Susan. "Walter Mosley on His Favorite Work." *Morning Edition* National Public Radio. June 26, 2001.

Streitfeld, David. "The Clues to the City of L.A.; Walter Mosley's Gumshoe Tracks Decades of Despair." *Washington Post* (November 10, 1992): C-1.

# Chronology

1952–70    Walter Ellis Mosley born on Jan. 12 in Los Angeles, California, the only child of Leroy Mosley and Ella (*née* Slatkin) Mosley. His father is African American and his mother Jewish. Both worked for the LA school system; he as a custodian and she as a personnel clerk. The family moves from Watts to West LA's Pico-Fairfield district. Mosley attends Victory Baptist Day School, Louis Pasteur Junior High School, and Alexander Hamilton High School.

1970–81    Until 1972 drifts through Europe and to Santa Cruz, CA. Then goes to Vermont to attend Goddard College, but lacking focus eventually drops out. Returns to school and finishes a BA degree in political science at Johnson State University in Vermont in 1977. Meets Joy Kellman, a choreographer and dancer. Moves with Kellman to Massachusetts for graduate work in political theory at University of Massachusetts at Amherst but leaves without a degree.

1982–84    Moves to New York City and works as consultant doing computer programming. While on a job for Mobil Oil Corporation, begins writing and decides to pursue creative writing full-time.

1985    Enrolls in creative writing courses taught by Bill Matthews, Edna O'Brien, and Frederic Tuten at the City College of New York (CCNY).

1987    Marries Joy Kellman.

1988–89    Finishes first novel, *Gone Fishin'* in which he begins to develop the characters of Easy Rawlins and Raymond "Mouse" Alexander who later become central to the Easy Rawlins mystery series. Publishers deem the novel commercially unviable. Writes *Devil in a Blue Dress* setting Easy and Mouse in a *noir* detective novel. His teacher, Frederic Tuten, submits *Devil* to his own agent, who proposes to represent Mosley and later sells the novel to W. W. Norton.

1990    Publishes *Devil in a Blue Dress*, the first in a ten-book Easy Raw-
        lins mystery series. *Devil* is nominated for the Edgar Award for
        Best First Mystery Novel and wins a Shamus Award for Best
        First Novel given by the Private Eye Writers of America. Over-
        seas, *Devil* wins the John Creasey Memorial Award given by the
        Crime Writers' Association of Great Britain (also called The
        CWA New Blood Dagger Award).

1991    Publishes *A Red Death*.

1992    Publishes *White Butterfly*. Presidential candidate Bill Clinton
        mentions Mosley as one of his favorite mystery novelists, spur-
        ring Mosley's popularity.

1993    Mosley's father, Leroy Mosley, dies. Mosley attributes his inter-
        est in language and storytelling to his father's influence. Leroy
        Mosley's Louisiana roots, his World War II experience, and his
        migration to Los Angeles contribute significantly to the creation
        of Easy Rawlins and his LA milieu.

1994    Publishes *Black Betty*.

1995    Attempts to turn *Devil in a Blue Dress* into a screenplay, but ulti-
        mately leaves the task to Carl Franklin who also directs the film.
        Writes screenplay, "Fearless," for an episode in the Showtime
        TV series *Fallen Angels*. Publishes his blues novel, *RL's Dream*
        to critical acclaim. A finalist for the NAACP Award in Fiction,
        it wins the 1996 Black Caucus of the American Library Associa-
        tion's Literary Award.

1996    Publishes *A Little Yellow Dog*, then takes a six-year hiatus from
        the Easy Rawlins series. Wins an O. Henry Award for the So-
        crates Fortlow short story "Thief" and the 1996 Black Caucus
        of the American Library Association's Literary Award for *RL's
        Dream*. Named the first Artist-in-Residence at the Africana
        Studies Institute, New York University (NYU). This appoint-
        ment begins a continuing relationship with the Institute that
        results in a lecture series, "Black Genius."

1997    Publishes *Gone Fishin'*, his first novel and a prequel to the Easy
        Rawlins mysteries, with W. Paul Coates's Black Classic Press in
        Baltimore. Works with Yolanda Moses, president of the City Col-
        lege of New York (CUNY), to create a new publishing certificate
        program aimed at young urban residents to increase minority
        employment in the publishing field. It is the only such program

in the country. Awarded the TransAfrica International Literary Prize for all of his work.

1998  Publishes *Always Outnumbered, Always Outgunned*, the first of Mosley's three books featuring the ex-con, street philosopher Socrates Fortlow. It wins the Anisfield-Wolf Award, honoring books for contributing to the understanding of race in America. Adapts *Always Outnumbered, Always Outgunned* as a screenplay for an HBO film, directed by Michael Apted. Publishes *Blue Light*, his first foray into speculative fiction.

1999  Publishes the second Socrates Fortlow novel, *Walkin' the Dog*. Edits *Black Genius: African American Solutions to African American Problems* based on NYU's Africana Studies Institute's lecture series.

2000  Publishes *Workin' on the Chain Gang: Shaking Off the Dead Hand of History*, a sociopolitical essay, for Ballantine's prestigious Library of Contemporary Thought.

2001  Returns to mystery writing with *Fearless Jones*, the first novel in the Fearless Jones series. Set in 1950s LA, it introduces second-hand bookstore owner Paris Minton and his best friend, war veteran Fearless Jones. Publishes *Futureland: Nine Stories of an Imminent World*, his second speculative fiction book. Marriage to Joy Kellman ends in divorce.

2002  Wins a Grammy Award for his liner notes accompanying Richard Pryor's *And It's Deep Too!: The Complete Warner Bros. Recordings (1968–1992)*. Returns to Easy Rawlins, publishing *Bad Boy Brawly Brown*. Publishes *What Next: A Memoir Toward World Peace*, his second book on contemporary issues.

2003  Publishes *Fear Itself*, the second novel in the Fearless Jones series, and *Six Easy Pieces*, a collection of Easy Rawlins short stories. Begins writing social and political commentary regularly for *The Nation*.

2004  Publishes *Little Scarlet* and *The Man in My Basement*, a novel of ideas.

2005  Expands his literary range by publishing *47*, a young adult novel that combines African American folklore and history with speculative fiction. It wins the 2005 Carl Brandon Society Parallax Award for best speculative fiction by an author of color. Publishes *Cinnamon Kiss*. Receives the Sundance Institute Risktaker

Award for his work. Also, awarded an honorary doctorate by CCNY.

2006     Demonstrates his virtuosity by publishing *Fortunate Son*, literary novel; *The Wave*, speculative fiction; *Fear of the Dark*, the third Fearless Jones mystery novel; and *Life Out of Context, Which Includes a Proposal for the Non-violent Takeover of the House of Representatives*, his third political monograph.

2007     Continues to defy classification as merely a mystery writer, publishing *Killing Johnny Fry: A Sexistentialist Novel*, an experiment in erotica; *The Right Mistake: The Further Investigations of Socrates Fortlow*, the third book in this series; and *This Year You Write Your Novel*, a common sense guide for aspiring writers. Brings the ten-novel Easy Rawlins series to an end with the publication of *Blonde Faith*. Wins the Wheatley Book Award established to recognize literary achievement that transcends culture, boundary, and perception.

2008     Having written for *The Nation* since 2003, joins its editorial board. Publishes *Diablerie*, another experiment in existential erotica, and *The Tempest Tales*, his homage to Langston Hughes's Simple stories.

2009     Begins the Leonid McGill mystery series set in contemporary New York City with the publication of *The Long Fall*.

2010     Crosses genre boundaries again, transforming *The Tempest Tales* into a play, *The Fall of Heaven*, which premiers to positive reviews at Cincinnati's Playhouse in the Park. Publishes *Known to Evil*, the second Leonid McGill novel.

Conversations with Walter Mosley

# Walter Mosley

## Thulani Davis/1993

This interview was commissioned by and first published in *BOMB Magazine*, Issue #44, Summer 1993, pp. 52–57. © Bomb Magazine, New Art Publications, and its Contributors. All rights reserved. The BOMB Archive can be viewed at www.bombsite.com. Reprinted by permission.

Novelist Walter Mosley, forty-one, already a cult favorite among mystery readers, suddenly appeared on television and in the papers in January when newly inaugurated President Clinton named him as his favorite writer. Mosley is the author of three novels: *Devil in a Blue Dress*, the tale of troubles caused by an illusory woman who forces people to cross dangerous taboos; *A Red Death*, which brings the '50s McCarthy witch hunts into the churches and Africanist meetings of black L.A.; and *White Butterfly*, the chase for a serial killer who does not interest police until a white woman turns up among his female victims in a black neighborhood. The books incidentally chart the lives of the unseen "blues people" in L.A. in the '50s and early '60s.

Mosley has of late become a hot lunch ticket for movie stars happy to meet a guy who could fill a shopping bag with adventures of a free-wheeling black detective named Easy Rawlins, who lives in South Central Los Angeles, with memories roaming from Depression-era Texas to wartime Europe, and all the space between. Easy also has a seductively dangerous guardian angel, his childhood friend Raymond Alexander, better known and feared by most as "Mouse." Mouse is a clean dresser who smiles when he kills.

Mosley was born and raised in L.A., leaving at eighteen to go to Goddard College in Vermont. He dropped out and stayed in Vermont for five years, finishing his BA at Johnson State College. Mosley now lives in New York's West Village with his wife, a choreographer.

**Thulani Davis:** In your essay in *Critical Fictions* you say that you got into writing mysteries because editors didn't respond to your other works. What other writing did you do?

**Walter Mosley:** Oh, everything. I was writing short stories, and I was studying poetry. I don't think you can write fiction without knowing poetry, metaphor, simile, the music of the language. I wrote a novel called *Gone Fishin'* about my two main characters, Easy and Mouse, when they were very young in the deep south of Texas. You could call it a psychological novel. Mouse was looking to steal from and kill his stepfather, and Easy was looking to remember his own father, who had abandoned him when he was eight. I sent it out to a lot of agents. They all liked it enough to send back intelligent letters. But none of them thought that a book of that sort would make it in the market. This was like '88, '89.

**TD:** So, Easy and Mouse have been around a long time?

**WM:** Mm-hum.

**TD:** Why Texas?

**WM:** Well, the books map a movement of black people from Southern Texas and Louisiana to Los Angeles. So, that's why Texas. A lot of my family and a lot of people that I know come from there.

**TD:** When you wrote *Gone Fishin'*, was your intention to write a series of books that mapped that movement?

**WM:** Yeah. I just didn't think they were going to be mysteries. Have you ever seen the movie, *The Third Man*? Great movie. I just loved Orson Welles's character. I read the novel, and in the beginning Graham Greene says that he was hired to write the screenplay, and he wrote the novel first, to work out the kinks. I thought that was such a great idea I decided to do it myself. Of course, I got about three chapters into *Devil in a Blue Dress* and forgot anything about a movie. I was going to City College Graduate Program in writing, and the head of the program, Frederic Tuten, asked me if he could see the book. To abbreviate the story, I came back from a trip and he came to me and said, "Walt, my agent's going to represent you."

**TD:** That was great!

**WM:** Yep. Wonderful.

**TD:** And now the novel *Devil in a Blue Dress* is being made into a film. What about writing the screenplay?

**WM:** I didn't do very well at it the first time. I mean, I want to try it again sometime. Carl Franklin, who directed *One False Move*, is directing *Devil in a Blue Dress*. He called me the other day, and he's asking all this stuff, which is nice. He certainly doesn't have to. His first three pages are like my first three pages. But what Easy was *saying*, he made *real*. For instance, Joppy's bar is on the second floor of a butcher's warehouse. So in the script, Carl has a guy with an apron and blood sitting next to Easy, saying, "I gotta get back to work." The thing is, to change everything into images. I have an idea of that now. I certainly am going to write screenplays again. It takes a long time to learn. Also there's a different emotional relationship. I think of it as larger than possible.

**TD:** What does that mean?

**WM:** Most directors I've met have incredibly large, irrational hearts. They believe in things passionately—did you see the movie *Hearts of Darkness*, the movie about Coppola making *Apocalypse Now*? He explains what he did by saying, "In order to make this movie about Vietnam, we did what America did. We took too much money and too much equipment and went out into the middle of the jungle and got lost out there." That's what he did. That's where that movie came from. That's what you have to do if you're going to do something that means something.

**TD:** That's what he does anyway.

**WM:** Yeah, but a lot of good directors do this.

**TD:** So, you're going to have a film noir?

**WM:** I don't think so. The one thing I love about Carl is that he understands what I am saying. My novel is about a man who is facing his fear and his ambition in a new world after passing through two very strange worlds. The first, you know, is the deep South. He was completely convinced that was reality. And then World War II, which totally blew everything asunder, and then didn't put anything back together. Now, here he is in California with a chance, with all that baggage. He's trying to face those fears. The novel is about that. The language is the noir language, part of it anyway, and certainly the time and the place—the fact that Easy is a reluctant detective. But, it's not really *that*. Carl's talent is character development—*One False Move* is a movie about characters.

**TD:** I thought that film was brilliant. I had never seen a black director deal with race from any number of points of view, and yet not make race the subject. Everyone had a way of dealing with it. So, with very few characters, he covered the spectrum of what a lot of us do: from using race, to being flexible about it, to responding to it. For me, as a writer, it felt liberating.

**WM:** One of the problems with talking about racism, the relation between whites and blacks, is that it eclipses what real life is for black people, which is just life among each other. But so much of our intellectual heritage, which is good on one hand, but baggage on the other, is the discussion being in racial/political terms.

**TD:** And whites frequently have the feeling that is what black people are doing all the time—relating to the world through race, if not actively protesting and complaining about it.

**WM:** And with very severe lines drawn. The thing that I really like about the genre of mysteries is that they're exotic, and you can write about things which are unknown. One of the things I adore writing about is the black community. This guy's a carpenter, this guy's the head chef of this place, and they all get together in this park or on that corner because it's sunny. They all have a drink together and they like each other. They're all middle-class working men, as opposed to whatever other image people, black or white, may have of them.

**TD:** The people who are in the periphery in a lot of movies—it is as though we are looking at *those* people. If there was a Chandler or a Hammett or a James M. Cain story and suddenly we see what was going on on the other side of town, in the same space of time. Easy does work for this police station with one black cop in it. Is that one of the reasons you picked the '50s? Because it was a time when the police really would have needed an outsider to go into this black world with which they had only superficial interaction?

**WM:** That's interesting. It happens to work out like that.

**TD:** It wasn't intentional?

**WM:** No. I mean, you still have the same problem. Black people are not going to talk to a police detective even if he's black. He's still a policeman, which means he's an enemy.

**TD:** It seems like an exotic world in '52, '53. The assumptions that the white characters make about blacks go unchallenged. And by having Easy do the detective work, they don't have to find out anything about that community. They're not concerned with the particulars, they just want the results. So it remains his turf.

**WM:** The way police treat black people in the community is not like, "I need your help." They're like, "C'mere nigger, I want to know something." We instantly don't want to respond to that. And as Easy says, the people they want to talk to are "the element." They don't want to know about the churchgoers; they want to know about the people who are out there in the street, who know what's going on, who might be doing something. These people don't talk to the police. But they do talk to Easy, because Easy's okay.

**TD:** Easy doesn't apprise the police of the black nationalist Garveyite's activities. He's a fairly amoral character in conventional terms. His principle is to leave black people alone who aren't interfering with the FBI or the police or whoever is important in the power structure. He doesn't expose them to a certain extent.

**WM:** Many people think the noir genre is simply a mood. But there's a lot of elements to it. The noir genre is like the white hope in a world that has lost its hold on the string that ties it to morality and goodness. It's a man in his forties who knows the ropes and is ethically defined. He has no mother, no father, no wife, no children, no property. He doesn't owe anything to anybody. If the police say, "We're going to put you in jail until you talk," he can go to jail. He doesn't have any kid out there he needs to feed. He doesn't have any wife that's going to find a new boyfriend because he's a damn fool. You know, he can do anything.

**TD:** This is emblematic of Western culture as well. The rootless man is on a quest for truth. . . .

**WM:** And for justice in an unjust world. Which Easy does do. But, Easy is so practical, and he's so pragmatic. He's always changing. My essay in *Critical Fictions* starts off talking about what you learn from poverty. My father told me this: you learn how to cook, how to sew, how to build things out of wood, how to wire things, how to plumb things. He only had a sixth grade education, but he could do anything he needed to do in this world. If his car broke down he could fix it, because that's the only way it got fixed. That's much more what the books are about.

**TD:** You say also that people knew what everything cost.

**WM:** Yeah. In both senses. They know how much beans cost, how much pants cost; they also know how much, at what point, they will give up their own dignity, their sense of right and wrong. And then they're always aware of things: when somebody's door is unlocked, or when it's quiet next door, or who's on the corner. These are manifestations, awarenesses of someone who lives in poverty.

**TD:** All of your characters have that—they don't miss anything. And they never volunteer what they know about anything.

**WM:** What they think.

**TD:** Because frequently, when we tell what we know, we learn nothing.

**WM:** Right. You can't give away anything.

**TD:** It's a blues sensibility. The characters in the book come out of a construction that is a blues world. Their codes of conduct are like the wisdom that is dished out in a blues song—the vision that you might not be alive tomorrow.

**WM:** The relationship in a black world, or a nonwhite world, to the whole world is so complex. I've heard Taj Mahal sing this lyric, "I woke up this morning/With the blues three different ways/One said go/And the other two said stay." That's the problem, you don't know what to say, you don't know what to do. You know what you're going to do, but it's going to break your heart to do that.

**TD:** Most of your characters are very rooted in the now. Easy stands out for continually attempting to make long range plans. By the second book, he is protecting his stash: his land, his house, and everything that it has produced. He'll say in relationship to Mofass, "Oh he doesn't have the big picture that I have." Yet he's prepared, in the samurai sense, to go down at any time.

**WM:** He has to be, because that's his life. That's what he's learned. He's seen people die all around him. The one constant in every manifestation of life is that people keep dying. He can never be confident of having what he wants, but he wants it anyway. It's like that blues concept you were talking about, "I know I'm not going to get it but I'm still going to try." One of the ways he does it is by incorporating different kinds of people in his life. One of the beauties about fiction is that the world is filled with so many different kinds of people, and we can talk about those people. So you have someone like Jackson Blue, who is the smartest person Easy has ever met in his life, but he's also small-minded, a coward, emotionally very unstable and irresponsible. Once you have a character like that, or you have a character like Mofass, or Odell, or Dupree, who ends up taking Easy's wife at the end of the third book, then you have an interesting world. My novels are really about these people. Each one of my novels has some subject other than the subject of the mystery. *Devil [in a Blue Dress]* is a man coming to know himself, and in *Red Death* it was the relationship between the oppression of white people throughout the McCarthy period, and what the oppression of black people is about. The discussion at the end between Easy and Jackson Blue, when Jackson explains, "Easy, you don't understand. You'd be better off on the black list, because if you were on the black list then you could get off the black list." Then you have *White Butterfly*, which is the conflict between men and women. Of course I realized early on that I couldn't write about the conflict between black men and black women because it's too complex an issue for a small novel to take on. But to write about a whole bunch of black women, therefore, all kinds of women, like Etta Mae, who are so rooted to the earth that they can lift boulders and trees grow out of their ears and stuff. Or the Caribbean woman, mother of the murderer, Saunders. She's a very strong and powerful woman who scares the shit out of Mouse, but doesn't have the strength to deal with her son, and is somehow afraid of him. It's so easy to choose sides in the fiction, but I don't want to, I'm writing about these characters that I love to death.

**TD:** A couple of people have told me they find Mouse fascinating. They love Mouse. In *Red Death* when he seems to be coming apart at the seams, he's completely scary, because you already know he'll do anything. But then you see Etta so glad to have him back. Why did you make him attractive?

**WM:** Because I love my father so much. My father just died on January 1, which is the worst thing that happened to me. My father gave me the feeling, when I was a kid, that nothing bad would ever happen to me. I knew that if the police came to get me that he would protect me. I knew that if somebody was trying to kill me, he would be out there with a gun, because that's just the way it is. In Easy's world, this is really necessary, because Mouse says, "Listen man, them white guys got people on their side, man, you'd be a fool not to have me."

**TD:** And you have that feeling about Mouse?

**WM:** Yeah. When the guy is about to kill Easy, and Mouse enters with a, "Good evenin' Frank," he says, "Oh shit, Mouse is here!" and then everything changes. When you live that kind of life, everybody's sad and depressed, and all of a sudden that person is there and everybody's happy.

**TD:** Is that really why so many readers like him too?

**WM:** One, he loves himself. One of the most constant problems in the black community is that there are so many names for black people: colored, negro, Afro-American, black, African-American—now those are the official ones. There's also brother, blood, soul, soul brother. Then there are the slurs, the slang: nigger, coon, jigaboo, but all used by black people, all of them. "Yeah, I saw that nigger came up here, I saw him." That means something. The Eskimos have thirty-seven names for snow. The names are always changing, and control over what we are named is important, which is why you can have a political leader who wants to change the name.

**TD:** But Mouse?

**WM:** Mouse is Mouse. He's not looking for a new identity; he's not wondering; he doesn't want to read about slave history or African history. He doesn't feel bad about white people. He doesn't feel inferior to them; he doesn't feel afraid of them. Easy says, "This white man got trouble." Mouse will say, "Where does he live?" But if it was a black man it would be the same thing. "I don't care. It's either him or me, and you know it ain't gonna be me." And that "you know it ain't gonna be me" is a rock solid certainty that most black people don't have. . . . Poverty brings up all those moral questions. "I know just how far you have to push me before I will go into that drawer and pull out my gun. I know just how far." Most people in the middle class, black or white, don't think about that. But ask a young black man in a working class on down community, "What would it take for you to kill somebody." He says, "I'll tell you. You mess with my sister, you mess with my mother, you offer me a thousand dollars." There's a whole list of things where "I will go get the gun."

**TD:** If you asked me that, I would say you would have to try to kill me.

**WM:** And that proves that you thought about it.

**TD:** I have thought about it. I've had somebody try to kill me, that's why I've thought about it.

**WM:** That's too bad.

**TD:** Yeah, it is. I think if you've had the experience of coming in contact with your feeling or desire to kill somebody, then you don't have to think about it anymore. It's an experience you've had.

**WM:** And if you face it everyday. . . .

**TD:** Chester Himes, did you ever read him?

**WM** Uh-huh. That's so funny—there're people I like, black male writers, mostly they're poets, it turns out. Somebody like Etheridge Knight makes me so happy I can't stand it. But it's more than just that. I try to think of what lineage is. It seems that so many black writers are always creating who they are in the world, because there isn't the kind of lineage that you have in Eurocentric white male literature, where people actually do come out of each other. You have a great poet and he has a great poet who studies under him.

**TD:** But the critics who write about us are not familiar enough with the tradition to pick some people to say we came out of.

**WM:** People say Chester Himes about me.

**TD:** Do they?

**WM:** They do. But, you see, I don't feel like I came out of Himes. He comes from a very angry, a very disenfranchised place. Life was very hard for him and he needed to get away from it. People didn't pay any attention to him. I don't live under the kind of racism that he lived under. And even though I think it made decisions much clearer for him, which in some ways makes things easier, I wouldn't want to trade it. I learned more from Chandler.

**TD:** Who was the first mystery writer you read?

**WM:** Ross Macdonald. I loved him. I still love him, as flawed as he is.

**TD:** How do you see yourself fitting in with your contemporaries among black writers?

**WM:** I was in Philadelphia a couple of years ago. Quincy Troupe was teaching a poetry workshop. I was just sitting in the back listening. It was a black crowd of people. Quincy was saying, "I want everybody to write poetry. I want all black people to be writing poetry and making poetry and living poetry and. . . ." You know how Quincy is, he said that again. He said, "In order to write poetry, you gotta write good poetry, you gotta write real poetry. You can't just be writing something and say it's poetry. Just because you have the right politics, doesn't mean that you're writing poetry." He said, "I hate Bush." He said, "That's right, but it isn't poetry." And it was wonderful. 'Cause, you know, Quincy is such a powerful guy. Everybody was looking up at him and they were very serious and he was saying the truth. And very often in black art and literature, the mistake is made that the correct political stance makes good art, when indeed the correct political stance has nothing to do with good art. Nothing. The only issue for me is good writing. The job of writing is to hold, somehow, in a crystalline form, the language of the time. When, a hundred years from now, someone reads this, they will know what life was like at the time. They won't need to look at a history book to understand what life was like. They can see it and feel it through the language and description of life in that book. The contract of telling a story is that the reader has to wonder, what's happening next? And then there has to be a subtext, there always has to be a subtext. I think I'm writing good fiction. I mean, I'm not saying I'm the greatest writer in the world.

**TD:** OK, let me ask you in a different way: Writing mysteries has given you a wide and widely mixed audience. But has the genre restricted you at all? I'm interested in you, but I'm not interested in studying the genre. So, do you feel that there's some other audience out there who has yet to find you?

**WM:** I'm being slowly, though not so slowly anymore, discovered by a black audience. The mystery audience is almost exclusively a white audience. I pressured my publisher for two years to get me into the various black distributors. They wanted to do it, but it was very hard for them. There was reticence, on behalf of the black distributors, to deal with Norton. They said, "Who else do you publish who's black? He's the only one and you want us to do all this work?" But I think black people are happy that I'm writing.

**TD:** Yeah, I think so. A funny thing happened. I was watching the news after the inauguration and they said that the new things that are in now that Bill Clinton is president are saxophone pins, and what I would call white soul food, and Walter Mosley. Were you surprised to hear that?

**WM:** Some people whose bookstore I always read at had given him my books, so I knew he had them. Clinton, not at all a stupid man, wants to reach out for the black community and the Latino community and the gay community and say, "Hey listen, I'm interested." Now, you could look at this with a questioning eye, which, of course, makes sense to do. But at the same time, I figure this: if he read my books, that means that black language and black life, at least from one point of view, entered his life. Even if it hasn't entered his life, it entered other people's lives who have said, "Let me take a look at this book" and "Wow, this is what he's reading?" So I like it, I'm happy with it, and not idealistically or unrealistically, I think.

**TD:** Well, it brought you some kind of notoriety. I read an interview with you in *Vanity Fair*, where you were asked a lot about being a biracial person. Is it a constant subject that people ask you about and therefore annoying?

**WM:** No, actually. I enjoyed the *Vanity Fair* piece for a variety of reasons. My mother is Jewish, and I was raised among Jews and blacks; my father, obviously, was black. And I'm in a world today where there's all this conflict between Jews and blacks. So, the fact that Christopher Hitchens wanted to concentrate on that, I liked, because it's a dialogue that I don't mind getting at. I was on the Staten Island Ferry once with a guy who I liked a lot, a Muslim, who turned to me and said, "Hitler didn't really kill as many Jews as they said he did, and he really shoudda oughtn't a done it, but the Jews had all the *guilder* and them Germans just wanted to be free." This is like ten years ago, but I just can't forget it. I don't like anti-Black Jews and I don't like anti-Jewish Blacks. It's not that I don't like them, I just don't like the stance.

**TD:** But frequently publications treat an interview with a black writer as a situation to talk about race politics, and they'll forget to ask you about your books. There's a point at which any writer would be annoyed at being interviewed at such length without anybody saying, by the way, you write books, don't you? Do you get much of that?

**WM:** Yeah, that happened, but I wanted to deal with it. I'm kind of easygoing. My books came out in England. Yours did too; in fact ours came out at the same time last year.

**TD:** They interviewed me about the L.A. riot.

**WM:** But they needed to know, they were asking, "What's wrong with these people?" I didn't feel badly about answering them because I really wanted to get this other point of view.

**TD:** But, see, no one ever asked me about craft, no one ever asked me questions about how something is made. They really were asking about narrative content and how it compares to reality.

**WM:** I often change the subject, even when I'm talking to you I do it.

**TD:** Let me ask you two more things. I take it Easy Rawlins is going to be around.

**WM:** He's going to live a long time. I think I'll keep him alive until maybe 1990, 1991.

**TD:** There's a lot of stuff about World War II in your books. It seems to have made a particular impression on you. And you were certainly interested in the black liberators before most people ever heard about them. Were images from the war, stories about it, vivid to you in your childhood?

**WM:** Yeah. Everybody, every black man was in the war.

**TD:** You knew that growing up?

**WM:** Yeah. And they're proud of it. They loved it 'cause this was the first time they got to do a lot of things. And it was worthwhile.

**TD:** And did you hear about the liberation of Dachau firsthand before you read about it?

**WM:** You know, I don't know. I don't really knock myself out over historical accuracy. I knew it but I don't know why I knew it.

**TD:** What I'm really asking, Walter, is what kind of information makes a larger impact on you, the oral, or something you've read, or are they equal?

**WM:** It's the oral, definitely the oral. Black history is oral history. The reason black literature is the most alive in America, which I do believe, is that it comes from oral history, and oral history has always this weight. For instance, I'm telling you stories, and I want you to remember them, so I have to tell them really well. I have to tell a story that you'll be saying when you're talking to somebody else. And that story wants to go on and live on. You want to breathe life into your fiction, and people who read that fiction are supposed to experience that life. There's a kind of terror or *elan* or whatever. Much more than political rightness or wrongness, because that's kind of secondary really. So certainly it's oral history. Even now, my favorite thing is to have people tell me stories.

**TD:** I met a guy who had liberated a camp, and it was a story he had not told, not in twenty years, for some reason.

**WM:** The concentration camps themselves, for black Americans, are so poignant, because, for black Americans in the 1940s, it was worse than America. This was a serious thing.

**TD:** And it was a sign that things could get worse.

**WM:** "You mean you're killing them 'cause they Jews? And you do this to us?" It's incomprehensible, even for a black American. Like Mississippi. Did you see that liberators' film? When the guy says, "What am I doing here, when people are dying all around me?" And then when he gets to the camps—he didn't say it, but it's like, "Once I saw that, I realized that no matter what my problems are, I have to be here, I have to be doing this. I can't help it." And again, that's like a blues mentality. You have to do certain kinds of things. And of course, when I'd write about Chaim Wenzler, who can say, "Well listen, I know what it's like to be burned and shot at and beat and killed and put in ghettos. We named ghettos."

TD: You told me you wrote another novel that's not a mystery. What's this other novel?

WM: There've been a few but the book I've finished is called *RL's Dream*. Those are the initials they used to call the musician, Robert Johnson. He was Robert LeRoy until he found out his real name. And that book is a blues novel, not so much about RL, but about a fictional character who once played with RL and is now dying in New York and is trying to come to grips with his life and his history.

TD: You said to me something about wanting to write about the music.

WM: Ah. Now I remember that discussion. The most revolutionary moment of the twentieth century is black American music. I believe that it knocked down the walls of Russia. I believe that it touches and transforms everybody. It certainly starts with the blues. I'm not a musician, but I want to write about what music means. The only way I can write about it. I want to write about a black musical life. Robert Johnson's life. A life that is so hard and painfully and specifically itself that my main character, Soupspoon Wise is his name, says that by leaving the Mississippi Delta, he abandoned the blues, because you couldn't play the blues without a blues audience. You just can't take the blues out of the South. That music belongs there. It belongs on the streets and the roads and the paths. It belongs to the people. He thinks that he abandoned the blues, but this is a realization much later. It's a realization that haunted him. He didn't realize it at the beginning, but he felt it. He felt it from the beginning. His life kind of disintegrated. Now, in his old age, when he's dying, one of the other aspects of the blues, he is trying to come to grips with it.

TD: Did you do anything in this book that you haven't done?

WM: It's written in third person, so there's that. That was very nice because I could deal with my female characters a lot more easily. I'm limited by Easy. Easy, I think, is a very broad big character, maybe bigger than me, in life, but not necessarily in language. In language I have to be careful how Easy talks and what he knows, whereas in third person, it depends on whose shoulder I'm on in that moment. My narrator is closely involved with the other characters, so he takes on the characteristics of whomever we're looking at from that point of view at that moment. So the language can be much more lyrical. I can do a lot more things. The language can reflect the mood. I can get really wild, and I do. I get really wild.

**TD:** That's good. And what next?

**WM:** About the near future, I have a four-book contract at Norton and that's three mysteries and this book, *RL's Dream*. We'll see what happens from there. So, my next four years are spoken for.

# The Other Side of Those Mean Streets

## Charles L. P. Silet/1993

From *The Armchair Detective*, 26, no. 4, (1993): 8–16. By permission of Charles L. P. Silet, interviewer, and Otto Penzler, publisher.

Walter Mosley achieved instant recognition with the publication of his first Easy Rawlins book, *Devil in a Blue Dress* (1990). The critics were uniformly complimentary about the novel. They loved his historical re-creation of postwar Los Angeles and the unique voice he had captured with his characters. *A Red Death* (1991) was equally well received. Mosley moved his time frame forward into the early 1950s and once again explored the Afro-American world of LA. The critics placed Mosley squarely in the hard-boiled tradition of Hammett, Chandler, and Cain, even though Easy walked down mean streets not explored before. Once again, the critics recognized the unique voice and perspective of his central character, Easy, a black man who expressed his feelings within the traditions of the crime story.

With the publication of *White Butterfly* (1992), Mosley arrived. It did not hurt sales when candidate Bill Clinton was seen carrying copies of his books on the campaign trail or when he told reporters that Mosley was his favorite mystery writer. By then the paperback editions of the first two were on the stands and selling. Once again the critics were highly complimentary. Easy's world was becoming better known. Mouse, Jesus, Mofass, the locale of the "other" Los Angeles had become familiar to a growing number of mystery readers.

Walter Mosley now has a four-book contract with W. W. Norton to deliver three more Easy Rawlins books, plus a non-genre novel, titled *RL's Dream*, which is about the world of jazz and explores the character of the legendary blues guitarist and songwriter Robert Johnson. His next Easy Rawlins novel is called *Black Betty* and is to appear in the summer of 1994, *A Little Yellow Dog* is to be released in 1995, and *Bad Boy Bobby Brown* [A title Mosley changed to *Bad Boy Brawly Brown*] is scheduled for publication in 1996.

Walter Mosley has said he hopes that his success will have a positive effect on young, black writers and encourage them to write genre fiction. His books so far have opened up the world of crime writing not only to a new voice but also to a new perspective. As Mosley works his way forward in history, he is presenting his readers with a uniquely ethnic vision, one that brings favorably to mind the writings of Chester Himes, until now the best-known black writer of crime fiction. Like Himes, Mosley celebrates his heritage, warts and all.

Mr. Mosley is also a highly articulate and thoughtful conversationalist about all manner of literary things, as readers will discover in this his first major interview. It contains revealing material about Easy Rawlins, crime fiction, Black history, and fame.

**TAD** [*The Armchair Detective*]: Let me begin by asking for some background information, where you were born. Something about your family.

**MOSLEY:** I was born in Los Angeles in 1952, Black father, white Jewish mother, lived in Watts for quite a while in south central LA, and then moved to west Los Angeles into that great vast middle-class ocean. Then, as soon as I possibly could, I left and went back east, first to Vermont, then to Massachusetts, and then to New York.

**TAD:** You said that your father was Black and your mother was Jewish. Did this present problems, was it an enriching experience?

**MOSLEY:** One of the interesting things which most people who are white don't understand is that the Black community is pretty accepting in general. So there was really no problem. I had a white mother, but it was just different, nobody made a big deal out of it. The neighborhood I was in was half-Black and half-Jewish, just like me.

**TAD:** Tell me something about your schooling.

**MOSLEY:** Actually elementary school was very important for me. I went to a place called Victory Baptist Day School which was the only private black elementary school in Los Angeles. It was a very poor school where mainly the teachers just loved you to death. I went back there just the other day and the school is exactly the same. Everybody is new but it hasn't changed one bit. The principal was walking through the schoolyard and she knew every little boy and every little girl and what all their issues were. One of the interesting things about education for children is children can't help but learn, they always want to learn, they can't stop learning. The problems are mostly of an emotional kind. We felt so loved in a real way. I think it was a great experience for me, a really wonderful experience.

**TAD:** Then you went on to high school?

**MOSLEY:** Yeah, I went on to junior high school and then high school. They were public schools, predominantly Jewish, where I learned a great deal but I wasn't very happy in those schools because it was more like a factory education.

**TAD:** Were you interested in writing at this point?

**MOSLEY:** Nope.

**TAD:** What about college?

**MOSLEY:** I went to a place called Goddard College in Vermont where I was actually asked to leave. It's almost impossible to be asked to leave from Goddard but they did. Then I went to Johnson State College, some years later. I studied political science, and then I went to political theory school at the University of Massachusetts at Amherst. I finally decided, "Hey, this isn't making any sense." So I returned to computer programming, that's the big thing in my life, returning to programming.

**TAD:** How did you get into programming?

**MOSLEY:** I had been in Europe with a friend of mine when I was about nineteen or twenty and we were staying with his relatives who were very wealthy and I realized that not only did I not have as much money as his relatives, but I didn't have as much money as the people they hired to work for them! On the way back to LA, I was thinking, "Ok, now, I have to have a job. I don't really want a profession; I don't want to be a doctor or a lawyer because I don't have any commitment to that stuff. So I need a craft." Then I thought of all these possible things to be and finally it got down to nurse or programmer because you could move around a lot with either one of those jobs. Then I thought, "Oh, God, I can't stand the sight of blood!" So, programmer.

**TAD:** At some point, you went to the graduate writing program at CCNY.

**MOSLEY:** After I left graduate school in political theory, I moved to Boston and then later to New York where I was a programmer for many years. I had written a series of letters to my wife and she said they were wonderful letters and other people in my past said I had always written wonderful letters. One Saturday I was at work when nobody else was there and I started writing these sentences and I really loved them and I thought, "Maybe I really could be a writer." That was in '85–'86. Then I studied writing with a guy in his office for about a year. He had a little workshop behind his house. After that, I went to City College.

**TAD:** How did you decide to write professionally?

**MOSLEY:** Well, I never did really. What happened was that I was going to City College in the writing program and it was kind of artistic. It was not a commercial base. But I was there and I was very serious about writing. I wrote a novel that wasn't a mystery and nobody seemed to be very interested in that book.

**TAD:** This was *Gone Fishin'*?

**MOSLEY:** Yes. After I wrote that book, I sent it out and nobody bought it. So, then, I started writing something else that turned out to be *Devil in a Blue Dress*. My plan was that I was going to go to school, get a degree, and after the degree get a job somewhere, not New York, as a teacher of creative writing and I would keep writing and one day I would be accepted as a writer. But I wrote this book, *Devil in a Blue Dress*, which I kept in the closet. The head of the writing program, Frederic Tuten, said, "Why don't you let me take a look at that?" This is abbreviated, but it's not much. So I did and I went away for the weekend and when I came back he said his agent, Gloria Loomis, was going so represent me, and she said, "This is a good book, this is good literature, and we're going to do something." And I've never been happier.

**TAD:** Where did you get the idea for Easy Rawlins?

**MOSLEY:** Oh, it came from writing like so many ideas. The way I write is I think you have a guy and the guy is going to the door and is about to open the door. He doesn't know what's on the other side of that door and neither do I. That's the way I write. When the door's opened, kind of magically we both see something at the same moment and I write it down. I was writing a short story about Mouse but from a first person point of view. It started out: His name was Raymond but we called him Mouse because he was small and had sharp features. It goes on and on explaining Mouse, and by page four, Mouse looks up and says, "Hey, Easy, how you doin?" and he was talking to my narrator and that's where he started. So Easy started from his relationship, his feeling for this guy Mouse.

**TAD:** Why did you decide to set the books back in time?

**MOSLEY:** It's a migration only rather than through space it's through time. The first book, *Gone Fishin'*, happens in 1939. Also it just turns out to be important because the books are really about Black life in Los Angeles, how the people got there, what they were up to. The big influx, not only for Black people but for everyone, was right after WW II. Then there are all these important events since WW II, contemporary, historical events which Black people have been edited out of. I'm talking about, for instance, in *A Red Death*, the juxtaposition of the lives of Black people and the lives of those people who were destroyed by McCarthy. So there's all this important history. Because real history, it seems to me, is held in literature not in history books; people simply don't read history books. The history as it appears in novels is always flawed but emotionally true.

**TAD:** What is this progression in time designed to do?

**MOSLEY:** One reason is to go through these moments of history of Black people. Then another is the moments of history of Los Angeles itself; and then America, like with the McCarthy period. I love the mystery genre, I really do, and that's the reason that I was able to work in it, and the genre itself is in flux, it's changing. It's worthwhile to take a look at it from an intellectual or scholarly point of view. The original characters in "hard-boiled detective" fiction were a kind of spirit, the sad spirit of Western humanity looking at how low we've come, where we are and what kind of moral and ethical world we live in. The characters were ageless and completely unanchored: no mother, no father, no sisters or brothers, no children, no property, no job. All they had was their moral life. In a way, it's beautiful and most beautiful in a book like *The Maltese Falcon* and also in the series of books by Dashiell Hammett on the Continental Op because there's no progression; there's just all this terrible, insane world. But as the genre developed, it was done to death; Hammett did it, Chandler did it, Macdonald did it. I think that there's really not much left to do. What else is Sam Spade going to do? He's static. What I'm doing with Easy, I'm making him get older and older, so the world around is changing. His mind, to some degree, is staying the same, and to some degree, aging, and his body is getting older, his friends are dying. He's much more of an everyman in that case rather than an overman which is the way I see Sam Spade or Marlowe.

**TAD:** Obviously you don't see much distinction between what we would describe as genre or crime fiction and straight fiction or literature.

**MOSLEY:** No, I don't see any difference in it. Of course, in the genre there are certain kinds of things that you have to do, but it's the same in a coming-of-age novel, somebody has to come of age. So you have to follow the conventions. Good fiction is in the sentence and in the character and in the heart of the writer. If the writer is committed to and in love with what he or she is doing, then that's good fiction.

**TAD:** Let's talk a little bit about some of the individual books. *Devil in a Blue Dress* was your first. What did you want to do with that?

**MOSLEY:** It's very interesting. The subtext of it is jazz language. The period of the book was a time of incredible hope. All of these very poor people from the Deep South, had left the South, which was even worse than the war, and had come to LA. This was a time of absolute possibility. We were going to make it. But there were built-in problems. There was the racism of the world around them and the limitations in themselves that they were carrying with them. That's how I went with Easy. I wanted to talk about him as this incredible, complex psyche who comes out of the Deep South into LA with all of these hopes and aspirations and what he can and cannot do for both external and internal reasons. Those were the dynamics I was talking about.

**TAD:** One of the early Chester Himes novels is about working in a war plant and it deals with thwarted aspirations.

**MOSLEY:** But that is very different from my characters. One of the things about Richard Wright, James Baldwin, Chester Himes, all of the characters at the end of their novels end up in Paris. Easy is not the kind of guy who would end up in Paris. He wouldn't know how to end up in Paris. So he does make it here in America. But how he makes it is flawed and scarred. I mean he gets money, he buys property, but he pays for it. It's such a complex thing that I can't break it down to any kind of social, political, or racial level. If you push against life, if you try to make it in life, then you create even more tragedy. It's not that you don't make it, it's that you realize that getting there wasn't what you thought it would be. And that really comes out of the *noir* genre, that whole idea of you can't really get what you want.

**TAD:** What do you want to explore in *A Red Death*?

**MOSLEY:** *A Red Death* has several things going on. One is the concept of friendship in this modern, civilized world. Easy finds himself working for the IRS and the FBI, and he hates them and they hate him. The other thing is, of course, the McCarthy period itself. Most Black people were poor and working-class and had nothing to do with Communist organizers. They were Black already. You don't need to be on a blacklist if you're Black. I just want to make that connection between the oppression of people.

**TAD:** You also talk about the church or a church.

**MOSLEY:** The church is a very important part of the Black community. It's different than a middle-class church where you go there on Sunday and you're part of the church but it's not really the heartbeat of the community; it's maybe like the conscience or something behind you whispering "Don't do that. Don't do that." But the Black church in the Black community is the heart of your life—everything goes on there. When I went back to Victory Baptist Day School, which I modeled my church after, they showed me an apartment building and said, "This is where all the elderly ladies go for the church wing, when they get too old to work and pay their rent." It wasn't like bragging or anything. It was this is what we do for the young people and this is what we do for the old people. Of course, whenever you have that much emotional weight on an institution you have some amount of corruption and some problems. So I just wanted to talk about that.

**TAD:** There is a dense texture to the social fabric of the novel.

**MOSLEY:** Yes, the book portrays a kind of life that doesn't exist in literature as a rule. Certainly most white people don't know it and therefore can't really write about it. One of the problems when starting to write about Black people is that it's very hard for those outside to understand our life because the way the media deals with us: we're drug addicts, we're welfare people. So when I sent out my book, *Gone Fishin'*, which is like a lot of other Black novels—it's not a mystery particularly—publishers were concerned about who would read this book. The book is about two young Black men in the Deep South following some kind of quest. The publishers weren't interested in this. It wasn't political; it wasn't about women; it didn't really work for an external audience. So what I was able to do in the mystery was to pull people in who are interested in the genre and still talk about the lives of Black people.

**TAD:** Let's talk about *White Butterfly*.

**MOSLEY:** I think all novels are failures. This is what I honestly believe: that a novel is an impossible art form. It's too large to attain perfection so what it has to do is have an intention and how close it gets to that intention is how good you think the book is, which is one of the reasons that people like crime books because you can always have a mystery and have the mystery solved. So you get a sense of resolution at the end of the book even though the book itself may not have been completely successful. In *White Butterfly* I was trying to talk about the relations between Black men and Black women and then have some kind of reflection on men and women in general and I completely failed, I think. However, in trying to do that, I brought out a lot about the relations between men and women. Easy's relationship with his wife, Mouse's relationship to women, women's relationships to him, and so on. The whole book is just men and women all over the place dealing with each other on all kinds of different levels. Easy gets older and as Los Angeles begins to change, he necessarily becomes more involved with the white community through his property investments, his motels. As he gets more involved, he becomes more aware of his limitations.

**TAD:** You mean limitations placed on him by the social world.

**MOSLEY:** Right. In this new book I'm working on, *Black Betty*, it's the same thing. Easy is more and more outside of his own world and also he tries to distance himself from his life. He's just not very happy with what he is doing.

Easy likes to do favors for people because he feels responsible, but he wants to be respected and he wants to be above board. He doesn't want to be like Mouse. He doesn't want to even be with Mouse. He loves Mouse because Mouse has saved his life too many times for him not to. He doesn't identify himself with that world of Mouse but the world itself won't let him go. So it's not only outside oppression from the world but inside he is really held back. The same thing happens with him and his wife, Regina. He was raised in a world where you don't tell people what you have. You don't let people know things and just because she's your wife doesn't mean you've got to open up. She had a hard life, too. Maybe she's going to take away what you got.

**TAD:** In *White Butterfly* your opening lines are about a man who is "rage-colored," and I thought about anger and I wondered if you had the recent LA riots and Rodney King in the back of your mind.

**MOSLEY:** When people start talking about the riots it's like this is the first thing that happened. The issue is the violence that happened to Rodney King but it's not particular to Rodney King. It happens every day in every city. You can be sure that there's some Black man or not-white man or it may be a white man too, who has come from poverty, being beat to death in some back alley by some cop who doesn't like him or by some cop who thinks he's doing the right thing which is even worse. That's the violence, that's the cost. Someone talks about how the riot costs us a hundred million dollars, think of the cost of that implosive violence happening every day to people, think of what happens to that guy who gets the shit kicked out of him in some back alley—sixty to seventy of them every day—that violence has to come back somehow. It's not like it just happens and it goes away. It's not like you can kick the shit out of somebody and then they just forget it and go back to their lives.

**TAD:** Americans measure the cost in terms of property rather than human suffering.

**MOSLEY:** Right. Exactly. There's been no understanding of it. None whatsoever as far as I'm concerned. People talk about Rodney King but it's Rodney King and the thousands of others like him. Everybody Black knows that you're always on the edge of this happening to you. It's the truth and it's frightening and you better not say what you think. When I'm talking about *White Butterfly*, Easy always remembers this: Don't say what you think, don't even let it show because if you do you're in trouble.

**TAD:** So Easy is a reluctant detective who doesn't want to get involved.

**MOSLEY:** Right, he doesn't want to. He's an intelligent man and he has a philosophical bent and so he realizes in *White Butterfly* even after he refused to cooperate with the police that then when a white girl gets killed, he has to become involved. So he recognizes that he, unwillingly, has become part of the racist structure.

**TAD:** Except as he says, the one thing he won't do is run down a Black man for the law.

**MOSLEY:** Right, as a rule. But he will do it and has done it. It's always that back and forth thing. This is so much more interesting and I think it's so much more what we need to do in fiction because I hate setting up heroes that we really can't live by. You know, real people make mistakes, have flaws, do the wrong thing, and you have to be able to deal with that.

**TAD:** Why did you have him get married?

**MOSLEY:** Because people get married, that's why. It's so totally the right answer for me. I just sat down and started writing the book and he was married. The genre has to develop. That *noir* character, who used to be outside of our lives is now inside of our lives. So instead of looking at him from (to use the title of your magazine) your armchair, I want you involved. I want Easy to be like everybody else. He's not the smartest guy in the world; Jackson Blue is the smartest guy in that world. He's not the toughest guy in the world; Mouse is the toughest guy in that world. But he's a regular guy, maybe a little better, maybe a little stronger, maybe a little smarter but he's a regular guy. He has children, he has a wife, that's the way life is. I'm not being critical of Ross Macdonald, Chandler, or Hammett, because they had a different project than mine but in today's world to write about a guy who doesn't have any responsibility or a woman who doesn't have any responsibility and so therefore can just make her decisions unhampered is a fantasy and it's a little too light for me. I don't particularly want to read it.

**TAD:** Who have you read both in crime fiction and in regular fiction that's had an influence on you?

**MOSLEY:** In crime fiction, I've read lots and lots of people. Charles Willeford, I just adore. Every one of his books is so deeply flawed plot-wise, but it matters nothing to me because he's such a wonderful writer. I was reading one of his books the other day about some old guy and his wife; he was seventy-two but looked older and she was sixty-three and looked older than him. It was so funny; just the way he wrote it. My God, this guy is fantastic! Hoke Mosley is a real guy. It's so right. I've read everybody. Gregory Mcdonald—I've read all the Fletch books, I thought they were wonderful. Parker, of course. Vachss, whom I adore because I think that he is so deeply committed to what he believes in. I feel the heart coming through it and I compare him to Dickens. Rex Stout. I've read almost everything Simenon ever wrote. The people I love for writing are the French: Malraux, Camus, Gide, for just the style of writing; it is almost the heart of fiction for me. And then the older guys: Proust; and tons of Black poets: Gwendolyn Brooks, Derek Walcott, Amiri Baraka. It doesn't matter who writes it, no matter their sex or their race or what period of time they lived in. I mean when you read Shakespeare, it's still alive today. It's amazing what a wonderful writer he was or whoever wrote that stuff.

**TAD:** You've been treated very well by the critics. How do you respond to critics?

**MOSLEY:** When they treat me well? I love them. I have been treated very well in two ways. Number one, I've been reviewed a lot therefore a lot people know my name, whether it's good or bad. I've also gotten a lot of very good reviews and I'm very happy about that. I try really hard to write well; I think I know my limitations. I'm a new writer, really. I'm not young anymore but I'm a new writer. There's a lot more that I could do a lot better and so the fact that people overlook flaws to see what's good about my fiction, I'm very happy about. I don't mind people criticizing, but it doesn't seem worthwhile to me to trash anybody in public no matter how successful they are. But I've been very happy about the criticism.

**TAD:** President Clinton has been very excited about your books. Any comments or responses?

**MOSLEY:** Well, I'm very happy about Clinton because of what he's done. The way I see Clinton is that he is reaching out for people who have been completely ignored before by the Oval Office. I'm really happy he likes my books, and I believe he does. But the thing that I'm even happier about is the fact that he would even say it. Partially for me, of course, because it's good for my publicity, and partially because Black people are out here, writing and doing work and trying really hard and changing the country in so many ways and people just ignore it. So I'm really very happy about what he's doing and I feel included in a way in the world. He recognizes that here's a Black writer in America doing some important work. That's certainly his position in the world and I'm very pleased, doubly pleased.

**TAD:** Let's talk a little bit about *Black Betty* and then what you have on the docket for the next couple of novels.

**MOSLEY:** *Black Betty* happens in '61. It starts off in a dream and stays in a nightmare. It's a book basically about the violence between Black men. The book talks about the dark side of hope. It's '61 and Kennedy's in office and Martin Luther King is marching down South and all of a sudden all of that unconscious Black anger and rage is concentrated. Easy is sitting there, a part of this world of bright hope, but feeling like he is the dark, shadowy underside of that hope. He's trying to work his way out of it. There's his belief that "If I can just save one person's life." But the only thing he can do is take somebody's life, he can't really give life. He comes to all these realizations throughout the book. I'm taking a chance with this book because I'm doing a lot of new things for me like having more than one mystery going on as once. Easy has children and he lives kind of far away from his basic native community.

**TAD:** What about Easy's children?

**MOSLEY:** They live in a house he rents, him and Jesus and Feather. Jesus is going to junior high school and everybody is happy. It starts off in a dream. In 1956, after *White Butterfly* was over, Mouse got into an altercation. Somebody said something he didn't like and he killed him. He was captured and sent to prison. So the book starts off with this dream of Easy remembering the death and how senseless it was and how horrible it was. Mouse gets out of jail and he's looking for revenge while Easy is looking for Black Betty. He has to keep Mouse from getting revenge and he has to find Black Betty and both of them are very difficult.

**TAD:** It sounds like Easy is back to juggling.

**MOSLEY:** I remember a long time ago I read a story about a woman who was on a telephone which had call waiting. She was one of three women who were good friends. One of the other women was on the phone telling her how the third woman was having an affair with her husband and this woman did not know if she was angrier at her husband or at her friend for this betrayal. On the other line there is this guy from Chile who is being kicked out of the country, but if he went back to Chile he's going to be killed because of his political beliefs and she was trying to help him. In the meanwhile, she was making dinner and the children are having some kind of discussion, which she is a part of trying to keep them on the right track; and her husband is coming home. So she's doing five things at once. I said, you know, this is really a woman's way of seeing the world because men are very linear, they go to work and they start laying bricks, not all men are like this but most male work is like that. But women have to deal with all kinds of things all at once and I started realizing that this is also true for poor people. You're always struggling to survive. If you're doing one thing and you happen to see something else which you *know* is important you've got to include it. So that's what I was trying to do with Easy, with what I call a feminine sensibility. I was thinking about that in writing this book. Everybody's in this book. Easy is trying to weave his path through it in order to get out of the nightmare, but I don't think he's successful. I promise he'll be happier in future books.

**TAD:** After *Black Betty*, you've got two more books lined up.

**MOSLEY:** Well, actually I have three. The next book is *RL's Dream*.

**TAD:** It's about Robert Johnson.

**MOSLEY:** Yeah, which I'm very excited about. I believe that it's some of the best writing that I've ever done. It's a blues novel and doesn't have anything to do with mystery or anything like that except maybe the mystery of life as Vachss says. Then I have two more Easy books. One I'm very, very excited about. It's great. I finished the first draft of *Black Betty* a few days ago, and I'm about to go back into it, but the thing that I love is that I've already planned the first chapter of *A Little Yellow Dog*, which is the next Easy book. It's going to be a love story, which I had never thought of doing before and I'm really very pleased with that. Then I'm writing a book called *Bad Boy Bobby Brown* which is going to be my homage to Malcolm X.

**TAD:** And these are going to continue to move forward in time?

**MOSLEY:** Yeah, definitely, '63 will be *A Little Yellow Dog*, and '65 will be *Bad Boy Bobby Brown*, and then I'm going to have to have something about the summer of love.

**TAD:** It's plenty to keep you busy for the next several years.

**MOSLEY:** Oh, yeah, it's so much fun to do. I love writing about Easy. I really do think along with Jerome Charyn that detective fiction is very important in this contemporary world. It really helps people to think and understand and open up. Crime fiction is very compelling to people; they want to know what happened, they want to know what happens next, they want to know why and they want to feel some sense of resolution.

**TAD:** Because of your success, you're breaking new ground as a Black crime writer. How do you feel about that?

**MOSLEY:** I feel comfortable, to tell you the truth, with myself which is a nice place to be in. I don't think that I'm the last word. I'm the first one who could give you a whole bunch of criticism of my work; what it does and what it doesn't do. One of the things that I understand, like understanding Easy, I can't do everything. I think that I have a good ear for Black language, not slang because slang is something that lasts for about six months and is gone. Black dialect has been with us forever. I feel like I'm doing something that's good and I guess important. It's important for me and my sense is that it's important for a lot of Black people in America and also a lot of white people who are interested in hearing and thinking and opening their minds to different things. So I guess the answer is that I feel comfortable with it.

**TAD:** You're opening up a whole view of a Black community that largely has not been accessible in large measure before.

**MOSLEY:** My favorite novelists are Charles Dickens and Mark Twain and the reason is they are completely open to the reader and that's really the thing I want to be. I'm not going to shirk from saying what I think my character is or what I think my character's world is like, but I want to write fiction that's really embracing, that will bring in people and people will want to read it. Like E. M. Forster said in his book, *Aspects of the Novel*, the main thing about a novel is the story and the story is what happens next. I want my readers to say, "Oh, wow, and then what?" and I want them to turn the page because that's what is most important about writing. It just so happens that because I'm writing about Black characters and Black people, the thing that I'm most interested in, that they'll be wondering what happens next in these Black lives, whether it's a white reader or whether it's the president, or some Black person who really knows this life and is happy to read about it.

**TAD:** Engaging your readers is very important to you.

**MOSLEY:** I met a guy in LA (I'll never forget this) and he came to me and said, "I read your first book and I'm going to read the next, too, because I want to figure out why Easy's such a jerk!" His personal thing about what Easy did with a woman was unacceptable to him. That's real! Easy is a real character for this guy! It's very funny, but I really like that. My characters, I hope, are real enough for people to respond to. My dream is to write the series and have it treated as one of those series in crime fiction which mean something. I would love to do that.

# Walter Mosley's Secret Stories:
# A Ride with a Mystery Writer
# Who Evokes the Uncliché d

## Lynell George/1994

From the *Los Angeles Times Magazine*, 22 May 1994: 14–17. © *Los Angeles Times.*
Reprinted by permission.

Midafternoon, and we are sailing. The wide span of Century Boulevard seems vast in its possibilities, a seductive expanse with room to roam or expand. At quick glimpse, it is sparkling, but a brief pause at a light reveals something quite different—a poorly patched facade, a wall of chain link encircling nothing, rubble from some long-lost decade left to rot or rust.

"Look at these giant streets!" Walter Mosley rides jump seat, taking in L.A. the way many Angelenos do, at 45-miles-per, the window raised, studying the blur of color and shapes skidding outside the windshield. We make a left onto Central Avenue, slowing enough to see features on figures sitting in Will Rogers Park. Picnics. A ballgame. Families, black and brown, taking advantage of the sun, the air carrying a cool mist that, with imagination, could conjure the nearby ocean. "These houses are nice—they're little, tiny," he says. "A lot of people come here and say: 'When are we gonna get to the bad community?'" The answer comes in a voice colored the softest shade of irony: "You're in it, brother."

At the tip of 76th Place and Central slumps the shell of a broken and singed mini-mall threatening complete collapse. The All-American Liquor Junior Market's marquee still advertises "Hot dogs $2.50," as if the building is only momentarily darkened, the owner under the weather or off on a brief vacation. And there are survivors—fish markets, a shoeshine parlor-cum-barbershop, a senior citizen center, the Universal Missionary Baptist Church, all grouped around empty lots strewn with trash and weeds.

Mosley grew up here, and he's been mining these broad streets, and their

**29**

smaller side arteries, for stories for nearly half a dozen years. But at first, he doesn't seem to register the damaged terrain. Or doesn't speak about it. He's busier reconstructing the past, letting the vacant lots spark a fragment of a memory, reading the symbols in piles of wood and iron.

"When I was a kid along [this stretch of Central], there was a White Front, a hardware store, a liquor store, little markets and bars, a shoe store, television repair shops, a whole economic community," he recalls, his voice moving with a bit of a rhythmic lilt. In moments, he erects filling stations in empty lots, replaces the nuclear-age post office with the old Goodyear plant and a parking lot full of gleaming tail fins.

Mosley's measure of fame comes from the detective stories he's astutely woven from that vanished place. His mysteries are period works, spanning 1948–1961 on these streets—Denker and Slauson and hot-lit Central Avenue—where dreams and hard work intersect. And Ezekiel (Easy) Rawlins, his reluctant private eye, navigates the hurdles of this world—the Police Department, the subtleties of discrimination, unabashed racism—with both feet planted firmly on the sidewalks banking these wide boulevards. A protagonist acutely sensitive to the mercurial nature of his world, Easy's not quite a social commentator, nor an island of a private eye like Philip Marlowe. Instead, he's at the center, struggling, hoping to make it through one day into the next.

Easy Rawlins is about to appear on film, played by Denzel Washington, as Carl Franklin (*One False Move*) directs *Devil in a Blue Dress*. *Devil* (1990) and Mosley's third book, *White Butterfly* (1992), were nominated for Edgar awards; *Butterfly* and his second, *A Red Death* (1991), were nominated for Golden Dagger awards (*Butterfly* won). President Bill Clinton has proclaimed Mosley his favorite mystery writer, and his works—which sell well but have not hit the bestseller charts—pop up on college reading lists with increasing frequency, surrounded by the works of Chester Himes, Richard Wright, and Ralph Ellison, his most frequently cited literary forebears. The latest Rawlins installment, *Black Betty*, set at the dawn of the '60s, four years before Watts blew, is due next month.

L.A. itself, you could say, comes to Mosley in a dream. He lives in Greenwich Village in New York, estranged from this city for more than a decade—L.A. was a claustrophobic web of the too-familiar and the unattainable, and he had to escape—but he's never stopped feeling the pull of the city's possibilities. It's a somewhat idealized L.A. that Mosley creates in his books, patterned after the close, culturally diverse South Los Angeles community of his youth, not the alienating vastness he felt navigating through the rest of the city. He re-creates that early community, those connections, those voices, with memory, history, and the grand stories of his late father, Leroy Mosley. The vision of Los Angeles that persists in his writing is a clever variation on the one he remembers but is worlds apart from the one he confronts on brief visits. Though the city inhabits his heart and head, "I don't get it from L.A.," he says. "I get it from how I stand in relation to L.A."

Writing about Easy, he says, "is in a way reclaiming experience." And in recasting the past, Mosley also lends a sense of clarity to the present—and possibly the future.

It is quintessential Raymond Chandler: "I went on out and Amos had the Caddy there waiting," Chandler's detective Philip Marlowe observes in *The Long Goodbye*. "He drove me back to Hollywood. I offered him a buck but he wouldn't take it. I offered to buy him the poems of T. S. Eliot. He said he already had them."

Amos, Chandler's "middle-aged colored chauffeur," is a shadow figure whom Walter Mosley would eagerly give flesh and form. With lyric grace, Mosley has evoked many of those who passed through in silence, subtly sketching faces and histories for figures that have appeared as ghosts in this genre.

It's 1948 when Easy Rawlins, in Mosley's first installment, is laid off from his aerospace job in Santa Monica. World War II had created a humming assembly line of defense-industry jobs that helped fuel a mass migration west to fill them. But when an exhausted Easy refuses to put in a little overtime after a particularly hard shift, his high-strung boss fires him, leaving Easy in a spot, unsure of how he'll raise his $64 mortgage payment. As he mulls it over in a neighborhood bar owned by an ex-boxer named Joppy, his answer sidles up to him: DeWitt Albright, a white man in a flashing white suit glaringly out of place in these environs, who knows a little too much about Easy's private affairs but offers him fast money to a find a white woman who "has a predilection for the company of Negroes." It's Easy's chance out.

"Working for Joppy's friend was the only way I saw to keep my house. But there was something wrong, I could feel it in my fingertips. DeWitt Albright made me uneasy. . . . I was unhappy about going to meet Mr. Albright because I wasn't used to going into white communities like Santa Monica to conduct business," says Easy, "but the idea that I'd give him the information he wanted, and that he'd give me enough money to pay the next month's mortgage, made me happy. I was dreaming about the day I'd be able to buy more houses, maybe even a duplex."

Easy is the tangible, full-coverage insurance, the safety net, for his clients, Mosley explains. "The idea about Easy is, who will be there for you when you really need it? And this is not whether you need $10, this is like when you come running and somebody's after you. Easy is not the kind of guy who figures, 'Well if I do this, I'll get killed.' He says: 'I'll do this, and I might get killed but I'm going to do it anyway, because this is where you have to stand up.'"

When Mosley speaks of Easy, it's as if he's relating the escapades of an irascible cousin or the brother with the gold tooth who always gets the barber chair with the best light—a figure he knows inside and out. In the stories, Easy emerges as the sort of black male figure that so much of popular culture has collectively erased from public consciousness or has yet to find a place for at the dinner table. There is a familiarity about him, a human softness that despite the unrelenting violence of his life allows him to be sickened by the sight of a corpse or to open his heart and arms to children, whom he takes in like strays. There are friends to answer to, comeuppance to be paid. He, unlike Chandler's Marlowe, is irrevocably tied to his world, his community, the landscape. "He has a lot of commitments in the world. These people are people he knows and he's responsible for. I don't understand how somebody like Marlowe could live," says Mosley. "He had no friends, no lovers really. No children, no parents, no job. I mean nothing."

Easy's universality, his human side, appealed to Jesse Beaton, who is producing the film version of *Devil in a Blue Dress* with Gary Goetzman; Jonathan Demme and Ed Saxon are executive producers. Browsing at a West Hollywood bookstore, Beaton, who was eager to find another project to tackle after *One False Move*, pulled the book from the mystery shelves a few years back. She was taken by it for a couple of reasons. "There's so little documentation of that period in L.A. We know a lot about Harlem, what a rich, lively, vital world it was. Unfortunately, so much of that [L.A.] world is physically lost. Burned in fires, riots, rezoned, crashed down, empty lots. Very little of Central Avenue remains. The Dunbar [Hotel] is there, but what was surrounding it is not." On a personal level, she emphasizes, "I was about to lose my house. I thought, in this world we live in, people who feel that they would never have anything in common with someone like Easy Rawlins do. We all are trying to hold on to that bit of the American dream. I felt that whoever you were, you would understand this. I lost my house," she says with a chuckle, "but Easy kept his."

Easy Rawlins has friends to spare, in more than one city. "He sort of represents that mass movement out of the South and into L.A. during the war," says David Fine, editor of the anthology *Los Angeles in Fiction* and professor of English at Cal State Long Beach. "Watts is filled with displaced Southerners. There is this sense in his novels of people living on the edge, being uprooted and displaced. I don't know anybody who writes about South-Central that way. He's got a real sense of life lived exposed, raw, right on the edge of existence."

What makes Mosley's work sound authentic to many black readers' ears is that he never uses the shorthand "South-Central" in his writings. He steers clear of sweeping generalizations, working to create an image so clear one can see its pores or recognize the voice in the dark. Many a behatted church lady will be happy to tell you that before the '70s, "L.A. Negroes" lived on the east side or the west side of a city efficiently divided by Central Avenue. "It was wonderful," says Mosley's childhood friend Kirsten Childs, "to see [in Mosley's books] this place that's not a caricature and not smaller than life. Not meaner, not nicer. People live here, grow up, and die here. It was like this whole world was created as I remembered it."

Some, like Richard Yarborough, associate professor of English and Afro-American studies at UCLA, compare Mosley's simple yet vivid landscapes to those of filmmaker Charles Burnett, who directed *To Sleep with Anger* and *Killer of Sheep*, both about black life in Los Angeles. Their manner of revealing the unclichéd complexities of life in black L.A. is often elegant, even in its grittiness. Yarborough sees the most striking similarities in the way Burnett's and Mosley's work shows big-city life in the postwar decades merging with the superstitions and pace of the South. And Mosley, he says, "captures the oral tradition right in the movement from the one site where it grew up to the other where it is changing. Easy can speak quote-unquote, conventional English, or he can speak black English. In *A Red Death*, he is reading about Roman history, yet he has Army experience and is part of the street."

Easy finds his surest footing as a black everyman—someone's father, brother, cousin, lover—with bills to pay, marital problems, feuding friends, and an insatiable lust for a life that is seldom anything less than hard. He's not a formal detective with a license, he's a "utility man" who does favors; in his part of town, he knows where to go, what to ask, and how to ask it.

"I felt a secret glee when I went into a bar and ordered a beer with money someone else had paid me," Easy confides in *Devil in a Blue Dress*. "I'd ask the bartender his name and talk about anything, but really, behind my friendly talk, I was working to find something. Nobody knew what I was up to, and that made me sort of invisible; people thought that they saw me but what they really saw was an illusion of me, something that wasn't real."

There are many who might lay claim to being Mosley's paradigm for Easy. Neighborhood cronies. Back-room prophets. It's Mosley's father who's most often cited. But, says Mosley's friend Childs, "I know that Easy is based on a lot of different people, but there is a part of Easy that is definitely Walter. This major vulnerability. There were certain things that were letting you see part of Walter's soul, part of Walter's mind."

On one level, a pretty air-tight argument can be made that Easy's progenitor, a man whose favorite color is gray, is just as elliptical as the character he so impeccably created. Even though he would furiously argue the point, he, too, could meld with the shadows—if his eyes didn't skitter about so much.

"Easy *isn't* a shadow," Mosley maintains, and so begins the dance, the teasing smile in his voice. "You know what he's thinking, doing. . . ."

"But the people in his life don't."

"True."

"So wouldn't that make him a shadow?"

"Well . . . not exactly."

The debate is interspersed with a running commentary as we drive through vaguely familiar haunts, but if the conversation veers too close to the territory Mosley chooses not to discuss, he deflects questions with veils of jokes and riddles and anecdotes or turns inquiries inside out. The entire production is performed always with the most elated version of his smile, fully revealing a generous gap separating his front teeth. Shifting characters, maybe slipping into the voice of Easy's best friend Mouse, or giving voice to an anonymous man standing on the corner, Mosley's a mimic at the ready with quick, and many times acerbic, remarks.

"In the '40s, there was a time of great hope in Los Angeles," he says, his eyes lit with the momentum of a story. "It was a big place, it was a countrified place. It was a place where if there was a job, the job was digging ditches, it wasn't somebody saying: 'We're looking for colored people or Japanese people [to dig] ditches.' It was, 'We're looking for *people* to dig ditches.' So no matter what color you were, you were working there. And if you were a white man and said: 'I'm not working next to that niggah,' they'd say, 'Well, get outta here, because I got twenty niggahs working here and I need to dig my ditches.' There was hope and opportunity. And as L.A. began to redefine that hope, that possibility, the dream lost a lot of its glitter. Even though a lot of the dream came true—a lot of us who came through that time became lawyers and doctors—still, a lot of us are down in the boarded-up 'hood.'"

At once warm and veiled, there is the public Mosley: the raconteur, the debater, the banterer, the charmer, the wild and wide-eyed eight-year-old; there is a more contained Mosley: the thinker, the analyst, the inquisitor. He's as obsessed with the intricacies of *Married with Children* as by the stories of his orphan father's vagabond youth in Louisiana and Texas. He's a conundrum who pulls from Louis Armstrong and folk singer Mary Mc-Caslin with equal fervor and fascination.

"There is kind of an elusiveness to his soul," says Frederic Tuten, who was Mosley's writing instructor and is now his best friend. "I can't presume to say that I know Walter." This understanding seems only to deepen their connection. "We both have this kind of strange part of us that didn't grow up, so the world is always full of surprises. It's as if the two of us have been condemned to solitary confinement, and when we're let out, we are sort of amazed by what we see." What passes in Mosley's view this particular afternoon is not the often-resurrected image of a bombed-out war zone, although these communities and their collections of wide boulevards and tree-lined streets are struggling with their wounds.

"It's just a community of scarring," says Mosley. "It started in '65 and [then] just got more and more." We roll along, verbally sifting the remains, wondering about the cause of the damage: urban unrest of '65 or '92? Maybe a neighborhood fire or the earthquake or just plain old garden-variety urban blight?

"There's great wealth in the city, but there is a kind of disintegration going on," he says, still watching, recording the image, possibly filing it away. He readjusts himself in the seat. "You have to understand the character of these people from the inside, not from the outside. I don't know who this fellow is," he says, gesturing toward a stout man in a three-piece suit, glasses, Bible in hand, his black hair powdered with patches of silver. "He's not walking like he's nervous, you know what I mean?"

Mosley believes, as do many African-American educators and pundits, that what rests at the core of this community's unraveling has less to do with absence of monetary riches than it does with historical amnesia. "An identity has been misplaced, and that's one of the things that I'm a very small part of. Everything that happens to black people in America is not talked about. So we lose it. It's not written down." Countering this loss within popular fiction, Mosley suggests, is like chasing a remedy with that proverbial spoonful of sugar. "It's an adventure," he says with a coy laugh, "because most of the things that Easy does are kinda fun."

On this stretch of road, the juxtapositions are jarring—the crumbling detritus of some once-fetching 1940 storefront squats next to a circa-1980 convenience structure of glass and concrete. The ragtag collection plays tricks with time and place.

These darkened doorways inspire brighter memories. "Even though most of those stores were owned by white people, at least there were stores in the community where people could go shopping, where people could get jobs. There was a relationship developing with the community, and that's really what's gone. And that, I think, is analogous to a physical reflection, in a negative sense, [to] the hope that is also gone from the community." His voice goes soft, loses speed. "But a lot of the people are the same. They're still here."

And 76th Place itself pulses on. For ten years, the Mosleys lived here, near Central, in a white wood-frame house edged in green, with a small front porch that provided a perfect stage for stories. Today, it's a street of single-family dwellings, pastel duplexes, rose bushes, birds of paradise exploding askew. A woman, on her knees, polishes the knob of her iron screen door while children, mostly Latino, command the center of the street with balls and bikes.

Near the corner, a large wood-frame court of bungalows painted crisp white, its property line marked off by a tall iron fence, sparks something. Mosley leans forward in his seat to frame the picture better. "Right here is the court—Poinsettia Court—they're all over L.A.," he says, finger jabbing at the glass. "That's where I imagined Easy living."

It all comes back in a flood. An easy smile moves across his sand-colored face and large, sad eyes.

"My father raised me in this neighborhood and he had high hopes for me. It wasn't: 'Walter can get a job at the garage, maybe, if he's lucky.' He was saying, 'My son is going to make it, 'cause I'm going to make something out of my son,' which he did."

What might be absent physically is made up for by what has failed to dissipate spiritually, Mosley notes. "This community is still really kind of wonderful because when you really look directly at people, people are kind of smiling a lot and telling each other stories. [But] it's kind of a funny [feeling]. It's not like what I remember physically, but then again, it *is* what I remember physically."

The unfolding scene plays tricks with one's memory. With the notion of memory itself. Vaguely familiar backdrops, partly familiar players. This lively tree-banked street next to Central Avenue, where life persists despite its new ghost-town feel. Beauty parlors specializing in a "Texas press and curl" and soul food cafes now coexist with *discotecas* and *mariscos* and taco stands. And behind it all, lending a somewhat surreal backdrop, the downtown skyline hovers like Oz.

Down the block a little farther, Mosley points out a house stripped, he says, of its former character. His full lips return to a gentle pout. "That's my house right there, but it's not the same anymore."

This little strip of small homes, duplexes, and bungalow courts was, Mosley believes, much more of a neighborhood than could be found elsewhere in the basin. He remembers a community that often disregarded color, religion, and ethnicity, possibly important for a child whose father was black and whose mother was white and also Jewish. He grew up relating the struggles of his black forebears to those of his mother's Eastern European lineage. He speaks of fleeting crushes on the Mexican girls who lived nearby and was fascinated by them because they were "so Catholic." This community that "got along" was perhaps a built-in comfort zone for Mosley.

"Everybody knew one another. People are still living there who lived there when I was a little kid, and that's not the way you think of L.A. The *real* Los Angeles, the Los Angeles I lived in, there was no Hollywood. One thing," says Mosley, his voice drifting like a whisper, "even though you couldn't find a way out, there was a great sense of possibility."

Ella Mosley kept a sentinel's watch on her only child. She and her husband met at a local school (she was an elementary school clerk, he was a plant manager), and Walter Ellis Mosley was born in 1952. "I always worried about him, and you don't want to be that way, but you can't help it," she says. "Walter wanted to walk down the street one time to the store, he was six maybe, he had never done that before. There was nothing that could have happened to him, so we let him, but I'm walking on the other side, trying to keep out of sight."

About the time Walter was ready for junior high, the family moved across town to a comfortable four-plex just off the western stretch of Pico, a new retreat that Leroy Mosley, who collected property as others do stamps, made a hideaway by planting an exotic array of vegetables, fruits, and flowers.

Drifting back to his adolescent years, Mosley recalls most clearly the ache at the pit of his lungs from the air that so often smudged the skies ocher. He remembers feeling trapped within the flat, hot vastness.

He read voraciously. "I'm not sure that it was traveling through books. I love to read. I was reading Dickens, Hesse, that kinda brooding youth stuff. I was reading whatever I got introduced to in school that I liked, and stuff my parents had just read. My first favorite book was *Treasure Island."*

His intake later increased to include a steady diet of comic books and paperback sci-fi. Mysteries didn't enter into the picture until his twenties, and the only writing he was flirting with at the time didn't venture further than poetry.

"I was very unhappy," he says. "It seems to me like I wanted something, but the something was intangible; I didn't know how to get it. In L.A., that big middle portion of L.A., people don't walk on the streets, people don't come from the same background or the same area, so your connection with people is very tenuous at best." Once out of his little neighborhood, the connection was gone.

He cut it completely when he decided to attend Goddard, a "radical" arts college in Vermont. "I thought I really had to go someplace where people will be like me. Things that I will say, they will understand." But upon his arrival, Mosley wasn't sure he understood them. "They had a large black population . . . and they were all living in the same dorm, except me. It wasn't that the school wanted them to live there, it was the decision on their part. I thought, 'I'm going to search out a ghetto to live in? Nuh uh.'"

He drifted from one campus to another and from one set of adventures to still others without a goal, with not even the essence of direction. "I think I was informed by like the Kerouac and Ginsberg sensibility, and also by L.A. and the hippie movement," he explains. And what was he studying? Mosley pauses, then lets out an explosion that doubles as a laugh—"Who knows?"

Writing came a little later, like a storm out of nowhere. After receiving a B.A. in political science from Vermont's Johnson State College in 1977, he met Joy Kellman, a dancer-choreographer, while he was working on a Ph.D. at the University of Massachusetts at Amherst. They married in 1988. He'd shown talent as a potter and painter and some aptitude for computers. "I was sitting in a room, and I was working as a consultant programmer. It was a Saturday, and nobody else was there. I was writing programs. I got tired of it, so I started typing on the computer," he says. "I typed: 'On hot sticky days in southern Louisiana, the fire ants swarmed. . . .' I said—'Hey, this is cool. This means I could be a writer.' So I start writing."

In a few months, a manuscript, *Gone Fishin'*, under his belt, he enrolled in a graduate creative writing program at City College of New York. It was 1986. "He was writing these wonderful, beautiful stories," says Mosley's one-time instructor Tuten, author of *Tallien: A Brief Romance.* "The vividness of the characterizations, the very simple, elegant beauty of the prose. And there is a lyricism there that you don't find in much American writing today."

After Mosley had completed his instruction with Tuten and won CCNY's De Jur Award, he asked Tuten to critique a new manuscript. Excited by the power of the work, Tuten took it to his agent, who promised to sell the book—and did, six weeks later.

"He didn't give it to me with that kind of anticipation," Tuten says. Since then Mosley has weathered the blizzard of events, Tuten believes, with ego safely in check. "He's had plenty of occasions to play a big shot. He's never done it with anybody. I can't say that he's humble. He knows the value of this work, but he didn't become a writer to become famous. He didn't become a writer to become a celebrity. That happened, and I've never seen anyone else handle it so well as he."

Walter happy at last? Well, happy would seem a stretch. Contented but busy seems to sum up his demeanor, which at moments makes him appear as if he is leaning on a gilded railing of some grand balcony, watching it all unfold. Lately, his thoughts center more on the final tinkerings on his blues novel, *RL's Dream* (due next year) and testing his chops with a screenplay, his own take on the relatively nascent 'hood-film genre that he's been banging out on his laptop in his Santa Monica hotel room. With all the clamor surrounding him of late, Mosley seems to fly from vague disinterest to a quiet merriment when talk of his success rises in conversation. "He's very controlled," his mother confides later. "But being too controlled is not good. I always thought that his head would get too big, but he is just as easygoing. [He] never lets on that everything is great."

At its downtown source, Pico Boulevard, crowded with life, noisy with enterprise, serves as the vivid bridge, the wide road to the Westside. It's the bridge from Central Avenue to Mosley's teen years, the period in which he planned his grand escape.

"This is so L.A., these palm trees standing here, big wide streets, and all these completely innocuous cinder-block buildings. It seems like this place where nothing real is going on, which is why you can really write crime fiction about L.A.—because really behind all these things, there is all this weird stuff, and strange people who come from all over the place . . . and you don't know where they went after they left here.

"When you see something like this," he gestures toward the boulevard, "this isn't as real as what's in your head. In your head, you have the details," says Mosley. His gestures are careful, understated. His hands are reserved only for the most dramatic moment in the action, a crescendo. "When I was a kid, and this was before cable, black people got together and told stories. And storytelling is its own fuel. All you have to do is evoke a feeling. Sometimes it's just a word. A sentence."

However, unlike Easy, who has cast his lot with Los Angeles ("He's going to live in his neighborhood. And either he is going to get killed in that neighborhood or he's going to survive in that neighborhood"), Mosley hasn't.

"I wouldn't live in Los Angeles," he says. "The center of Los Angeles, though I am moved by it aesthetically, living in it, I remember being very kind of, I [didn't] know how to get out. There were no walls, but there was great distance."

He's tiring of questions or maybe of just coming up with serious answers to them. The eight-year-old peeks from behind the hedge, the trickster upsetting the balance, toppling the status quo. With a part-dreamy, part-devilish expression inhabiting his eyes, he takes a breather.

Roaming around his hotel-room carpet on stocking feet, he finally pauses to install himself in the love seat, to take advantage of its view of the very edge—the lazy Pacific as it curls and stretches eight stories below. He sits, legs pulled beneath him, dressed entirely, once again, in black: socks, jet shirt tucked into charcoal trousers. His calf-length cashmere coat, which he wears on the dust jacket of *White Butterfly*, and his Kangol hat (one of a pair he and his father purchased in London) are draped across the foot of the bed, suggesting that the pause is only temporary.

Over the course of the week, he's been busy with a varying collection of duties and diversions: lunch with his mother, a visit to his father's grave (he died of lung cancer late last year), a meeting with "the movie people," interviews, more pages filed away on the screenplay, and, of course, some time set aside to catch up with his favorite TV family, the Bundys on *Married with Children*. The room is cluttered with tools of his spare time: a Hilma Wolitzer novel, a copy of Ray Bradbury's *Fahrenheit 451* (for an essay he's working on), a flute, and sheet music. His laptop, folded away, rests on the room's only table. His morning writing ritual is a constant. With the jet-lag, it begins at 3:30; he quits at about 10.

"A novel, it seems to me, has to be larger than the mind of the writer," he says. The largeness of L.A., though daunting and "stultifying" to a younger Mosley, is now the precise dimension he seeks to replicate in his work. "The novel is based on a plot, and the best way to describe a plot to me is the structure of revelation. If you can hold it all within a small space, a space small enough for you to see and perceive, then you don't have the feeling of revelation, because it's too controlling. What you want is something big, where things surprise you, where things become."

He would like to avoid narrow pigeonholes or empty spokesman roles, despite the expectations of those of any hue.

"Expectations?"

"Well, you know if you're black and you make it, you should want to be helping other black people in ways that most people don't even help their family. And I think a lot of black people feel that responsibility. I know I do," he admits. "But at the same time, it can interfere with your work. People come up to you and say, 'Well, you have to write in African tones, my brother.'"

"'Well, you know, I'm writing the way I write.'"

"'But you see, your mind has been brainwashed by The Man, and you have to return to our true identity.'"

He tends to be more populist and universal in his thinking. "A good novel comes out into the world and grows as people read it. Other people, they see things, learn things, they get a little inkling of something that may make its way into something else [or in the] actions that they take in their own lives. I want black people to have a good time. I mean, I want black people to read the book and say, 'That's my language, that's my life. That's my history.' But I want white people to say, 'Boy, you know, I feel just like that!'"

Human struggle, failure, and the occasional reward of good fortune serve as the dramatic and emotional engines for much of Mosley's work. "I'm not really happy," he says, "with political writing as political writing. That kind of sociopolitical writing they do about black life—'The Black Man, blah, blah, blah, and the Black Woman, blah, blah, blah.' And then the white this and Jim Crow and all this other stuff. I mean I like mentioning it, because I think it's a part. But it's such a small part of black life."

"Politics?" I coax him toward elaboration.

"Well, politics is a big part of our life, and so is racism. But most black people are living lives, making love, raising children, listening to music, working hard, saving money, learning new skills in order to survive, watching television, telling jokes, telling stories—so much of life is that. And black life in America is really kind of a celebration. Even when people are really sad," says Mosley, eyes wide, hands painting vast landscapes, portraits, busy triptychs.

"And when they're sad, how do they celebrate it?"

The answer is sly, trademark-simple: "That's the blues."

# The Monday Interview: Walter Mosley

## Esther Oxford/1995

From *The Independent* 9 October 1995. Found at http://www.independent.co.uk/life-style/i-like-the-freeflowing-creative-chaos-you-get-from-being-black-says-the-urban-crime-writer-feted-by-white-america-i-dont-write-to-change-the-world-1576683.html (accessed 2010). By permission of *The Independent*.

The *Los Angeles Times* sees him as a preeminent spokesman for America's blacks. President Clinton is his most famous fan. The *New York Times Book Review* says he is "one of America's best mystery writers." British newspapers have referred to him as "the most important black literary figure since James Baldwin."

So what does Walter Mosley, forty-three, America's hottest black author, think of himself? "I don't feel like an idol," he says, wriggling his bum back in the chair and smiling pleasantly. "In fact, I feel kind of normal."

I want to feed him frozen date mousse and apricot sorbet to honour the occasion. That is what President Clinton gave him last time he was at the White House. But Mosley won't even accept coffee. "Let's just sit," he says, wandering from the reception of his Nottingham hotel into a draughty restaurant mall. So we do—sit—next to a veneered table.

"Clinton likes my books because they remind him of the South," he says. (Clinton has also made a point of popularising black writers: it was not only artistic merit that prompted him to choose Maya Angelou, a black feminist, to deliver the inauguration poem.) So has it helped his book sales being Clinton's favourite writer? "Don't ask me that!" Mosley says. "Ask me something else!" When I insist, he says: "I like the fact that he read my books, enjoyed them, and didn't try to hold that in. In fact, I voted for him."

Mosley's five books are about men. Black men. They are about slummy living conditions, about infidelity, death, love, compassion—all described in lush, lyrical words that rise like sculptures before your eyes. Holding the books together is Easy Rawlins, an unlicensed, unofficial, and very off-the-books detective. This hero-detective is America's new love. "Easy Rawlins is so caring. He is such a kind, compassionate man," says a white, middle-class, middle-aged American woman on the train to Nottingham (she and her companion are attending the international crime-writing jamboree at which Mosley is appearing).

They do not mention Easy's antipathy to white (middle-class) American women. "He is marvelous," they declare.

He doesn't fit in with the image I have of him. I expected to meet Easy Rawlins—a man who drinks in the afternoon, chain-smokes and woman-ises. Someone who looks weary and worldly. Someone with scars on his face and a wiry, ravaged body. After all, this man must have lived in the slums to be able to write about the slums. But no—Mr. Mosley emerges from his hotel room with the tousled, wide-eyed look of someone who sleeps like a kitten.

We meet as the O. J. Simpson trial comes to its climax. The trial has played out the themes of Mosley's books: the way white police are alleged to conspire against black men; the way that black men can abuse women.

Almost immediately, I make a mistake. I ask him a question containing the words "black people."

"There is no such thing as a black race," he says, sitting up suddenly, his burgundy-silky shirt falling in ripples. "We are so intermixed that there is no race. No pure race. The fact that you are labeling me black is a fact of rac-ism."

Mosley is half-Jewish. From then on I refer to "so-called black people." Mosley is happy with that. "You sound like Malcolm X," he says.

I ask him if he likes being "so-called black." "Yes," he says, "I like the free flowing creative chaos that you get from being black. . . . I like being part of a group of people in search of an identity." He also enjoys being part of "an incredibly powerful oral tradition." This theme comes up again and again in his books—how black Americans have their own language, their own sto-ries, music, folk tales and riddles, their own grammar ("I is" rather than "I am").

He also appreciates writing for a black audience. "They pick up on a note, a beat, a rhythm which I recognise as part of our shared history," he says. Black Americans know what Mosley is talking about when he describes the brutal treatment of blacks by white police; how the authorities don't care when black girls are murdered but they start caring when a white girl is murdered; how a lone black man can hardly walk round town without bumping into a gang of whites strumming for a fight. "Ninety per cent of black people in America experience what I write about," he says.

Women in particular love his books. His thrillers take them into the man's world that they hear about but cannot enter. But we are also forced to look at other women from a male point of view. The sight is not pretty: Mosley has sprinkled an array of female characters through his books, whose function is to strip, deceive, mislead, spread their legs, and please. He says "sex is just used as a metaphor." That hasn't stopped women from accusing him of "writing to titillate."

But then Walter Mosley is not noted for his willingness to appease. His life has been one of railing against accepted order. Brought up as the only child of a socialist, Russian-Jewish mother and black American father, his memories of his childhood have a political flavour. He remembers feeling irritated about how "nobody reacted" when "niggers" were put into "black dumb classes at school" and whites were put into "white smart classes. . . . They just said: 'Oh, OK,'" he says, still smarting thirty years on.

After graduating from high school in 1970, Mosley left the Watts area of Los Angeles, California, and headed for the East Coast. In 1977 he was awarded a bachelor's degree in political science from Johnson State College, Vermont. For a couple of years he floated through a variety of jobs, including making and selling pottery and operating a catering business. Then in 1979 his future wife Joy Kellman, a dancer and choreographer, walked into his life, and together they moved to New York where Mosley got work as a computer operator.

It was then that Mosley's interest in writing was kindled—by Alice Walker's Pulitzer Prize–winning novel *The Color Purple*—a story about a black woman living in the South. "I thought, 'Oh—I could do this,'" he explains. Shortly after that he wrote a sentence "about people on a back porch in Louisiana." He was so taken with that single sentence that he signed up to creative writing classes.

His first novella *Gone Fishin'* featured Easy Rawlins but it was not a detective story. The work was rejected by a number of publishers because of its subject matter: there wasn't a market for books about black men, he was told. Mosley rewrote the novella as a detective story, but the theme was the same: the life of Easy Rawlins. He called it *Devil in a Blue Dress*. The novel was published in 1990 and has just been made into a film. *A Red Death* was released a year later followed by *White Butterfly* (1992), *Black Betty* (1994), and most recently *RL's Dream* (1995).

Read in a block, the novels tend to blend together. They are all set in the urban jungle, in steamy stripper joints, underground clubs, housing projects, car parks, and shopping streets. Easy Rawlins grows up during the course of four novels—getting married, acquiring a mortgage, adopting two children, then losing the wife and the mortgage. But the theme is basically the same: Easy Rawlins beset by temptation, aware of his shortcomings, in search of the baddy and just a hint of moral deliverance.

"People read my books too fast," Mosley complains. "They are so eager to solve the mystery that they skim." But I didn't care what happened at the end of Mosley's books. I read them for their cinematic quality. It gave me a buzz to be swished through red rooms, blue alleys, to follow Easy Rawlins as he disappears into a brothel to visit Marla the prostitute, who sits with "her legs wide enough to expose a thick mat of pubic hair."

The scene in *White Butterfly* in which Easy Rawlins rapes his wife by forcing her to have sex "the way dogs do it" has been particularly controversial. "I get women coming up to me, saying, 'Why did you include that scene?' But I was not proposing that men should rape their wives. I put it in to encourage people to discuss rape within marriage," Mosley says.

So does he have any qualms about titillating readers in this way? No, he says. The novels are just a reflection of real life: "That is what poor people do—they eat sweet foods or salty foods, they drink or get high and they have sex. If I were to ignore it, to pretend it doesn't happen, then the book would be a lie."

Mosley says he has made every effort to make sure that women are not misrepresented in his novels. "Yes, Easy Rawlins does appreciate women sexually—but he also recognizes strength of character, intelligence, and the ability to do things that he can't do," he says. Elsewhere in his books, Mosley is careful to ensure that for every female character who is humiliated or hurt there is another female character who is given a positive role. "That's what is important. If a man is given character and a female is given character then it can't be sexist," he says.

In one chapter, for example, a young woman "plump and the colour of a dusky orange" is watched by two men as she parades naked before a window. If that woman was the only female in the chapter then yes, her nakedness could be seen as gratuitous, says Mosley. But there are three other female characters in the chapter, all of whom are portrayed as hard-working women struggling to make a difference, he points out. They are not victims. They are not objects. They are tough.

"I don't write to change the world," Mosley says, stretching like a fat cat. "I'm not here to give answers either. I just want to raise the questions." He starts gathering together his belongings. "Ask me one more thing," he says. I think hard. "How did you find out about seedy caverns, fear, about the way people kill, the sad side of sex?" I ask.

"Let me put it like this," he replies. "I didn't have to go far to figure it out."

# Walter Mosley Writers Institute Seminar and Evening Reading

## Donald Faulkner/1996

Transcription from the Visiting Writers Series Archive of the New York State Writers Institute at the University at Albany/SUNY. Copyright © 1996 New York State Writers Institute. Printed by permission.

Note: The following interview consists of the transcript from two events held on February 20, 1996. The first part records the interaction between Walter Mosley; Donald Faulkner, the Director of the Writers Institute; and an audience of writing students, faculty, and some members of the general public. The evening session records the question and answer session between Mosley and a general audience after his public reading.

**Donald Faulkner:** I want to say that Walter Mosley is a man of his word. He was willing to come and visit with us last fall, and that afforded us a great opportunity to have an advanced screening of *Devil in a Blue Dress*. It was the first event in the Writers Institute's fall 1995 series, and it was also my own inaugural event with the Institute.

Today's event is also special. I first met Walter a few years ago at Yale, where I previously taught. Walter's visit was one of the most memorable readings and discussions that I had organized there.

Walter Mosley is the author of four Easy Rawlins mysteries. I say frequently that genre writing is not what his book is about, and that his writing, like all good fiction, has at its heart the exploration of a mystery: Something is hidden, something is discovered, a secret is revealed.

Walter has broken out of the Easy Rawlins voice and has continued to break out of it in yet another collection. He has become a very energetic writer in a very short space of time. Most recently in the fall, in the novel *RL's Dream* which centers its action on the old blues musician Robert Johnson. I remember describing its contents to William Kennedy as a couple of people

**47**

down on their luck trying to help each other out and trying to explore the dimensions of that. He said to me, "Gosh, that sounds familiar, it sounds kind of like a plot that I pursued at one time." Needless to say, the work is as different as the two authors are different.

Walter is here today with us to answer your questions and to explore, in terms of craft, some of the concerns you have or some of the reactions you might have to his work. Okay, I'll leave it at that. Please welcome Walter Mosley.

[applause]

**Mosley:** Hi. I must seem odd, huh? I feel odd, so I have to seem odd. I was being driven from New York, and I was sleeping in the back of the car. All I can say is I really was sleeping soundly because I woke up thinking about what I was going to talk about tonight and I decided the topic should be death. I woke up thinking that death is really the defining factor right now for the way that I think about anything I'm doing. One of the things that I've been thinking about is writing, and the other day I laid out everything that I know I want to write, and I laid it out in relation to when I'm going to die. I'm very psychological, very, on the outside, psychological. My father died when he was seventy-six, but he smoked, so I think, well maybe I'll make it to seventy-nine. So I'm forty-four and I really think that the reason I was thinking about that was because I was sleeping so soundly; it's like I was dead. So that's why I feel odd, but I feel like I'm coming back to life in some kind of way. So coming here, I was really thinking about reading tonight, but are there any questions? Anybody read anything I ever wrote and brought anything that they might want to ask about?

**Audience:** When you wrote *Black Betty*, it seems Rawlins brings over the preacher and Albert because he knows that Mouse has to kill somebody.

**Mosley:** Well see, he doesn't have the preacher over to mock. You think he does, but he doesn't. I got interviewed about this. It was very funny and it made me very sad about writing tricky endings to books because you think that he's going to turn in Albert.

**Audience:** Oh no, I was going to say it was out of character for Rawlins. . . .

**Mosley:** To anyone who hasn't read the book, the real plot of the book is about Easy's good friend who taught him things when he was a kid [and who] is dying of cancer—of which my father was dying then and he has just died. He was very miserable because he [the character] was so sick he couldn't kill himself, and he wanted to die. He asked Easy to kill him and Easy, you know, says he'd be in trouble for murder, he'd be prosecuted. At the same time, Mouse is out of jail and he has to kill somebody because somebody turned him into jail. Part of Easy's energy in the book is spent trying to find out who actually turned Mouse in because Mouse is going to kill these people. He finds out that it's this guy, this crazy kid, a self-proclaimed minister who creates scenes from the church in his front yard. When he finds out, he turns in Martin. He goes to Martin and says if Mouse comes here and asks you a question, you say, "Yes, I did that." And Mouse kills him, which I liked very much. But I had a problem with that because it was hard for me to get an interview in the *Chicago Tribune*.

When *Black Betty* came out, they [the *Chicago Tribune*] said they had somebody who wanted to interview me. So I see this woman, and we're having this interview, and toward the end of the interview, she asked me that same question. This woman was very full of herself. I tried the nicest way to tell her she'd made a mistake. So I never got the thing [the interview] because, well, she didn't write it because she was embarrassed. It was very funny.

**Audience:** Why don't you tell us something about how you go about the actual writing. Do you outline your plots first? Do you write in long-hand? Do you rewrite seven times? What do you do?

**Mosley:** When Edna O'Brien was here did you ask her these questions? [audience laughter]

**Audience:** I ask everybody the same question every time I'm here.

**Mosley:** So did you ask Edna? Did you talk to her?

**Audience:** Didn't talk to her.

**Mosley:** Edna's the greatest with this. I like her story much better than what I do. Edna writes everything long-hand, and then she sends it to a typist, and then she gets it back and makes corrections and sends it back—which sounds so wonderful to me. I really want to do it, but I can't. I just can't write a book in long-hand, I just can't do it. I write in the morning, when I wake up, usually for two or three hours, maybe four if I feel really good. Then when it's over, I go about my day. And I do that every day.

My first draft is always on my computer. The only thing I demand of myself is a first line, and it's usually the only thing I give myself. Sometimes, like in this new book, the first line is funny, because usually the first line is the first line in the book. This new thing is that I came up with this first line that I love, but it didn't fit, until page one hundred ninety something. It was a great line, for me. It's this line in my new book, "It was the dog's fault." I really liked that line. It really tells me everything I need to know about the book. I just put it on a free page at the beginning of the book, and then you turn to chapter one. I write the first draft on the computer, and then I print it out, and I read it, and I make changes, and I put it back, and I print it out, and I make changes, and I put it back, and on and on. There's a point in your writing when you can no longer read the words that you've written because you're too familiar with them. So you read them, but you don't really read them; you read what you think you're reading. It becomes crazy. I realize that at that point, the best thing to do is to read the whole thing out loud into a tape recorder, which I do, which is really deadening; it takes forever, like a week. I read the whole thing out loud into a tape recorder and then I listen to it a couple of times—often I fall asleep listening to it, but I listen to it a couple of times. Then, I go back to the process of printing it out, putting it back, printing it out. . . . As that process goes on, more and more comes long-hand writing. As I realize that parts are going to go out, I may sit down and write twenty pages in long-hand, in a section, so I have to add the section here, and I'll write twenty pages and then type that back into the computer. For me, writing is all kinds of voices, it's reading out loud, it's sometimes reading to people, it's typing in the computer, it's writing by hand, it's listening to it all on a tape recorder—everything possible.

**Faulkner:** You mentioned Edna O'Brien, and I can remember you saying that she had given you an assignment that you have been trying to do ever since. Do you remember that?

**Mosley:** Oh yeah. I remember I've said a few things. I studied with Edna at City College. She said a couple of things to me. I wrote a play and her criticism of the play, which I thought was wonderful, was that it didn't make her cry. She said, "Well, Walter, you know, it's fine, there's nothing wrong with it, but it didn't make me cry." So then I said I have to make Edna O'Brien cry. It's the funniest thing. I didn't succeed, but I kept trying.

The other thing Edna did for me, I think, was that she read a line from E. M. Forster's *Aspects of the Novel*, which says a novel is fifty thousand words, more or less, of spongy prose. I loved it, because poetry is made from diamonds, and then short stories are like diamonds and platinum working together, and then a novel is a sponge. I really liked that idea, that I didn't have to work so hard.

Workshops are funny anyway because workshops are created not to do what they say they're doing, because you can't actually write a finished piece of work in a workshop. You can just workshop it to death. Short stories, a lot of the criticism makes sense. Like, why would you say, "She had blue shoes?" Of course you want to say, "Because she had blue shoes, so what?" That gives you an idea that people are making connections, that blue means sad. But no, she's just wearing blue shoes. Every line means too much. In a poem, every line means twelve things, and in a short story every line means eight things, but in a novel, a line could mean only one thing every once in a while. Often, three or four things, but it doesn't have that much weight on it. So, Edna opened me up to that. Also there's a question of economics. Who buys short stories? I don't know why people like short stories either.

One of the reasons I feel like I could talk about them is because I've been writing them lately. I'm writing this series of short stories. All of the stories are connected. They're all about one character, a guy named Socrates Fortlow. Somebody had asked me to write a short story, and I had no intention of writing one. It was a short story about Edward Hopper of all things. I'm not concerned with Hopper, but there's this woman I wanted to go out to dinner with, but she wasn't going to go out to dinner with me. So, I said, "Listen maybe I'll write this story, but could you take me to dinner," and she said, "Yeah, I'll take you to dinner, as long as you're going to write the story." I decided I wasn't going to write the stories, but you know the thing was that I felt guilty three days beforehand, so I wrote this story about Socrates Fortlow, a very wild guy who murdered people indiscriminately in his youth and spent many years in prison and has now come out. And now, he's really thinking there's some value to life for these people who live under the template, underneath the justice value of this system, and he wants to figure out how we can do the right thing in our society. Well, what happens is that I gave the story to the woman and she liked it, so I published it. Then I started to think about it, and I said, "Well, you know, this is a very good theme." It is kind of like a novel, this story, but it's much easier because I know who the character is. In a novel, you could say everything you need to say, but in a short story only the tip of it shows. Underneath there's this whole mountain that you have to know of the story. If you write a bunch of short stories about the same character, about the same place, then you have that mountain. Nobody asked me this question, but I like answering it. [laughter]

**Audience:** Did you have to do much research to use description, or do you commonly hide in basements and know how to break into an office by breaking into the adjoining office?

**Mosley:** I didn't do any research for those things.

**Audience:** [incredulous] You made it up? [audience laughter]

**Mosley:** It is true that you pick up these things in life, every once in a while. I'm not interested in police procedures because I think the police are corrupt, or overworked, or just inept. I don't think anything good about them.

**Audience:** That sorta comes through.

**Mosley:** I think that when people write about police procedures, what they're writing about is a comic ideal; they're not really writing about what really happens. I was writing in this book the other day that there's a piece of evidence and a police officer is holding it, looking at it, and the copyeditor changed it so that the police officer was bending down, looking at it. I understood that he thought that police officers actually follow police procedures, but we all know they don't. I mean, if you watched the O. J. Simpson case, it was like, "Did you do it?" "No I didn't." "Bullshit, did you put your hand in the blood, did you bleed in the blood?" "Yes. I did, I just didn't think it mattered." [audience laughter]

This is something I do a lot: you put yourself in the situation. There's a dead man in your house and for whatever reason, you don't want to turn it [the crime] into the police; you need to get rid of the body. We could just cut his body up into pieces. Really, this is what most people do. No, they're not weird, it's just easier to carry out an ankle than it is to carry out a whole body. We don't want to do that though, because it's too—ugh! So what do you do? Ever see *Paris Is Burning*? One interviewee, an older cross-dresser, died recently. His friends went in to clean up the apartment, and they found, in about fifteen garment bags, completely covered with baking soda, pounds and pounds of baking soda, a dead body—mummified. They figured that he'd had a lover that was abusive about twenty years before, and he killed the guy, in his little apartment in New York. So he probably said, "Oh I know, I'll put him in a whole bunch of garment bags, and I know if I put enough baking soda in there it'll suck up all the odor. . . ." And he just left him there—for twenty years! Okay, so you're going to keep him—why you're keeping him is another story—how you're going to keep him from starting to smell? Well, you put him in ice! It's the same thing you'd do to any meat. It does so happen that I know lime decomposes organic material. So yeah, what you do is, you just sit and work through it as if you were having the problem. That's what I do; I love figuring this kind of stuff out, because I'm not going to do it in my real life.

**Faulkner:** You wrote one time in a piece of yours that I really respect about how poverty teaches you things. You learn about the ways in which you have to move deviously. It sounds like that's what you're thinking about in presenting a problem; if somebody has some particular problem and has been there at one point or another in their lives, he will have some kind of knowledge that the average reader doesn't.

**Mosley:** Poverty, I think, is a thing that makes Easy Rawlins different from a lot of detectives. Most detectives are detecting crime and Easy Rawlins is, but there's something else in his method that is not unique but is not the usual one in the genre, because poverty makes you pay attention to a lot of things. You pay attention to when the door's open and when the door's closed; you pay attention to how many locks there are on the door; you pay attention if there's noise going on next door, you pay more attention if there's no noise next door. If you're about to go out, you know who's on the street and you know what they're doing and you know what they might be doing. Also, you enter into a moral dialogue. At what point is something wrong and is something right? For instance, you go out in the street and you don't have any, let's say, cutlery in your house and there's a guy selling knives on the street—good knives. He selling them for twenty-five dollars and you know they cost three hundred dollars over at Home Goods, but twenty-five dollars you can afford. Now you know that if you pay someone twenty-five dollars you're paying somebody who stole them. Do you see? You think about that, you know you're contributing to crime by doing this, and you're aware of that, and then you have to make the decision of whether or not you're willing to do it.

One of the wonderful things about using that as the base, rather than using police procedures, or rather than some other kind of detective method, is that you can enter into moral codes at the same time dealing with the puzzle or the fantasy or the fiction. A lot of times, you'll read all kinds of fiction where people have moral questions but they aren't real. They kind of make them up—well you could be thinking about this moral and you could not be. If your characters are based in a reality that's forcing them to make decisions, then you can believe in those decisions that they're being forced to make.

**Audience:** Who are Easy Rawlins' adversaries?

**Mosley:** Who are his adversaries? It's the little yellow dog. If you come tonight, I'm reading the first chapter with the little yellow dog. It's a major adversary—major adversaries are nonhuman creatures.

He has a lot of different people whom he fights, but I think mainly it's the spirit of the crime. There are a lot of ways me and Easy are alike in our struggle, but in that way we're absolutely the opposite. Easy is completely kept out of the crimes by a variety of things, like his own mind. He's been so conditioned to think of himself in a certain kind of relationship with white people and to the white man's world that he often doesn't allow himself to make decisions that will be beneficial to him. So if you're reading the book and wondering why he doesn't do this or that or think, "All he had to do was say yes, or say he owned this or believed this . . ." and he didn't. If he did say something to his wife Regina, he could have kept his relationship with his wife but he couldn't tell her because he couldn't trust her, because that's where he comes from. So, I wouldn't say that his main adversary is himself; I think that all of the things that made him, that make his world, because he has these inculcated senses of racism and because he lives in a racist world on top of that, he's one of his archenemies—and the little yellow dog.

**Audience:** I'm thinking about black detectives, and I can get a whole list of them and most of them are written by white people, but I think they're entirely different because, as with Chester Himes, what you've got is the same idea that the so-called law means nothing at all. I mean his heroes are all cops, but they don't follow any of the standard cop procedure. I find it interesting—are there any other black mystery writers?

**Mosley:** One of the few things I can kind of settle up—you know how a lot of people want to say, "I did this?" It's easy to. I could say that I wrote a lot of books. Beyond writing my books, I can't say, "I get it." When I started writing, there was one other black mystery writer working—well not just working, he was getting published. Then I got published and *Devil* did very well on a whole bunch of different levels. Some of them were fantasy, like a lot of people thought I made a lot of money off that book, which I didn't, and I made less on *A Red Death*, the second book. But the book got out there, people knew what it was; maybe they didn't buy it, but they knew about it or maybe they didn't read it but they saw it, or they didn't read it but they read about me in the *New York Times*. Whatever it was, it had a big effect on the world. So, now, there's at least twenty-five black crime writers writing and publishing, and they come from all walks of life. You know, maybe a black lesbian writer writes about a black lesbian detective. There's a wonderful book, I can't remember the name, but I remember the character's name is Blanche. [most likely referring to a Barbara Neely novel]

One of the things that Angela Davis says is that race is a consequence of racism. There is no race; there is racism and then there is race. You think that it's a wonderful statement and you wonder if it's true, and then you look at it and think about what a black person is. So you can look at me and then you can look at the way my father looked which was about fourteen shades darker than me and had features much different from mine, and then you look at someone who is completely different, like someone who is black but then has red hair and freckles. All of these are black people. Well, what defines them? It's the features. Well what exactly does that mean? It's the color of the skin.

You look at these twenty-five different writers, like Chester Himes and myself, very, very different writers. He comes out of a richer life; I come

out of rags and ruins. It's very exciting, I think, to see black mystery writers. There's a problem with people complaining about how somebody has
already written about a black detective. Well, yeah, there's more than one
white detective, too, but that doesn't seem to be a problem. Being black is
like a trick! It's not that interesting. Then you have the internal issue, which
is that black people aren't writing—about anything. The problem is about
discovering what race is. Within art and also within ourselves, our lives.
I think that I can help in there. People say that I can still be real and write
about something I like.

From the Question and Answer Session, "Walter Mosley Talks on Writing,"
following Mosley's evening reading. The transcript for this session may be
found at http://www.albany.edu/writers-inst/webpages4/archives/olv1n1
.html#mosley.

Affable, witty, and always ready to slip into street slang, Mosley entertained
questions from audience members after reading from *RL's Dream* and *A Little Yellow Dog*. Mosley's steady informality belies his serious thought about
writing as an African American, the politics of culture, and the deeper issues that lie beneath his popular writing. A number of questions refer to
both the novel and film *Devil in a Blue Dress*; the film was then in general
release. Mosley begins by talking about the differences between his "literary" novel and those in the mystery genre.

**MOSLEY:** *RL's Dream* is much more serious than the other book *A Little
Yellow Dog*. I like it, but I don't read from it as much anymore. Bill [Ken-
nedy] and I were talking about going on tour—you go on tour and you read
your books until you hate them. I haven't read this in a long time. I'm kind of
partial to it; it's my little move outside the genre, which I think is something
healthy to do. Otherwise you get stuck in commerce, you know.
   "When's the next Easy book? Well, we can up that advance."
   "Well, I'd like to write a book about the blues."
   "Oh, really. And who's going to publish that? You going to give that to a
university press? It's a history, right?"
   So, [to audience] any questions, thoughts, declarations of love, offers of
money? There's a hand.
**Q:** Why do you use colors in the book titles?
**A:** I'm often asked that question, and I always have the same answer, which
one guy actually got angry at me about and wrote me a five-page letter, re-

buking my answer. But my answer is, there must be. You see, I wrote a book, called *Devil in a Blue Dress*. I thought it was kind of a catchy title. People said, "Ooh, yeah, yeah, I'd like to read that." They wouldn't know why exactly, but they'd think so. Then *A Red Death* is kind of like a send-up, you know— "Masque of the Red Death," Edgar Allan Poe, the discoverer of the detective novel in the American world. So I'm working on the third book and my editor, Jerry Howard, says, "So what's the color of this one?" And I looked at him and said, "The color?" And he goes, "Yup, blue, red, got to have a color." And I didn't have a bad reaction to that. I said, "All right, *White Butterfly*." That's good. I was going to call it Papillon, but he didn't say I *shouldn't* use a French name. I was going to call it Papillon Blanc, and [then] he said, "No, no, no, no, no, we don't like the French that much in this country. When they translate it, they can call it that." And I've liked it since then.

I was going to write *Bad Boy Bobby Brown*. [laughter] No, honestly, this was before that became a popular phrase. Now I'm afraid I'm going to get sued if I use that name, so I'm going to have to change that. Then the next Easy book after that, I'm going to call Ruby, which I really love as a title.

You see, I believe that most things are not what they appear to be. I believe that most reading is talking about reading. You read a story, somebody else reads a story, and you talk about that, and that's where learning comes in. I believe that most of the things that we write as novelists and poets and essayists come from unconscious places, and what our real process is to organize the unconscious in a way that seems to make sense on one level, while making a completely other kind of sense, that you don't quite understand, on another level. And so, the same thing with my titles. See, that was a little question. Nobody ever asks me a big one. Is there a question back there? [question inaudible] What about what? . . . Blacky girl? No, I have *Black Betty*. Well, you know, "Black Betty" is the title of a song by Leadbelly:

*Black Betty had a baby*
*Wasn't none of mine*

I think those are all the lyrics he ever says in the whole song. Goes on for a while. And [for me] it was a nostalgic feeling. But again, you know, I don't know. Had to have a color. Liked *Black Betty*, quite a bit. . . . Yes?
**Q:** Can you comment on the places and times that Easy Rawlins lived?
**A:** The times and places that Easy Rawlins lived? You know, he was born in the deep South, lives in the deep South, in a place that's almost magical in

its best and worst senses. I wrote a book about that. It hasn't got published yet, but it's going to be published in about twenty-four months, about Easy and Mouse when they were nineteen, twenty years old. It's a coming of age novel. You know, you write a coming of age novel about black men in 1989, and you get this kind of response from the publishers:

"Now, wait a sec, are they in politics?"

"No."

"Are there black women?"

"Well, there are some, but you know, it's about these two black men."

"Well, are there white people in it?"

"Not really."

And they say, "Well, is it about the Revolution, or is it about Civil Rights?"

"No, none of that stuff. It's just two young black men living among other black people."

And they say, "Well, you have to understand. White people don't read about black people. Black women don't like black men. And black men don't read." I once went to a bookstore where I was talking about that once, and I pointed to all of the black men in the audience and I said, "You know, you guys must have all thought you were coming to a video store, right? But that video store's across the hall in the mall." Nobody left, luckily.

I'm trying to write about that wonderful kind of under-discussed migration of black men and women from the deep South after WWII. America— like if you sold a banana in South America, America got a piece of it. If you sold a pound of rice in China, America got a piece of it. America got a piece of everything. We were rich. We were the Mob. We had everything. And so we needed to build more and more things so we could make more and more money, and there were jobs available. So black people were moving up North, moving into California, moving everywhere, so they could work. Because, you know, all the jobs were taken in the South, and the South was still depressed over the Civil War. So all these black people moved out. They moved to California so they could get jobs so they could work. And that's what I want to talk about, because nobody talks about it. You know they have these maps, these mystery maps? You know, Philip Marlowe was here [in L.A.], and Continental Op was here, and so and so was here, and the one time Nero Wolfe ever came to California he was here. But when you see South Central—one time Philip Marlowe was on Central Avenue, and that was it.

One of the things is, historically, we [African Americans] haven't written a great deal of popular fiction about our lives, and about our movements, and it's something that needs to be done. So that's why I've done it. But you know, it's like '48, migration, '53, McCarthy, '58, who knows what happened in '58? Then we get into the '60s and we start talking about black violence, we start talking about black revolution, etc. I want to bring Easy up to the '90s. He can go through two riots. I like that idea.

**Q:** What did you think about the movie of *Devil in a Blue Dress*?

**A:** Well, I didn't make it, so I wouldn't change it. It's Carl's [Carl Franklin's] movie, and I loved it. I thought it was a wonderful movie. It's too bad that we didn't see more of the Daphne Monet character, and that we didn't get deeper into her character, for a few reasons, I think. But you can't do everything, and I think it's a really good movie. And a movie that will stand the test of time. I don't think it will become passé. I was very happy with it. It didn't do very well. But, what can you say?

**Q:** Where did the story of *Devil in a Blue Dress* come from?

**A:** You know, who knows? Speaking again about the unconscious, one time, in *Devil in a Blue Dress*, I wrote about a guy, owned a bar, was married to a woman. He was messing around all the time. He mistreated her, he had all these girlfriends. And then he got sick, diabetes, lost both of his *legs*, lost both *legs*, and the wife puts him in a room, and every night she comes in and she sets down a fifth of whiskey in front of him. Then she goes into the next room, next door with some man, and then she has loud sex with that man all night long. Maybe a couple of men. And I thought that this was kind of a wonderful thing.

Well, my father read the book. My father reads that part and he says, "Walter, you know that part, where they were having, you know, the woman and the sex and the man with the *legs*?" And I said, "Yeah, dad. You like that?" He said, "Yeah, I liked it, but how did you know that?" And I said, "Well, what do you mean? I made it up."

He said, "No, no, no. I knew that man. I knew that man. He lived right down the street from me." You know, it's an amazing thing, the amount of knowledge that you have. Thing is, I wrote this chapter [of *RL's Dream*]. It's the first thing I wrote in this book. It was Chapter 11, the first thing I wrote. And I didn't do any research at all. None. I just wrote it. And then I went through it to see what was wrong. Like I would talk to people from Mississippi, and I would talk to my father, who is from Louisiana. I'd talk to them and say, "Does anything sound like, wrong, in this?" I think a couple of things were off, you know, and I added the smells, but as a rule, I just wrote it. Because fiction is an amazing thing. Not only is 90 percent of what you learn from fiction what you talk about it, but also, most of what the audience gets is what they bring to it. Your problem is not to mislead the audience. Your problem is to open a world to them, and let them bring their information to it. All you have to do is not lie. And so my research has always been a kind of backwards research. To make sure that the things I said are, one, evocative, and, two, not wrong.

**Q:** Your characters seem less black or white than simply human. How conscious are you of race when you write?

**A:** Well, you know what Angela Davis say: Race is a consequence of racism. But believe me, you and I are not the same. We know that in the world, that to be black in the world is to be black in the world. It's not what you look like. It has nothing to do with what you look like. You say, "Well, that man look like a nigger to me." "What's that mean?" "Well, I don't know exactly. But that's a nigger." And that's kind of the way it is. It's the kind of illusion that can get you killed, you know. And when an illusion gets so deep that it can get you killed, it starts becoming reality, I think.

**Q:** Do you write your father and mother into your books at all?

**A:** My mother kind of made some appearances in *A Red Death*. She definitely made some appearances there. And Easy is not becoming like my father. My father's more like Mouse than Easy really. I know you're supposed to write autobiographically, and I've heard very important people say that we all do it, and who else could I be writing about really, than who I know, and me. I mean, who else could I be writing about? Who do I live with? But the thing is that Easy is Easy. He's like a guy I could never be.

**Q:** Easy relies on Mouse even when he knows Mouse is bad. What's important to Easy about friendship?

**A:** Yeah, Easy has a thing about friends which is good, I think. But you know, when you come from that rural background and you come to the city, what people do is they relied on friends. Not having money wasn't as important in the country as it is in the city. If you don't have money in the city, you're going to die. You don't have money in the country, well, if you've got friends, what difference does it make?

**Q:** Do you prefer first or third person narrative?

**A:** Well, you know, most of *RL's Dream* is third person. And I didn't feel bad about it when I wrote it. And of all the myriad criticisms that I got for it, for instance—that I didn't like my characters, I don't know the blues, the blues is not the devil's music—of all the criticisms that I got, one of them wasn't that I didn't know how to do third person. I like third person, but when you're writing a mystery, it's very good to have a . . . central character, you've got his voice. It's a very hard thing to do, first person. It's easier to write third person.

**Q:** Some of your language is very poetic. Where does that come from?

**A:** Well, I studied poetry for about three or four years with Bill Matthews, the poet. And I studied very seriously, with my very bad poetry. The one thing that poets have still is a mastery of the tool, of metaphor, of illusion, of condensation, of meter and of music. They master that. A good poet has to master all of those things. And a good fiction writer, may not [be a] master, but you've got to know it pretty well. So I studied poetry in order to write fiction, but again I'm not consciously going out and saying, "Okay, I'm going to use this thing." I know there are a couple of rhymes, for instance, in the way Soupspoon talks in that chapter [of *RL's Dream*]. And they came out naturally, and I left them, because sometimes people do talk in rhyme, especially that oral history. It's like we were talking earlier about Raymond Chandler—I think it was Raymond Chandler. It could have been a Ross Macdonald line—where he said, "He was calm, like an adobe wall in moonlight." That's a very poetic line, but it's also very true. It hits you, and it's like something you probably hadn't thought of before, even though you've seen it, you know?

**Q:** I wanted to ask you about your feelings about the adoration of Bill Clinton?

**A:** My feelings about it? It doesn't hurt. I always say that you know I'm very pleased that it wasn't George Bush who liked my books, because I'd have to say—I mean, I'd be nice—I'd say, "Well, at least he has one bit of taste in his life." One bit of non-criminal activity. I've been very happy about it. It's a very interesting thing. I'm a very technical guy. I think technically. People ask me a question like that and I think I have to answer it technically—"What was Bill Clinton's effect?"—as if like I'm my publisher's accountant? "What was his effect on your career?" And I know. I figured it out. Because it didn't sell that many books, really. It's steadily gotten better, but the reason is . . . people in America, they're not illiterate, but they don't like to read. It's just a thing. People in America, they're not dying to go out and read. The people in Germany read as many books as they do in America. People do other things in America. And everybody is a victim of this. And it's funny, you know, but actually black people read more than white people, which is a very weird thing. You wouldn't expect it to be true. Of course, black people have more to learn about who they were than white people think they have to learn. But the thing is, the media, they don't read, or they read what they like.

"So, what do you read?"

"Well, I read Mary Higgins Clark, and I read Marquez."

"Well, do you know about this other writer?"

"No, I don't know about any other writers. I read those two, and nobody else."

"Well, what about Clinton?"

"Oh, Clinton. He reads Walter Mosley."

And so every media person in the country knew who I was, because Clinton read me. And so whenever I have to ask for something, or whenever they have to respond to, "Oh, Clinton—books? Walter Mosley." Or I come to town and they say, "He's a writer, yeah. Well, I can ask him about Clinton anyway." You know what I mean.

**Q:** Where do you go to learn about people for your books?

**A:** I live in New York. I live in the West Village, and I get around on the subway, and I go walking around. New York is one of those equalizer places, like everybody is the same, and you can't even think that you're special, you know. Because they'll say, "Like who the fuck you think you are man? Shit, get out my way. I'll cut your ass." And you go, "Okay, excuse me. I'm sorry. I wrote a book." "Yeah, so what." It's a funny thing. Everybody's there in New York. I think it's true everywhere in the world, though. Some people like to elevate themselves. We won't go into who they are, but some people like to elevate themselves and remove themselves and have a stance in the world and that's fine. That's cool with me, but mostly all you have to do is live life and you see people and you know people. I wrote a tiny little ten-page script about a scene I saw once. I was in a subway and there was a very neat little black couple, very neat. Two very neat little kids, very neat. We were going to Harlem, and we stopped, and a big woman comes in, black woman, big, big, with these kids that were, like, wild. And the very neat little kids went, "Oh, my God."

And the neat little couple did, too. They looked at the woman and said, "Martha? Hi." And Martha came up to them. "I haven't seen you since you move out the projects." And she came up and sat down with them and they were talking about their kids and school, and she said, "You know I can't even have my kids in school 'cause I got to go down to the court and they got me on trial," and they said, "What's wrong?" And she said, "Well, you know, I was going to cash my check, and these three niggers, they must have been watching me through the window, 'cause I come out and they grabbed me and took the money right out of where it was. I took my knife out and I got two of the motherfuckers, but the one with my money got away." And then she said, "When the cops come up, I said, 'Get him, get him,'" you know, with the knife, right, "And they arrested me." You have this image of this woman with the blood dripping and these guys dying in front of her, and she's still confused. This is months later and she's still confused. "Why did they arrest me, when the man who stole my thirty dollars was running?" But that's what life is like, right? I mean, we're all there. It's not that far away and you realize, you know, "I'm not going to steal that woman's money, or say anything mean to her, either."

**Q:** How did you come to write *RL's Dream*?

**A:** You know, I wrote it first to get out the idea of what I wanted to write, like who was this guy, Soupspoon. Because you see, I wanted to write about Robert Johnson, because I think Robert Johnson was one of the great men of this century. I mean, he was a bad guy. He wasn't a nice guy. But he was a genius, in the same way that [Christopher] Marlowe was a genius. He took a form that already existed and raised it to a level of genius. He was a rebel. He was a sexual revolutionary. He was murdered in a bar, in his twenties. He and Marlowe were like the same guy, just in different centuries. And I thought about him and I thought about him and I thought about him and I said, "How can I write about this man?" and I realized that I couldn't, because to try to write about who his girlfriend was or what he did right or what he did wrong would diminish him and you wouldn't see his greatness. And so what I decided to do was to write about this other character, Soupspoon, who now is himself dying, and trying to remember what it was that he had when he was a kid, and the major event was knowing Robert Johnson. And so that's why I wrote that chapter, and that's what I was trying to get there, and I figured it out by writing that chapter.

**Q:** Will Easy ever find out what happened to Daphne Monet from *Devil in a Blue Dress*?

**A:** It's very hard to say, because I discover books as I go along with them. I know he'll see his daughter again. I can't keep him away from his daughter, but I don't know about Daphne. I'm kind of thinking about putting together an outline for a screenplay that would follow a Daphne-like character, because I'm very interested in her racial thing. It's so funny. You know how people like to get mad at you—it means that they like you. My father used to tell me that when I was in school. That the girl who used to hit me in the back liked me. And I'd say, "I wish she didn't like me so much, Dad." I've had a lot of arguments with black women, who say, "Well, he didn't even like her after he found out she was a black woman. He only was with her because he thought she was white." And they'll be mad at me, looking at me. "But it's not true," I say. "He wanted to marry her. He wanted to go with her. He didn't care that she was black." But people wouldn't believe me, you know. That racial question is so tight—it's like a little ball of anger. So I would like to deal with it, but I don't think in the Easy books, because you can only do so much with this particular genre, which is one of the reasons I wrote *RL's Dream*. Some things the genre does wonderfully. Your editor comes to you and says, "You know, you're spending ten pages and all I got is sociology here, Walter. What's going on with the murder?"

**Q:** What's your perspective on black men as presented by black women writers?

**A:** Well, it's interesting, you know. We were talking about Terry [McMillan], Toni [Morrison], Alice [Walker], some others. A lot of the time black men argue like, "Well, I don't like the way she talked about it." Well, the first thing is, it's true, right? There's nothing they say which is beyond the realm of imagination. There are a lot of things that their imaginations don't even reach out to. I have an image in my mind, and I have never seen this, but it's there in my mind. It's a guy kind of dressed like Bobby Brown, right, and a woman who works in a hospital, black woman. She's wearing her white thing. He's come up to her, she's just coming off work, and he's saying, "Baby, can you let me have twenty dollars." She's saying, "Why don't you go out there and get yourself a job and make you twenty dollars. I work for my money and you should be working for your money." And he's saying, "Oh, baby, I need that twenty dollars. Give me twenty dollars, I'm gonna go to JoJo, and then we got something together and something gonna be happenin'; we gonna have some real money, I gonna make some," and you listen to this, and she keeps on telling him he should work, and you're kind of on her side. But the thing is, she always gives him the twenty dollars, always; and she always complains about him taking her twenty dollars. It's not the first time it happens, it's the fifth that I'm interested in, and that a lot of times when I read these books that you're talking about, I don't see that fifth time. And I would like to. But, I'm not criticizing, because there are a lot of really wonderful women writers now, a lot of wonderful books getting deeply into the characters of women, sometimes deeply into the characters of men, and I think it's wonderful that they're doing this writing. And if I'm going to complain, I should just be writing my own book, and trying to deal as well as I can with that issue, you know.

At the same time, you see a lot of men complaining, "Look at Toni," like she went to the store and said, "Don't buy Walter's book. Buy my book. Buy my book." And she doesn't do that. I've seen her in bookstores, and she doesn't do that. She says, "Buy Walter's book." Terry McMillan actually says,

"Oh, I love Walter's books. Go read them." It's too bad more people don't listen to her about that.

But the thing is you never hear black women actresses complaining about black men actors having all the jobs in Hollywood, though they do. Whoopi Goldberg is the one star, and then there's a lot of other black women, you know, Angela Bassett, and quite a few other people who, you know, they're working, but they're barely working. They're really struggling out there. But they don't say, "Well, the men are taking our jobs." So I don't feel that either. I do like to enter that dialogue that we're like kind of co-dependent. We're both causing each other's problems. And I think that that stuff is more and more being discussed and talked about, so I have no complaints.

**Q:** Have you had a lot of criticism for your portrayal of racism in your books?

**A:** You know, it's funny. Not too much. It's odd. I don't know why. Every once in a while, somebody will write me a letter—I have a letter that I haven't yet answered. A woman wrote me about *RL's Dream*. She said, "Well, it's a very good book, but all the white characters are evil in the book." Which is not true. It's just not true. Kiki, this white woman, saves Soupspoon's life, and is a positive character. She has trouble, but everybody has trouble in the book. So I'm going to respond to that letter. But usually people don't do that to me. I don't know why. I have a good lawyer? I don't know. Two more questions and I've got to go.

**Q:** Do you feel stereotyped as a mystery writer?

**A:** It's not just the publisher. It's the genre and the people who read the books. And I agree with this. There are a lot of black mystery writers today, about twenty, twenty-five. Some of them hate the genre. They hate it. They say, "Oh, I'm writing this book, but I have a really serious book I want to write." And I go, "Well, maybe you should be writing that book and not messing with this." And you find as they go on in the genre that they'll have like thirty pages about a community where black people are living and there are issues, da da da, and the plot's just not there. In mystery, you have to stay with the plot. That's why people are reading the books. And it doesn't matter who they are. It's not like black people read my books because they're interested in a lot of sociology. They're reading it because it's fun. They can go read something else if they want to learn something. They're reading my books because they want to see what Easy's going to do next. They want to see how he gets out of the troubles. Because the identity becomes Easy and his moral stance, his issues, so I can do character development on him. I can do sociology on him. I can do where he lives and the people he knows, but as soon as I try to get out of that I'm going to leave the plot of the book. And I don't think that's good. And I think if I want to do something like that, I should go to another genre, which I do, you know. Like in *RL's Dream*, the plot is very simple: there's a man, he has cancer, he once played with Robert Johnson, he's dying. He wants to remember. Okay, fine, three hundred pages of that. If you like that, you can read it. And if you don't like that, you can read something else. One more question.

**Q:** Do you have any interest in reading your own work on audio?

**A:** Interest. I would like to do it. Audiotape people need a movie star. Really, because what you're trying to do is sell it. I wrote the book, and then they get Paul Winfield to read it. Paul Winfield read four of the Easy books. He did a wonderful job. Gregory Hines read *RL's Dream*. People may not like me, but they like Gregory. And they may not like me, but they like Paul Winfield. So it will be a while before I do that. I might read the short stories. I have some short stories coming out.

Well, anyway, guys, it's been really wonderful being here and visiting with you. [applause]

# Walter Mosley, 1998

## William Mills/1998

From *Index Magazine*, Sept/Oct, 1998. http://www.indexmagazine.com/interviews/walter_mosley.shtml (accessed 2010). Reprinted by permission.

It's a Tuesday evening. Another New York City day lowers to a livable pitch. Walter Mosley, the acclaimed mystery writer, sits behind a large wooden desk in a chair that resembles a medieval oak throne, talking with loud inflections that bounce off the walls. Mosley is the king of all his imagination, an imagination that has produced the vivid whiskey-laden scenes of *RL's Dream* and the character Socrates, and the Easy Rawlins series, which includes *Black Betty* and *Devil in a Blue Dress*. Talking with Walter Mosley is like having an afternoon conversation in a barbershop on Jefferson Street in my native Tennessee.

With *Gone Fishin'*, Mosley switched from a large, well-known publishing house to an African American press, allowing for a non-mainstream publisher to capitalize on his loyal and diverse readership. According to Mosley, "Here is a black man, Easy Rawlins, having a whole bunch of bad experiences as a black person, but the book itself is completely framed in a white economic and cultural framework. There was no statement in that. I had to go a step further and at least try to use the power I have. I thought it was necessary."

Now, with his first science fiction book, Mosley is setting out to conquer new territory. The story, set in San Francisco during the 1960s, is about a brother named Chance and his interactions with people struck by a strange "blue light" from outer space. The book, *Blue Light*, will be released next month.

**WALTER:** Where did you grow up?
**WILLIAM:** In Nashville.
**WALTER:** In Nashville, people call Mississippi the South. [laughing] No one ever thinks of gradations of the South outside of it. "No man, he's from

Texas." That man is from the South. "He's from Alabama!" That's like the deep South.

One of the things that the Easy Rawlins series is about is the migration of Black people from southern Texas and Louisiana, into Southern California after World War II. People came back from the war and they didn't expect racism to be gone, but they expected a job. It's like: "Listen, I know you're going to hate me; that's all right, but I need a job. I just came back from the war and at least I can have a job."

**WILLIAM:** And this is when you were brought up?

**WALTER:** Yes. I'm born in 1952, and I'm aware of things from '57, '58, '59. My whole family, from Texas and Louisiana, all moved to L.A. So I'm around all these people who are in their twenties to mid-thirties, who all came from the deep South.

You know, when I was a little kid, I was on the Art Linkletter show, *Kids Say the Darndest Things.* I was seven years old. I had the deepest Southern Texas drawl you could imagine. He said, "What are you going to talk about?" "I'll talk 'bout Noah and da Ark." It's like, wow. I like listening to it sometimes.

**WILLIAM:** You can hear it now in west coast rap. You hear it in Snoop Doggy Dog. They definitely have that twang.

**WALTER:** Yes, you just inherit it. Everybody I lived around was from the deep South. So it was like I was from a suburb of Los Angeles called Houston, or Galveston. That was my neighborhood. We ate soul food and barbecue, and that was it. "What you going to be cooking?" "Well, I'm cooking some gumbo. Do you want to come on over?" Nobody ever said, "I'm going to throw on some steaks." So everything I knew as a child was deep South. As far as I'm concerned, that's where I was raised, in the 1930s and 1940s, in Texas and Louisiana.

**WILLIAM:** And that's how you learned about the blues?

**WALTER:** I found the blues because I went to the Victory Baptist Day School where they sang gospel. I lived around people who had a blues sensibility. *RL's Dream* is not so much about the blues and music as it is about that sensibility. I was raised around that sensibility, going to church. And then I heard it again in the music in the '60s, with Jimi Hendrix.

**WILLIAM:** Which was coming from the blues?

**WALTER:** Oh yeah. I could stop on Jimi for a long time. I haven't finished with him yet. From Hendrix to Taj Mahal, who kind of reappropriated all this, they sounded like people I grew up with. And that music—Blind Lemon Jefferson, Sonny Terry . . . all the way back.

But in the late '60s, when I was listening to Hendrix, black kids would say, "Man, that's white music!" I said, "No, it's the blues." It comes out of that sensibility.

**WILLIAM:** Can you describe it?

**WALTER:** It's about Mavis Spivey painting her whole house white and mourning the loss of her child, you know, fifty years after the kid is dead. That sensibility, when accented with the blues, is alienation. When you start thinking about who blues singers are, people didn't like them. The church people didn't like them, nobody did.

**WILLIAM:** The juke joint and in the church. Those were two places to find it. When I was growing up, my dad had a 1977 Cordova and would listen to Bobby Blue Bland 8-tracks. My mom was ready to crawl out of the car. They were two different people.

**WALTER:** Even though you can hear the similarity of the music, or even the similarity of spirit, it's the specific content in it. So you didn't think God said it to you, you said the whiskey said it to you. [laughing]

**WILLIAM:** How would you say this blues sensibility influenced your writing?

**WALTER:** It depends on what I'm writing. You know, it's so hard to be raised in a ghetto, any kind of ghetto, because you start to define yourself by the ghetto. Do you know that incredible skit where Eddie Murphy dressed up like a white guy?

**WILLIAM:** On the bus?

**WALTER:** Yes. And when all the black people get off, they start serving cocktails, talking about philosophy, and listening to classical music.

**WILLIAM:** Right.

**WALTER:** In the ghetto you think you're stuck because you don't realize that everyone has their ghettos. When people introduce me they say, "This is Walter Mosley, the mystery writer." And I'll say, "Well, I'm a writer." But once I'd written some stuff that wasn't mystery, they'd introduce me as "Walter Mosley, the mystery writer who is also very good at writing urban, gritty . . ." blah, blah, blah. So now they can say I'm the one who does that so well that it sometimes transcends the mystery.

**WILLIAM:** And now you've just written your first science fiction novel.

**WALTER:** Yes, and I had all kind of troubles. I sent it to all these publishers, and they said, "There are black people in it, but it's not urban, it's not gritty." I think the first line is: "A streak of blue light barely fifteen seconds long hurdles a deep silence into the den of radiance from Uranus."

Now, that's a line I wrote, but there is no blues sensibility in that line. I think that parts of my work are very much influenced by that sensibility. Certainly Easy Rawlins and the sad life around him. Certainly the little book in *RL's Dream, Always Outnumbered, Always Outgunned. . . .* Maybe even the science fiction novel.

**WILLIAM:** Whatever the genre may be, is there something that you're always aiming for?

**WALTER:** The idea is to talk about the highest form of human art, and—this is my opinion—the highest form of human art is tragedy.

**WILLIAM:** Why?

**WALTER:** Because we are, maybe, the only creatures who are intimately aware of the fact that we're going to die, even when death is not imminent. We know death is waiting for us, and death is a fearful thing. But other creatures fear it when it's there; a big gaping jaw is about to eat them. Us humans will just be sitting there, and all of a sudden you might go, "Oh shit, I'm going to die."

In every century you find it in opera and in theater and sometimes it's in music, but certainly in the twentieth century, the blues is the apex of the appreciation of tragedy, of loss. That's what the blues is about. You know, I'm going to get up this morning, and I'm going to put on my shoes. [humming] The idea that I put on my shoes in the morning is the hardest thing in the world.

**WILLIAM:** Having to deal with another day . . . again.

**WALTER:** Right. The sun could be up, but if you had to pick cotton. . . .

**WILLIAM:** Yeah, it had to be like the worst shit. [laughing]

**WALTER:** But blues musicians had dignity. In a way—and not to speak overly highly of myself—*RL's Dream* is a reclamation. Although I'm not reclaiming something in the form, I'm not picking up a guitar, because that doesn't work anymore. That's other music and we want to move on to James Brown, Snoop Doggy Dog, Tupac. To have someone talk about his life, which is disintegrating, which is just being lost all around him and there's nothing he can do about it—that's the blues. And I just love it. The blues has changed the world.

**WILLIAM:** Did you do a lot of research for *RL's Dream*?

**WALTER:** I had been living in New York for about fifteen years. So I knew where every place was, but I had only been to Mississippi once before. I remember I wrote a thing, it was about a guy at a barber shop that was also a juke joint. It had a barber shop in the back and there was a one-eyed cat out front.

After I had written the book, I went down to Mississippi. I went to a juke joint and they had a barber shop in the back and a one-eyed cat in the front. According to the story, there was supposed to be a train, and there I was and a train was passing by. I was going, "My God!" So there are things you know, and you have to rely on your self-knowledge.

**WILLIAM:** Did you always know you were going to be a writer?

**MOSLEY:** I only started when I was about thirty-three or thirty-four.

**WILLIAM:** What did you do before then?

**WALTER:** I was in computer programming for fifteen years, on and off. It wasn't interesting, necessarily. It wasn't like, my heart. You know, that idea of becoming a lawyer or a doctor meant that I would have to put my whole heart into it. I thought I would rather get a trade or a craft than a profession. See, you can apply your trade. You don't have to be married to it.

**WILLIAM:** And what prompted you to start writing?

**WALTER:** I wanted to go back to something that I really liked, and I always loved literature, reading, philosophy. So I just started writing. I wrote a line: "On hot, sticky days in southern Louisiana, the fire ants swarm." I love that. I thought, this could be a book, and then I started writing on that.

**WILLIAM:** How do characters come to you?

**WALTER:** That's a hard question to answer. I never really know. I understood once, about two or three years ago, that I write about Black male heroes. I said, "Oh, I see"—I had written about three or four books then [laughter]—"I'm writing about black male heroes. That's what I'm doing."

It seems to me the one thing that Black male heroes need to do is they need to solve problems, and the problems are very interesting.

**WILLIAM:** For instance?

**WALTER:** In one story, some white cops are rousting Socrates for no reason other than the fact that he's poor and black and walking around at night. He thinks to himself, "I can kill these motherfuckers. Grab this one, kill him; knock that one down and kill him. I could do it. I've done it before." But he doesn't do it. And that was an interesting solution to the problem. You give him the power to do something and then have him not do it.

When I'm writing, I'm just writing because it's a lot of fun. The brain is constructed in a funny way. It's not really direct. So it's fun to write.

**WILLIAM:** Can you talk about how you work?

**WALTER:** What you do is you think of doing something, and then it echoes through something else. "What is this? Oh, I see. Yeah, that sounds right." You feel like you're no longer doing what you started out to do, but it feels good. That happens a whole lot with me—most of the time, actually. Which is now why I just kind of trust myself.

**WILLIAM:** Being from the South, when I read *RL's Dream*, and looking at the character, Kiki, I thought she was black.

**WALTER:** When I went into the South on tour for *RL's Dream*, it was the first time that a lot of women asked me anything, and they were all white women journalists. They all said—either really meaning it, or as a kind of a blind—that they knew a woman just like Kiki. They would say, "You got it!" But like, half of them, it was them, you know what I'm saying? So it's an interesting thing. There are a lot of black women like Kiki, but there are a lot of poor white women like her too . . .

**WILLIAM:** Sure.

**WALTER:** . . . who live in their own little silenced ghetto where their brutalizing mothers and fathers are destroying their lives. They have no life, and they have no self-respect, and they go off trying to find it.

**WILLIAM:** Now, in terms of choosing to work with a black publisher, you wanted to show other writers—white and black—that you can be successful outside the larger mainstream?

**WALTER:** Yes. We can be in the mainstream. But for me, it's just not enough to say I'm black and then to put some words in a character's mouth. When you have a book, you're making 20 percent of the profit, and all this other money goes to the publisher. So my income is 20 percent, but my power is like 60 percent.

**WILLIAM:** And you can play off that.

**WALTER:** Yes, because if I give the book to a black publisher, they're making the profit, they're distributing to black bookstores, working with black designers—not that other publishers don't, but as far as I recollect, they don't hire too many black people. So giving my book to a black publisher was important because the important thing is for us to *own*. We can sell. We've been selling our bodies and minds forever. But to own property, to own a business, and to control it.

**WILLIAM:** You must have felt like you were taking a huge chance?

**WALTER:** Well, I was a little nervous because I was the only one doing it. The only one. But I'm not saying that other writers shouldn't publish where they do, because most people, their business is very tight. If you make $10,000, that's what you live on. If you make $10 million, that's what you live on. So you need the next $10 million, you know what I mean? And it's true for everybody.

**WILLIAM:** So you were the only person saying . . .

**WALTER:** . . . that mainstream publishing is almost completely white. They don't have people of color as editors or as salespeople.

**WILLIAM:** Why do you think that is?

**WALTER:** Because it's a closed industry. It's not visible to the public. Industries that are visible to the public have to hire people who live there. But if you're behind closed doors and you're not supported by government contracts, you don't have to think about it. So people naturally—and not in an avid, racist sense, but naturally—hire their friends.

**WILLIAM:** Well, I worked in a publishing company, but of course the pay was very low. A lot of people there were trust fund babies, who could hold out until whenever. . . .

**WALTER:** The people I know in publishing, some are rich and some are not. But there are no Puerto Ricans. No Dominicans. Very few South East Asians. It's like they don't exist! There are a lot of Filipinos living here, but how many Filipino editors do you know? And how come the head of the division of Spanish spoken word at some publisher doesn't speak Spanish? Things like that. . . . Sure I left them.

**WILLIAM:** Didn't you help set up a program to get students into publishing?

**WALTER:** Yes, I went to City College and I met with the president, and I said, "Listen, let's have a program like this." I had a little bit of money, just enough to pay salaries for some people for a few months. And now they have fifty-eight students, most of whom are people of color, all colors. And we're going to all the various publishers saying, "Give us some money and hire our people and pay them." Because who wants to struggle through that world for $16,000 a year? [laughing] They'll say, "I can work at McDonald's and get $16,000."

**WILLIAM:** Right.

**WALTER:** But even though you don't make a lot of money, you have a great deal of power. Publishing is like the cultural backbone, not only in America, but the world.

**WILLIAM:** So the doors open up a little. . . .

**WALTER:** The people who go into publishing and art are also going to be the people who change the world. And it's a world that needs changing. Because nobody's paying attention to the reading habits of black people.

**WILLIAM:** Although a lot of books have been coming out—Terry McMillan, Jill Nelson, Tavis Smiley. All of a sudden, white publishers saw that black people read.

**WALTER:** They had no idea what they read.

**WILLIAM:** But they saw the money coming in.

**WALTER:** Right.

**WILLIAM:** How do you think we're going to gauge this period in terms of black writers and what's being published? Is any of it good? Is some of it mediocre? What of it will last? I don't want to say there's a big canon arising from all this, but what do you think?

**WALTER:** I think there are a whole variety of canons that you need to pay attention to. Right now, it's an interesting time. But you have to keep in mind that publishers put out books to make money. If people are reading horror books, publishers will bring out as many as they can. But as soon as people stop buying them, it's over.

**WILLIAM:** That's how it works.

**WALTER:** Let's say black books are selling, and they feel great about it. But as soon as they think they're not selling, which has happened quite a few times, they're gone. So even though we know they don't spend money on books that aren't selling, the problem for me is that the people in publishing were never connected to it. They don't know who those writers are. They don't know if they're good or bad.

**WILLIAM:** They just put them out to make money.

**WALTER:** Yes. And if you have no black publishers, no black editors, no black sales force, nothing, then all those writers are going to be forgotten completely. That's the problem. You might have had a great writer there.

**WILLIAM:** They need more room to be nurtured.

**WALTER:** Or at least to be remembered. So it's important that we're everywhere, but we won't be everywhere if we're not in a position to make decisions. And I mean democratically, where everybody will talk and they will all be friends. The only possibility is to make history live. And the only way to make it live is to have people working.

**WILLIAM:** I don't know what's going to happen in the next century, but for African Americans, this was our century.

**WALTER:** Right, we did it. We did everything. But now it's kind of losing it. I mean, we had so many interesting heroes. A hero is not somebody you're supposed to like. It's somebody who represented you. Your father's a hero when you got a bike. The guy down the street is a hero because he saved your sister in the fire.

**WILLIAM:** It's someone you actually know.

**WALTER:** Right, and you love that man. The only reason I'm talking about this is that I think it has a lot to do with my fiction. My fiction is about people who make decisions. A lot of these people are larger-than-life characters. Just think back to Miles. There is no black man in the black community who lived at that time that you could say that about except Miles Davis. The police, if they had to go see Miles, they always called for backup. They'd say, "We're definitely going to need some backup here." "Well, what's he doing?" And they'd say, "We think he's asleep." "Then why do you need backup?" And they'd say, "Well, you never know. . . ." [laughter]

**WILLIAM:** You don't get much of that anymore.

**WALTER:** You know, I was in LA recently, watching television, and there was a black cop and a white reporter, and two young kids from the 'hood— gang bangers, let's say. The police chief was also there, and the reporter was asking, "Well couldn't you people use the chief here as a role model?" They said, "Shit man, how am I going to use him as a role model? Is he going to put food in my mouth? Is he going to put money in my pocket? Is he going to turn the heat on in my mama's house?"

The reporter said, "But he's a very successful man. Don't you know what's going to happen to you?" And one of the kids said, "Yeah, I know what's going to happen to me. I'm either going to be dead or in jail by the time I'm twenty! But that's just the way it is." And then the kids walked away. The reporter turned to the police chief and said, "What do you think about that chief? It's a lost generation!" I was watching this, and I was thinking, who is this for? Am I supposed to believe what they're saying? The kid was the one who told the truth.

**WILLIAM:** And it was based on the fact that the man couldn't or wouldn't help him.

**WALTER:** Yes. He wasn't even mad at the police chief. The kid could have said, "How can I have this man as a role model? He's trying to kill me." But he didn't say that. He said, "This man can't feed me. This man can't put money in my pocket. That's what I need. I need money and I need to eat." So if you want to make a change, you can't just be a role model.

**WILLIAM:** You really have to do something.

**WALTER:** The idea of saying, "I'm going to be a role model," is ridiculous. What does that mean? "I'm going to be a role model." Some kid is worried about people shooting outside his house at night, and imagine someone saying, "Think about Walter Mosley—you could be like him." [laughter] And the kid saying, "I wish I could be with him right now. Is anybody shooting at Walter Mosley's house? Could I go live with him?"

# Interview with Walter Mosley
# January 1999

## Samuel Coale/1999

From *The Mystery of Mysteries: Cultural Differences and Designs*. Madison, WI: The Popular Press, pp. 200–210. © 2000 by the Board of Regents of the University of Wisconsin System. Reprinted by permission of The University of Wisconsin Press.

**Sam Coale:** You have said that you wrote a single sentence one day which spoke to you and that that got you started as a writer. Could you explain this in more detail?

**Walter Mosley:** I was working as a consulting programmer at Mobil Oil, not as an employee but working on my own. I was there on a weekend, so nobody else was there. And I was writing programs. I got tired of doing that, so I started writing this sentence: "On hot sticky days in southern Louisiana, the fire ants swarmed." And I thought, "That sounds like the first sentence in a novel." I'd read lots of novels, and that sounded good to me. So I decided to keep on writing. I was about thirty-four at the time.

**SC:** Had you always wanted to write?

**WM:** No, I hadn't. At various times in my life I'd taken a poetry workshop or something, but I'd never ever considered prose, before that day actually. It was a voice that I understood and that I could write in. I'm always a little leery of "it" speaking to me. When you say "it," it's like the id. If you want to go in that direction, okay. I wrote the sentence, started writing, and took a workshop again, but after several workshops, it wasn't working. So I went to City College and studied poetry with a man named Bill Matthews for about two or three years. I was working. I had left Mobil but came back, then I sold my first novel, *Devil in a Blue Dress*, and then I quit.

**SC:** Why did you pick the mystery form to write in?

**WM:** The first book I wrote was *Gone Fishin'*, but nobody wanted to publish it, not because they were against the writing, but they couldn't figure out who would buy the book. Who would read this book? It's kind of an interesting notion. The publishing industry is incredibly Eurocentric and also white-thinking. The idea was that the people who bought books and read books were the people the publishers knew. Seeing that everybody in publishing is white, the idea that black people would buy books that were already being published was beyond them.

**SC:** So it is similar to Toni Morrison who worked at Random House and helped cultivate a black audience while she was writing the books that they would eventually buy.

**WM:** Yes.

**SC:** Did the publishers suggest to you the mystery form?

**WM:** No. Nobody suggested it to me. Everybody said that there was good writing in *Gone Fishin'*, but it wasn't commercial, and come back when I had something else.

**SC:** But why the mystery form, which is essentially Eurocentric and white?

**WM:** I'm not sure it is. Let's get rid of your caveat. What happened was that I read a lot of mysteries, and the mysteries that influenced me were of three different kinds. Political, which I find Dashiell Hammett to be; funny, which Rex Stout is; and then that kind of exotic world, which, I think, Arthur Conan Doyle portrays, bringing people to the exotic realms of the British Empire in his work. I've always loved those three different kinds of mysteries, where you're going into this new, exotic world or laughing at the voice that's telling you the story or becoming aware of the political nature of a narrative. I started writing definitely not knowing that I was beginning to write a mystery. It was only when I was about halfway through it, I said, "Well, it is kind of in that genre." And when I was finished with it, I realized, "Yeah, it is." So that was it.

Now of course there's also an economic issue involved. To begin with, when I wrote my first contract with Norton, it was for two books. The reason I wrote the next one is that they had already paid me for it.

**SC:** You had held on to *Gone Fishin'* until later, until you were established.

**WM:** Yes, after *Black Betty*.

**SC:** Which was a great thing in the way you gave it to Black Classic Press to publish.

**WM:** Yes. It was a wonderful experience for all involved. We were all happy about it.

**SC:** When Hillerman writes about the Navajo, he has to fit them into the mystery formula. He makes Jim Chee caught in the middle of two distinctly different cultures. Did that same thing occur to you in terms of black culture?

**WM:** I have a notion in my head that novels are plots. There are other things that they are, but they're also plots. They're stories which are based on plot. I also think that the finer quality of story-telling is plot. People are sitting there listening to your story. They have to be excited to find out what happens next. Plot for me is the structure of revelation, how things are revealed on the pedestrian level but also for revelation on another level. For me the mystery is not alien to any other form of fiction. It's part of every form of fiction. For instance, *RL's Dream* has no mystery to it. That was a very hard book to write because of that. I'm interested in what happened and why it happened, though you still have the "what's-going-to-happen next" in that book.

**SC:** You also seem very interested in moral questions, in the choices your characters have to or are forced to make. The mystery formula can be relatively simplistic when it comes to morality, the good guys vs. the bad guys, but you conjure up a world which is much more complex than that.

**WM:** I'm less interested in the simple concepts of good and evil. It's not true, for one thing, so it's hard to believe in. In an important way it doesn't really satisfy a reader who has any sophistication whatsoever. When I was a kid, I'd read a book, and Winnie the Pooh was always good, and the good princess and the prince wearing light-colored clothes would make it. That's fine, but if there isn't any gray area, then the reader has no way to identify with and understand the characters and the world they're struggling with. Mysteries, especially nowadays, help people with their own struggles with right and wrong in the world.

**SC:** Do you see yourself as in some way subverting the traditional mystery form?

**WM:** Well, no. Dashiell Hammett did that. The Continental Op was a guy who was always involved in a world where good and evil blended. You couldn't destroy one without destroying the other. I don't think I'm subverting anything, at least not from that particular perspective. When you have a country that denies its genesis and denies its roots, you have a country that's based on successful genocide. You have a country that's built on the concept of slave labor. And it's still going on today. It denies the black blood in its veins, the black and the red and the brown and the impoverished labor that built it. Then if you make a hero like Easy Rawlins, to some degree and at some level, that's subversive. I feel like I'm telling the truth, and it's hard for me to call the truth subversive.

**SC:** Even though we figure out who did what to whom, there is still this whole question of racism and moral ambiguity in terms of Easy's role and the society he's in. Maybe subversive is the wrong word, but your complex plots open up or break down the simplistic idea of good and evil.

**WM:** It starts dealing with other issues outside the issues of dealing with the mystery. I think that I do do that. When you start talking about good and bad, you think, how bad can this guy be, if Mouse is standing on the other side of you? Mouse is evil. He's other things, too, but he's evil. He does some really bad things. And Easy has to deal with him. So how bad could anybody else be?

The issue isn't if somebody's good or bad. There are the problems that Easy's trying to solve. He's trying to live in a world where there is no law. He's trying to impose some sense of justice in a world that has no sense of justice.

**SC:** The very environment he's in practically denies his ability to make moral choices.

**WM:** Any choice that he makes is condemned on one level or another. And so is everything he does. Now this is not untrue in the rest of the genre. The thing is you have to remember that this is always the point. This is the point, for instance, of Philip Marlowe. He is always walking in that gray area, doing things that the law might think is wrong, but we think is right. Same thing with Ross Macdonald and Lew Archer. Archer often has to make decisions which don't necessarily go along with right and wrong and the law. Even Sherlock Holmes does that at times. Sometimes he lets people go, sees that they've done something but decides to do nothing about it.

It's how I'm using it specifically with this kind of racial-political bent to it that makes the mystery different, but it's not a new thing in the genre. As far back as you go, you'll see that the detective, especially the hard-boiled detective, is questioning the laws and the rules of the society that we live in.

**SC:** It is a balancing act, however, to both play within the formula and create an environment that is so nightmarish and hard-boiled and racist that whatever happens within that environment opens up all kinds of different possibilities.

**WM:** Easy's job is different from the regular detective. When he's representing someone or trying to help someone, he's definitely going to be at odds with the police in ways that other detectives like Marlowe or Archer aren't. But the other thing that's amazing is that everybody's doing that all the time. Everybody in their lives is having to hide, having to lie, having to do things which makes him or her invisible or opaque to the law. You have to break the law in order to survive, because the law is against you.

**SC:** Do you buy DuBois' sense of double consciousness, both inside and outside the culture at the same time?

**WM:** Like Ralph Ellison in his *Invisible Man*. I've said before that Easy is a kind of concretized invisible man. And has to be because of the very nature of things.

**SC:** In the Rawlins' mysteries you cover the period of history, so far, from 1948 to 1963. August Wilson has done something similar in his plays. How did you decide to do that?

**WM:** That was my intention from the first when I wrote *Gone Fishin'* to follow that migration of black people to Los Angeles and to show what went on with them in L.A. as time went on, as people came from the deep South and moved up there.

**SC:** How much of Easy's history parallels or reflects your own family's history?

**WM:** My people, maybe; my family, not all that much. There are some aspects that cover my family. My father was a supervising custodian, and that's where Easy is right now. My father owned property and managed it, and Easy does that. It seems to be telling, but there's not much depth to it. All my father's side of the family came from Texas and Louisiana.

**SC:** It's similar then to the way James Lee Burke treats his family's history. Where does your mother figure into this?

**WM:** Partly because I'm writing it, my mother fits into it. As far as the Jewish side of my family, in the mysteries you have characters such as Chaim Wenzler and Saul Lynx who are major parts of books but not fifty percent of the books. Wenzler was a Communist union organizer. Saul Lynx is a Jewish detective married to a black woman. I guess that's where that side of my family comes from.

**SC:** How do you feel about the many critics who refer to Easy Rawlins as a black consciousness?

**WM:** What does black consciousness mean? Easy is a black man, and he sees the world from the point of view of a black man. The world sees him as a black man. Because of this, a lot of people will see a world either that they never suspected existed or that they have experienced their whole lives but never seen in literature. In that, it is a black consciousness. Not *the* black conscience or consciousness, not the only way to see the world, but a way to see the world which comes from the other side.

**SC:** So blackness is very much a social construction from the historical world you're writing about?

**WM:** Yes.

**SC:** Do you see any progress from 1948 to 1963? I see progress with Easy in terms of getting his act together, becoming more stabilized.

**WM:** Do I see it in the books? I'm not sure. We'll have to see as it goes along. There's some progress and some backsliding. We'll see more in the next Easy mystery, *Bad Boy Brawly Brown*.

**SC:** Does your interest in music and the blues help to explain the qualities of voice in your fiction?

**WM:** I've always been good at dialogue. Period. I'm good at writing from particular points of view, not necessarily just black. The way that people phrase words, use words, leave words out—that kind of stuff. There's that. And I think that's a mark of any good novelist. When I was with Toni Morrison once, she got introduced as a novelist, and I got introduced as "the mystery writer." But I don't see myself just in that category at all. I'm really interested in black life in America.

**SC:** Your newest novel, *Blue Light* (New York: Little, Brown, 1998) is science fiction. Where did that come from?

**WM:** I've always wanted to write science fiction. I love it. My whole life I've read as much science fiction as I've read mysteries. The book on Socrates Fortlow [*Always Outnumbered, Always Outgunned*] came out of a very specific desire to make sure that people understand that they know what philosophy is and that it comes out of the black community. We have a way of thinking about and seeing the world.

A lot of people want to see American history as just European history with some exotic spices, some Native American spice, some African-American spirituals; they know how to hum to God. That kind of stuff. But really the understanding of the world comes from everywhere. I'm not trying to denigrate European history and the advances in science, but America is so crazy. If you were going to get an operation, they would rather give you medicines that might kill you, rather than use acupuncture, which works just as well. I have a friend whose father died from anesthesia. When he went to get the operation, the anesthesia killed him. But they'll say, "We're the most advanced in the world!" No. In this particular thing, acupuncture is more advanced. You should be using that. The thing is you have a culture that denies history, so writing about Socrates or writing something even like *Blue Light*, which is a very philosophical book itself. . . . I'm not only thinking about being black or about being the victim of the white world or whatever. There are all these other things. Some things fit inside of writing mysteries, which is why I like writing them, but in a mystery every few pages you've got to check back into the plot.

Writing science fiction frees you up to think about the world. Sometimes you start looking at so-called literary novels, and they're about the guy who's waiting at the bus stop and got on the bus and saw the woman, and he remembered his father from long ago. And then he got off the bus, and he went to work. Sometimes it's brilliant, but when it sings for me—*Remembrance of Things Past, A Hundred Years of Solitude*—it goes way beyond things that you know or even believe. But you still believe them, even more, when you read them. I find it really exciting when you can ask, "What is the soul?"

I feel that there's an edict from the literary world, and that edict is that black people are best suited to address the nature of their own chains. But if indeed that's the only thing we ever do, then we'll never be free. You can't be free, looking at yourself as a victim or talking about the history of you being a victim. You have to be thinking about something else. So part of it was just writing a book that went way way out there, and started talking about, "What if we were not alone in the universe, and we were related to all other life? And what if we were equal to everything around us—mosquitoes and trees and jellyfish—that there's nothing really all that special that separates us from those around us? How would that compare to what we could be?" I thought about it and decided I'd put a black character in it, but it's not really a book about that. It's a book about race but more in a general sense.

**SC:** Does *Blue Light* relate at all to the American incarnation of voodoo, called hoodoo? The belief in a higher power or life force, the worship of the ancestors like Orde in your book, divination and prophecy, animism. Are you aware of that at all?

**WM:** I think it does, but it's not like I do some serious study of it. Right now when you called, I was reading this book on Plato. I'm interested in Plato. I read stuff like that. But I don't make copious notes on it. And I don't usually talk about it. It just usually becomes a part of you. I'm very involved in various organizations. I really got a lot out of being in Cuba [Mosley had just returned from a visit to Cuba with such luminaries as Danny Glover, the actor]. It kind of comes in, and it settles, and it simmers, and it comes out again. I'm not really trying to make an argument for any particular divination system. But they're there. And they're part of a dialogue. I see myself as the kind of person who opens dialogue. I think that's what novelists are. We open dialogue. If we do it right, the dialogues continue. People read about them, consider them, think about them. Either they talk about them or they write about them or they make music about them. But it goes on. The most successful person who does that in the English language is Shakespeare. I think that's wonderful.

**SC:** Is your writing part of a process of self-discovery?

**WM:** It is, but I wouldn't want to limit it to writing. Self-discovery goes on in a lot of things. It goes on in conversation. For instance, I was very fortunate when I was in Cuba with TransAfrica. The last night Castro called us all to the presidential palace. We went to see him, and he kind of lectured us for two or three hours. It was wild, because a lot of stuff he was saying was completely new to me. And a lot of it was things that I have been thinking about. Which led me when I came back home to reading Plato. I thought about Plato's *Republic* and all of its good and bad aspects and how it has its reflection in Cuba.

And also as you start to think about it, when you're talking to the person next to you, ideas come up. I think it's very concentrated for a writer. If you sit there and say I'm going to write a mystery—the bad guy is this criminal who runs his empire without anybody knowing it; the victim is Little Nell; the hero is the detective, Charlie Proudfoot; this is what happens—the whole plot is worked out, and then you write it down. You'll probably sell a lot of books that way, but the thing is you're really not going to find out anything about yourself, because basically what you're doing is just structuring things. Some things don't fit when you first write it. That's what rewriting is. But it feels good.

**SC:** Were Chance's experiences at Berkeley in *Blue Light* like yours?

**WM:** Some, but not much. I used to hang out in Berkeley. I knew what it was like, and I like to talk about it. But it's very different from my own experience. I went to Vermont in 1971, and I was there. I went to Goddard College originally. I lived there for about four or five years, and then got into the state college finally. Then I moved down to Massachusetts, went to the University of Massachusetts for awhile, studied political theory. Didn't really like it. I liked political theory. I wasn't very interested in teaching. I was a cook, and cooks usually cook more than they talk about theory. Or Socrates for that matter.

**SC:** Do you feel that you are in a unique position because of your background, both inside and outside the culture?

**WM:** I don't know. One wants to be special with a unique view of the world, but the reality is that there are very few black people in America who are only black. Almost everybody has some Native American blood. There's Irish. Look at people's last names. They're not just made up things. Mc-Something or other. There's some Scottish in there somewhere. Somebody owned somebody, and there was some mixing. The languages we speak, the schools we go to. So the idea of me having a special view of the world—sure I do, but most other people do, too.

**SC:** Some recognize the multiplicity of identities, but our national politics seems to be moving in another direction. I find that scary.

**WM:** It is scary if you don't accept who you are. A lot of people probably are incapable of accepting it. One of the things I was amazed at in Cuba, when you talk to political leaders, they told us, "We all have black blood in our veins." You'd never see a so-called white leader in America saying that. So you have people who are denying their history, and, therefore, they're denying not just me but so many others.

I'm a writer. I write novels. I think the Easy Rawlins books are novels just as much as *RL's Dream* or *Blue Light*, and even my collection of short stories has that feel to it.

**SC:** Is *Black Genius* (New York: Norton, 1999), the new collection of essays, based on lectures that you and others, such as Spike Lee, Melvin Van Peebles, bell hooks, and Angela Davis, gave at New York University?

**WM:** Each of them wrote an essay. I put together the thing. I wrote the introduction. I gave one of the talks. I just finished a book for Random House for their series on ideas of contemporary thought. I wrote a piece for it, called "This Blue Earth: Contemplating Our Chains at the End of the Millennium."

It's not like I'm experimenting. It's like I'm a writer. If I've done something once, I've done it.

**SC:** Are you ever afraid of being typecast?

**WM:** I'm going to be writing about black characters mostly. Certainly in *RL's Dream* I have a major white character. In *Blue Light* there are many different characters of many different colors. You wouldn't come up to Bernard Malamud and ask, "What are you going to write about?" I'm not that interested in drifting that far away from my basic subject. I don't think that novels are purely entertainment. They are entertainment, but I'm also trying to do something. This is a way of crystalizing and holding the culture and also examining the culture and letting other people examine it while they read it.

**SC:** Where did *Gone Fishin'* come from, your first book?

**WM:** I was learning how to write then. Part of it was trying to write a novel in the worst way. I was taking a class with Edna O'Brien, and she said to me, "You have to write a novel." And I said, "Okay, Edna. I'll do that." And I wrote that book. It didn't take me long. It was about three months. I was very excited. It was the beginning. It was me working it out. It wasn't me coming back and trying to explain anything.

I get up every morning and write. I didn't write at all when I was in Cuba. I had a few hours every morning that I could have written, and I decided for the first time in ten years not to. When I write, everything points toward that writing. The whole world outside shuts down. And I didn't want to do that in Cuba. I wanted to see Cuba.

I'm writing a new detective series. I have a new detective named Archibald Lawless, Anarchist at Large. You're always looking for a new kind of twist. I figure that an anarchist is a perfect detective. But I'm writing this book, and I'm discovering that it's really about something else completely, which is shocking to me. I really thought I knew what I was writing about.

I'm going to come back to Easy. There's no problem with that.

I have all these books. I've written a book called *The Man in My Basement*, which is a literary novel. I've written the next collection of Socrates stories, called *Walkin' the Dog*. That'll come out next fall. I really love writing.

It's funny, because we live in this English system, and English is big, but it's not everything. The writers who really move me very much are the French—Zola, Balzac. Balzac wrote like a hundred and eight novels. Simenon wrote eighty Maigret novels, and then eighty other novels. If you write, that's what you do.

**SC:** Do you have a feeling that you're making up for lost time, since you came to writing relatively late in your life?

**WM:** It's not that, but the thing is that when you have a choice of what you're doing and where you're going and who you're doing it with, the real important thing I know is that I'm a writer. That's the thing I do that's important. I'm continually drifting in that direction. What would I like to do? First I'm going to get that three hours of writing in.

**SC:** Many mystery writers started out just writing mysteries. I have the feeling that if I were to interview you ten years from now, first of all there would be seventeen more books, but secondly the mystery would be only one part of the spectrum.

**WM:** It is a big problem for mystery writers, because they're defined by it. I saw a woman once in a mystery bookstore, and she'd walked to the door, opened it but didn't step across the threshold, and looked at the owner, and she said, "I have two questions. Is the new Parker a Spenser?" And the owner said, "No." And the other woman said, "Oh, well, there's only one question." And she left. She didn't even walk in. My God! Because the new Parker at that time was a crime novel. It wasn't a Spenser. But the woman wasn't even interested in him writing another crime novel. And it's true, because I'll sell many more Easy Rawlins novels than I will *RL's Dream*, for instance, or Socrates. But if all that you were worried about was how much money you made and how many books you sold, you should go into real estate. That's where the money is. John Grisham makes a lot of money, but he doesn't make as much money as Donald Trump. Go into real estate! Buy buildings! People never get tired about buying real estate. They might get tired of your characters, but they never get tired about buying houses!

I really believe that my career is on an arc. If you're a real writer, you're writing words that are worth reading on their own account, not because of anything else but just because of the sentences. And the sentences help shape the structure of the story. Then you have a career, and that career has a long arc, forty years, fifty years.

**SC:** When you wanted to publish a book besides mysteries, did your publishers grumble?

**WM:** Grumble?! Oh, my God, grumble! Norton refused to publish *Blue Light*. It was what it was. They said we can't sell this book. And I asked, "Is there something wrong with it?" We don't sell science fiction. Which is not true. The other day I saw that Norton has an anthology of science fiction! I went to Little, Brown.

I just write. I feel that I've been pulled a little far afield, and I'd kind of like to get back to write the next Easy. I really do like the classic guys. I like Chandler, Hammett, and Ross Macdonald I think is a wonderful writer. But I also like Archie Goodwin's life. I don't care about the mystery; every plot is exactly the same. It doesn't matter really, because just reading his voice and his view of the world is more than enough. Archibald Lawless isn't exactly like that, because I always have a dark side to my work, but just to write a voice is fine. Lawless is not the narrator. He has hired a guy as his scribe, and the scribe is actually telling the stories.

Of course, writing in the first person is a very strong thing, especially for the hard-boiled detectives. I could write *RL's Dream* from a third-person point of view, and it was fine. I could never do that with one of the mysteries. With Easy you want to believe in him, and the first-person narrator helps make that possible.

# On the Chain Gang

## Elizabeth Farnsworth/2000

From the PBS Online NewsHour. April 6, 2000. Found at http://www.pbs.org/newshour/ gergen/jan-june00/mosley_4-6.html (accessed 2010). Reprinted by permission.

**Elizabeth Farnsworth:** The new book is *Workin' on the Chain Gang: Shaking off the Dead Hand of History* by Walter Mosley. His first nonfiction book, it looks at what he calls "the chains that define our range of motion." Mosley has written, among other books, seven critically acclaimed mysteries, featuring a reluctant private eye named Easy Rawlins. One of those novels, *Devil in a Blue Dress*, became a movie starring Denzel Washington. A story collection, featuring a character named Socrates Fortlow, an ex-con who's a kind of moral guide in South Central Los Angeles, became a movie on HBO. Walter Mosley grew up in Los Angeles, went to college in Vermont, became a computer programmer, and then wrote his first novel in his mid-thirties. His books have been translated into twenty languages. Thanks for being with us, Mr. Mosley.

**Walter Mosley:** Thank you.

**Elizabeth Farnsworth:** What are the chains you see? Who's still working on the chain gang?

**Walter Mosley:** Well, we're all working on the chain gang. I mean, that's what I wrote the book about. I was originally going to write a book about black people in the twenty-first century, and as I started to study and to think about and wonder about the problems that black people had, it blossomed out to cover everybody. So it seemed to me that even though maybe not everybody is aware of it, that we're all in the same boat, that we're all laboring under that margin of profit.

**Elizabeth Farnsworth:** Okay. Keep going. What do you mean we're all working on the chain gang, margin of profit?

**Walter Mosley:** Well, you know, the idea that . . . most of us are stuck in our labor, that we're three or four, maybe five or six paychecks away from poverty and homelessness, that it's almost impossible to pay for good edu-

86

cation for more than one or two kids, that it's hard for young people to buy a house, to make enough money to pay for both eating and the rent, all of these things that come together in America: America, you know, which is the land of plenty; America which is the richest country in the history of the world. It seems that if you're in the working class, which most of us are, no matter what kind of class we want to call ourselves in, it's a big struggle. And the struggle is getting harder; it's not getting easier.

**Elizabeth Farnsworth:** And you think the profit motive is to blame for this?

**Walter Mosley:** I think that the way that capitalism works and the way that it is understood is the problem. I mean, a lot of people think that democracy and capitalism are the same thing when they're two very different things. You know, it's a very simple book. . . . I'm not saying things that haven't been said before. I'm not talking about some kind of new system or some kind of scientific way to get out of problems. I'm just trying to say, "Listen, we're stuck inside of this margin of profit. . . . The only place really to make money is off the labor of the people working for you, and so we're the one who pays for it."

**Elizabeth Farnsworth:** And I was struck by how careful you were to say that you didn't propose any other kind of system, especially any system that's utopian or too idealistic, as you put it.

**Walter Mosley:** The people all the way back, 2,000, 2,500 years to Plato who tried to come up with theories or ideas about how society will grow, necessarily, from *The Republic* to *Das Kapital*, they always end up saying, "Well, for a little while we're going to need a dictatorship. For a little while we're going to need the few dominating the many." I don't want that. I mean, I think that we live in it today. I don't want it here. I don't want it any other time. I want us to come together. I want us to work in a democratic way, in a democratic process to try to change the world.

**Elizabeth Farnsworth:** And how? How do we all get rid of our chains?

**Walter Mosley:** Well, you know, it's so difficult to talk about, and certainly to be certain about. And in this book, you know, you have to understand, when I talk about a nonfiction book, I usually think that nonfiction books lie . . . because they're trying to convince you of their argument. I'm not trying to convince anybody of my argument. But what I'm trying to say is that we need to cut out the distractions, the spectacles and illusion. It would be nice to give up television and drinking and big arena sports for twelve weeks, let's say; just to sit down in your house and think about who you are and what you are and where you are—from that point, to begin to start to list what are the most important things in our lives. What do we need to do? What do I think the most important thing is? And then to ask questions. I mean, simple questions like, "Who can become president?" You know, when I think of it and when somebody asks me, "Well, who do you think could be president?" I say, "Well, I can tell you . . . I don't know who's going to be, but I can tell you that it's a him, that he's white, that he's over thirty-five and under sixty, that he's tall, that he's handsome, that he speaks well, that he's probably wealthy, that he's straight, that he's married. You know when you finish describing who can be president, you realize, well, you don't live in a democracy, because only 1 percent of the country can be president.

**Elizabeth Farnsworth:** Mr. Mosley, do you think that being a novelist gives you the imagination to see things as they might be, and that's one reason you can write a book like this?

**Walter Mosley:** Well, I think that in order to change what America is, we need imagination. I don't know if being a novelist, or being a photographer, or a painter, or a journalist or. . . . You know, there's a lot of creativity in a lot of different people in America, but in order to change America, we need to be creative, and we need to reject the creativity that's boxed and sold to us like on the television and radios. We need to say, "Well, maybe there's something better than getting on a game show and winning $1 million" or, you know, stripping down to my underwear and maybe attracting somebody for $1 million.

**Elizabeth Farnsworth:** At first I thought this was a departure. It's nonfiction. Your other books are mysteries. But all your work seems to me to be about morality when I look at it again. Socrates—after all, the name—Fortlow is the moral philosopher, even though he's an ex-con. Where did this strong interest in morality and moral dilemmas, really the solving of moral dilemmas, come from?

**Walter Mosley:** Well, you know, it's really interesting. When I was traveling around talking about my Easy Rawlins novels here and there around the country, a lot of people would ask me—you know, my mother's Jewish, my father's black—a lot of people would say, "Where does your Jewish side come from?" Or "Where's your white side," not thinking that that's Jewish. And I'm going, what do you mean? They say, "You know, we see Easy doing all of these things that we consider black, but now that we've seen him reading books, intellectual books, we think, "Well, that's where the white side is: The part that reads." And I look at these people, and I say, but you know, black people read, and black people think. But it was very hard to convince them. That's the reason I wrote about Socrates Fortlow. And I guess Socrates led me into writing this book. The biggest thing in black America is that we're solving problems. We're always solving problems, because we're faced with moral dilemmas all the time. Do you want to do wrong in order to make it? Do you want to do right and suffer instead? There are all kinds of problems that we face, and now you have to understand, I think that it's not just black people, I think it's all people in America. You know, from far right white movements to far left or radical black movements, everybody's worried about how can they get good medical care for their family and their children. Everybody's worried about having a good job and making sure that they and the people that they love can do well in their lives. And the reason I wrote the book is to say, "Listen, we come together." When Malcolm X says, "You have been bamboozled," he's not just talking to me. He's not just talking to black people. Everybody in America's been bamboozled. And we have to back away from that, look at it a little closer, and then wonder how we can do better with this nation.

**Elizabeth Farnsworth:** But I'm really glad you brought that up, because you write in the book that the chains might be more recognizable in the black experience, but they chain us, they restrain us all. And you do feel that African Americans have something to teach other Americans in this? Explain that.

**Walter Mosley:** Well, one of the problems with being marginalized, black people being marginalized, is that it's easy to say black history is a special thing; it's an elective, it's the month of February, it's not something important. But really, black American history speaks to all of America. To begin with, it is American history. The organization of labor, the labor of black people, is the foundation of how labor is organized in America. When black people were freed, the way that they were kind of re-chained to their labor, you know, becoming sharecroppers instead of slaves, is the way that almost everybody relates to their labor in America. And the way that we fought it, through the civil rights movement, through the Black Panthers, through the Black Nationalist movement, through the Congress, everything that we've done is a way to teach other people how to move ahead and how to fight against oppression in America. And indeed, there is oppression in America, as much as people don't want to think there is.

**Elizabeth Farnsworth:** Are people listening? Are you pleased with the reception you've gotten so far?

**Walter Mosley:** Well, you know, I'm very happy about it because young people, between eighteen and maybe twenty-five, thirty, have really enjoyed the book. People who are older, people who have been brought up in the system of the twentieth century, which means to say that political systems should have answers—you know, if you do A, B, and C, then it will work. No matter what it is—you know, if it's democracy, or communism, or fascism, whatever, those people, the older people have some problems with it [*Workin' on the Chain Gang*]. They say, "Well, you wrote all this stuff. You didn't give me an answer." I say, "Well, the answer lies within us." We have to find the answer in ourselves, and we have to find the connection between us in order to make things different.

**Elizabeth Farnsworth:** Well, Walter Mosley, thank you very much for being with us.

**Walter Mosley:** Thank you.

# Eavesdropping with Walter Mosley and Colson Whitehead

## Colson Whitehead and Walter Mosley/2000

From Book: The Magazine for the Reading Life/2001. © Barnes & Noble. With permission of Barnes & Noble.

Lured by the dual promises of a midday meal at a famous Brooklyn eatery and the opportunity to meet an admired colleague, Colson Whitehead and Walter Mosley accepted an invitation from *Book* to dine at Junior's Restaurant a couple of months before Whitehead's second novel, *John Henry Days*, a rumination on the legendary black folk hero, was released.

Walter Mosley, forty-nine, the award-winning author of six Easy Rawlins mysteries and half dozen other books, arrives punctually and hangs up his fedora and overcoat before sitting down. Whitehead—whose debut, *The Intuitionist*, was a critically acclaimed genre-bending novel about an elevator inspector-cum-detective working in a retro future in an unnamed New York—walks in a little after 1 p.m., having recently awoken. "You know what you're having?" Mosley asks. "A salad," Whitehead says, which elicits a "Damn" from Mosley before he orders ribs, fried chicken, a cup of matzo-ball soup, and three small Perriers. This is their first meeting, though the two have been paying attention to each other for years. Mosley made a strong impression with his first book, 1990's *Devil in a Blue Dress*, and hasn't let up since as a novelist, essayist, critic, or filmmaker; besides Easy Rawlins, the reluctant detective who was played by Denzel Washington in the 1995 screen adaption, he's also written a series of stories starring Socrates Fortlow. His new lead character, Fearless Jones, appears in June. Whitehead, thirty-one, was hailed as a next big thing by critics, reviewers, and blurb artists—including Mosley—when *The Intuitionist* was published two years ago; *Fearless Jones* has been eagerly anticipated. The two shared opinions on topics ranging from Ralph Ellison to Spider-Man. And Gina Gershon got name-checked as well.

**MOSLEY:** Why is John Henry important to you?

**WHITEHEAD:** I guess I just always really dug him, in elementary school.

**MOSLEY:** Me too.

**WHITEHEAD:** And just as a kid, he was the first black superhero I knew. I grew up in the early '70s, and one day—I think it was third or fourth grade—the teacher said, "We're going to see a movie," and it was a half-hour cartoon about John Henry. It was really moving. It was a black family in a cartoon; they were dynamic. John Henry is a superhero and he's fighting a machine.

**MOSLEY:** How did you feel about him losing to that machine? Because that made me cry.

**WHITEHEAD:** I didn't cry.

**MOSLEY:** I was so upset.

**WHITEHEAD:** I didn't know what to make of it, which is why I guess I had to write about it later on, because does he win or not? Does the machine win? *Or,* do the dehumanizing forces win? Is he affirmed or is it a useless gesture?

**MOSLEY:** So now, many years later, what's your answer?

**WHITEHEAD:** I still don't think I know.

**MOSLEY:** I guess I don't either. But I always felt bad about it. But he did win, right?

**WHITEHEAD:** He actually wins the race, yeah.

**MOSLEY:** Then he dies. A blood vessel breaks in his head.

**WHITEHEAD:** Yeah. So I think a lot of *John Henry Days* is about how do we interpret that. The book jumps around in different decades, different people: a blues man in the '30s, a sheet music writer in the 1910s, sort of struggling against their own personal machines. Can we win? What does winning mean? So I think it will provide a lot of different answers. You can walk away thinking, Yeah, John Henry wins, or, No, John Henry loses, and it would be OK with the book.

**MOSLEY:** One of the things I like about your work is that I don't really feel like you're trying to tell me what to think.

**WHITEHEAD:** I think you can read a book when you're ten, twenty and thirty, and fifty and sixty, and have different interpretations of that book. And that's what's great about art.

### On Being a Black Writer

**MOSLEY:** If somebody says, "Colson Whitehead, the black writer," what do you think about that?

**WHITEHEAD:** I always thought it was great. When I was in college and

I was trying to find what I couldn't find in course classes, in the black section, there're all the people you heard about that you were supposed to read. There are all sorts of interpretations you can put on being a *black* writer. Are you not being put in the same category as white writers?

**MOSLEY:** It is an interesting question. The other night I went to Toni Morrison's seventieth birthday party. It was a big thing, five hundred people. Rita Dove and I were the emcees of it. Everybody was there. Now somebody got up there and had to give a speech, and in this speech said Toni Morrison is the first black writer—no, first black woman writer—to be awarded the Nobel Prize. This person went on to say she was the first black and the first black woman to do a series of other things, and I didn't like it. I didn't want to hear it and I didn't want to hear someone talk about Toni like that. Damn. She wins the fucking Nobel Prize, and I still have to say, "Well, you know, but she's a black woman"? Come on. Really. At some point or another you have to say, "Damn." I'm looking at *The Intuitionist* and I would say this is a major literary event in American letters. I wish to claim you as a black writer on some levels, but on other levels, I don't want to; and really, I don't mind. When people say, "Walter Mosley, the black writer," this is fine, I don't mind. I don't care. You know, I am a black mystery writer, I'm a black blah-blah writer, or whatever kind of black writer I am, it's all right. But on some levels, I get upset. And I especially get upset for other people, not so much for myself.

**WHITEHEAD:** It's like the "N" word. It depends who's saying it. I feel like I'm trying to face black literature, I'm trying to extend the canon of black literature, and I'm a black writer doing this.

**MOSLEY:** Who do you see as your audience?

**WHITEHEAD:** The people who show up really change from venue to venue. When it first came out, and people hadn't read the book and they heard it was crazy elevator inspectors, I got a lot of sci-fi and comic book fans. Then when I read last week, it was mostly middle-aged women who had book clubs.

**MOSLEY:** Did you lose that original audience?

**WHITEHEAD:** No, I think they'll be back for the reading at the hipster bookstore. I'm always surprised at the faces who show up and just grateful that there is an audience, to tell you the truth.

**MOSLEY:** Anybody. I don't care who you are, just come. That's really true about being a writer. "Aren't you upset that there are only white people in the audience?" No. They were buying books and I was very happy to see them.

**WHITEHEAD:** I feel like my ideal reader is me at sixteen, or someone like me, who has just been reading the usual high school stuff and hasn't been exposed to some kind of freaky postwar black literature—when I was sixteen, I was reading Stephen King. . . . Last week I did a thing for this Writer in Schools program in D.C. The teacher had taught the book two days before and I went in and talked about the book and the kids were incredibly smart and thoughtful. They seemed to get the book. They didn't ask the same sort of questions I usually get. . . . They see me as the novelist guy, which I still have a hard time seeing myself as. I guess I am a novelist but they see me as a Novelist with a capital "N."

MOSLEY: You do well not to see yourself—or anyone else—in that way, because all of a sudden you start to sound like a baritone. [Deep voice] "Well, you know, I was thinking just the other day," [normal voice] and that's just awful.

## On Movies, Comics, and Agents Who Quit

MOSLEY: Have you done any writing of screenplays?

WHITEHEAD: Ten years ago I had this crazy thing. I was in college and I wrote a script for this small production company. It was the most horrible experience.

MOSLEY: Did they pay you?

WHITEHEAD: Yeah—very little. Meanwhile, it's this *Risky Business* meets *House Party*, some sort of black teen genre thing. It was so ridiculous and dumb. I'd get these notes: "How 'bout the main character gets in jail and has to rap his way out of being attacked by other prisoners." Aaaah, I signed a contract and I'm totally debasing myself.

MOSLEY: It's really true, though. It's the same as writing articles for a magazine. It's not so much beforehand they tell you what to write—it's after you've written it, they start cutting things out. . . . Films—what are you thinking?

WHITEHEAD: When the elevator inspector book came out, I got a lot of calls from big-name people who were like, "We love the book," and we'd have lunch and then they'd read the last fifty pages and realize there isn't a big car crash at the end of the book and I wouldn't hear from them again. And they'd also realize that the main character is a black woman, and we can't get funding for a black woman detective.

MOSLEY: Can we make her a man?

WHITEHEAD: Yeah, or make her Gina Gershon or—

MOSLEY: —Jennifer Tilly, hey. Shit. That's a movie right there. She could be black. You know, Larry Block had a character, the Burglar, I forgot his name, but they made the movie. It's a white, Jewish guy who's a burglar and they made it Whoopi Goldberg. So it's a black woman with a Jewish name—that's close—which I think was kind of wonderful. But that's what happens.

**WHITEHEAD:** I have a cousin I'm very close to, and he's a young filmmaker, and last summer he says, "Let's make some crazy action movie we always wanted to make when we were kids after reading comics and watching *Alien* and *Road Warrior* ten times in a row." We're working on it on and off. We'll see what happens. You know, it's fun making it up; it's fun to have the kind of rapport where you can say, "Let's rip off *Spider-Man 178* where Electro does this," and the other person knows what you're saying.

**MOSLEY:** You read Marvel [Comics]?

**WHITEHEAD:** I was a Marvel guy, yeah.

**MOSLEY:** I have this gigantic collection, it's like 30,000, and I've been lately accruing the first hundred *Fantastic Four*s. I have no end of love for it, no end of love.

**WHITEHEAD:** A couple years ago my parents were cleaning out a storage space that we had and they said, "Come get your stuff," and I was like, "I don't have any stuff in there." My brother shows up one day with about ten boxes of comic books I hadn't seen in years, so I read half of them over again. It was such fun, such kicks.

**MOSLEY:** It's still kind of wonderful for adolescent boys, and also for young black men—the whole notion of a need to become so much more than you are in order to just get what a normal everyday person gets. I have to be Spider-Man. I have to be the Thing. I have to be as smart as Reed Richards. I can't just be a normal person and go to school and get out and expect shit, because nobody has anything. I think for young black men there's also a desire to go further than yourself: I can jump up on top of that building and swing from place to place, and if somebody came up behind me, I could sense it. You can never sneak up on me. I can tell danger. The whole idea. I find it really interesting. . . . So you're working on your third novel? And you're a novelist, but not with a capital "N"—

**WHITEHEAD:** No, not yet.

**MOSLEY:** —But, you'd be dead if you have a capital "N" in your name. Is there anything other than that that you want to do?

**WHITEHEAD:** I'm really digging this lifestyle. It's been a strange five years from when I first sent the [first] book out to people. No one liked it. Then my agent actually dumped me.

**MOSLEY:** Really?

**WHITEHEAD:** Yeah. So I had to start over again from scratch when I finished *The Intuitionist*. I sent it [the first book] out to about twenty-five publishers. No one really liked it. After six months I got a call from my agent, and she's like, "Later for you."

**MOSLEY:** We want tunas that taste good, not tunas with good taste. That must have been really depressing.

**WHITEHEAD:** It was, because you have all these rejection letters and the person who you thought was your one ally is like, "So where do we send these manuscripts? Put them in the garbage? You want them back?" I think being dumped by the agent was actually beneficial because it was like, no one gives a crap, no one cares. I had to keep doing it, though no one cared except me.

**MOSLEY:** What did you do once you had *The Intuitionist* done?

**WHITEHEAD:** With this one I was like, I'm gonna chill, I'll get a day job, I'll revise it really slowly. And someone who read my first book said, "Oh, I heard about your agent dumping you and I know this woman who you might get along with, so when you're done, why don't you send it to her?" I sent it to this new agent and she liked it, and from then on it was a different story.

### On Philosophy and Forgetting

**MOSLEY:** Do you consider yourself working within a genre?

**WHITEHEAD:** I wish. I think it would give me more stability. So far, each book is really different.

**MOSLEY:** I think so also. I think it's wonderful. America doesn't have any working philosophers. The closest thing to philosophers in America are novelists, and most novelists are not. But I think that in your work you're looking for the meaning behind actions and behind character and behind even closed doors in some ways. You're looking for reasons. There're existentialist qualities to it. I think you're the first voice in a coming chorus— what I think will be a large chorus—and I think what interests me so much in your work is how thoughtful it is, and how incisive it is about not only human motivations but the intelligence behind those motivations. And I do see you creating a genre. When I see you compared to Ralph Ellison, I'm not unhappy with that comparison—

**WHITEHEAD:** Me neither.

**MOSLEY:** —Because, he's a great writer and all that, but also, you know what he's trying to do, honestly and almost without ego, which is interesting—because when you try to understand why things are, you have to remove yourself from it. I think you're very good at that.

**WHITEHEAD:** If you're going to try and talk about the world, you have to step back. And I think that half of being a writer is being outside all the time, but then the other half is trying to bring the world back to the people you're talking about, to your reader, bringing back your reportage—

**MOSLEY:** —to the people who are listening. People are listening in on your world.

**WHITEHEAD:** And then the fact of making real characters, real situations. The distance you've created you're erasing, by trying to make it real for you and real for the reader. So I find it's always this doubling effect where I can stand back and say, "Oh, that's a *really well* executed chapter *technically*," and then a couple days later, "Oh, I've actually kind of gotten to something about me or about people that I hadn't thought about."

**MOSLEY:** I think the writer writes some small percentage of the book, let's say 20 percent or maybe more, maybe less, depending on how many people read it. Like Shakespeare wrote maybe 2 percent of his books, and the rest of it we've made up over the centuries. Sometimes people come up to me and they'll say, "When Easy or Socrates or whoever went here and did this, I see what you were saying. I interpret that as what's being said is—" and then they outline something, and what they outline is really good. And it's really true and you can see that, hey, that really works, but I didn't mean it. Do you have that feeling ever with your work?

**WHITEHEAD:** All the time. I think that with *The Intuitionist*, which gets very abstract and was purposefully open to interpretation in a lot of different ways. People will say, "Oh it's a really great satire on work relations." And I'm like, "Yeah, for twenty pages, but that's not what—"

**MOSLEY:** But once you started it, they made the connections from then on. I had written four Easy Rawlins novels before I realized that one of the subjects of my books is black male heroes. I mean, I just never thought of it before. I never thought of it, I never tried to put it down, I never considered it. But one day, I realized, Oh, I'm writing about black male heroes. And then it helped me reinterpret the previous work, and it also sent me in a direction on future work: Even outnumbered, stick to your guns. . . . The first book I wrote was *Gone Fishin'*. I sent it around and, pretty much, people weren't interested in it. They said, "It's good writing; please send us something else—but people are not gonna read this," because they didn't see who the reader was going to be. They said, "You know, white people don't read about black people. Black women don't read about black men and black men don't read, so what are we going to do with your book?" They're wrong—and part of the proof that they're wrong was that the book was written—but that's a whole other thing. And so then I went on and wrote *Devil in a Blue Dress*, and some years later, I published *Gone Fishin'* [1997]. But the thing was, I had an idea when I started writing it: I wanted to talk about the migration of black people from the western South into California, like anybody else talking about their people, their family. One of the ways I see fiction is, you're telling stories of your people and your life.

**WHITEHEAD:** As I look back over *John Henry* and *The Intuitionist* and my first unpublished manuscript, I see a lot more of my upbringing and my experiences begin to take over these weird abstract concepts I start off with. My first manuscript I sent around was a black Gen-X tale that incorporated a lot of pop culture, and a lot of publishers didn't know what to do with it—because it was black twentysomethings hanging out in New York City, and apart from B-boy and romance novels, no one is writing this kind of fun, pop-culture material. When I finished that, I thought, people aren't going to get what I'm writing, so why not just do a crazy elevator inspector book, which is what I want to do, and forget about the whole, "Will publishers like it or not like it?" You just have to do what you have to do. It worked out OK.

**MOSLEY:** It worked out fine.

# BookMuse Interview
# with Walter Mosley

## Gail David-Tellis/2001

From BookMuse.com. July 2001. Found at http://www.bookmuse.com/pages/resources/ int_mosley.asp (accessed 2010). Copyright © BookMuse.com and reprinted by permission.

**Gail David-Tellis:** Thank you for talking to me. I have some questions and some are kind of longwinded, so feel free to do with them whatever you wish. OK?

**Walter Mosley:** Ohkeydokey!

**GD-T:** Paris Minton's determination to open a bookstore in Watts in *Fearless Jones* is the most obvious and recent example of how much you endorse reading in your books. Who is your favorite writer? What writers are you currently reading?

**WM:** I don't know. The idea of having a favorite writer. . . . The problem with having a favorite writer, is if he or she wrote a book you didn't like, what would you do?

**GD-T:** I'd still love her.

**WM:** But not that book. Steinbeck has written books that I like, but some of them are unreadable. I love *A Hundred Years of Solitude* but I can't read everything that Marquez wrote, not by any stretch of the imagination. Same thing's true of Melville, James Joyce. *The Stranger* by Albert Camus is a wonderful novel. *Man's Fate* by Malraux, *Their Eyes Were Watching God*, Zora Neale Hurston; *Simple Stories* by Langston Hughes. I really like Colson Whitehead the novelist, I've read a lot of sci fi, a lot of literary fiction. Lately I've been reading Robertson Davies. There's something brilliant about some of his writing. *The Fifth Business*, the first book. He's really in the head of that kid as he grows up.

**GD-T:** Interesting that you bring up Joyce and Davies as writers you admire because both are writers (it seems to me) with a lot of technical precision but not much heart—which goes to a question that I have. One of the things

I admire about your work is that you'll go along doing the thriller plot, you get me all caught up in it, then suddenly stop and go into a topic so intimate, so painful that I'm jolted out of pop experience into the deepest kind of empathy (I'm thinking here of Paris as a boy getting shut out of the library or of Easy Rawlins getting dumped by his wife Regina). Are these moments planned or do you let them happen?

**WM:** They happen, but I suppose there are other moments that happen that I come back and take them out because they interfere with the plot. So they're not planned, but everything in the novel is planned ultimately. You may not plan it before you write it, but after you write it, they have to fit.

**GD-T:** So you go back and pull things. How did you plot *Fearless Jones*? Was it outlined or did it happen spontaneously—or both?

**WM:** I rewrote it. The first time it didn't work. Writing is rewriting. I had two or three extra characters that were unnecessary. I don't outline at all. I just start writing. Write, write, write.

**GD-T:** Another thing I've noticed about your ongoing endorsement of reading material: how you name central characters after mythological (Paris = Troy), legendary (Fearless = Tristan), historical (Socrates Fortlow), or Biblical (Easy = Ezekiel Rawlins) figures. Do you expect your readers to make these connections? If one doesn't know, for example, that Paris Minton plays off of Paris Prince of Troy, can the book still offer enjoyment? How do you feel about the failure of the NY critics to notice that you're applying a myth to this book?

**WM:** Yeah, yeah. Any good book works on a lot of different levels and each level should work on its own right. On the level of a mystery or a crime novel, I think *Fearless Jones* works. I mean, at the level of mystery, I could change the character's name to Joe. It would still work—on that level. Same with the Socrates stories.

**GD-T:** Then it doesn't matter if the reader recognizes their historical significance?

**WM:** Yeah, though the names have ramifications when read at another level, having echoes of myth and legend, but the point is that each level should work in its own right. . . . It's like reading *Huckleberry Finn. Huckleberry Finn* is a boy's book but it's also a deep indictment of American racism. But you don't have to read that in the book and I think that's good.

**GD-T:** So by writing a book at more than one level, you can attract a variety of readers—which (as one of the country's most popular writers) you clearly do.

**WM:** Yeah, that's the other thing about working in a genre, you can do a lot of different things and certainly I do in the book but people often find deeper meanings in my books that I didn't even know were there.

**GD-T:** As in my review of *Fearless Jones*, where I take that Paris-Troy pattern and push it as far as I can? I'm outraged at the *New York Times* critic who completely missed that.

**WM:** And everything else. He didn't want me to be writing anything. The review said I shouldn't write books, if you read it the way it was written, but that happens sometimes. People don't like you for whatever reason. I don't like to get bad reviews, but you go out there with your work, you can't expect everyone to be thinking the way you're thinking. You know, they have their own reasons. They think they're important. You have to accept it.

**GD-T:** This is a long question. Nostalgia for the lost southern all-black community recurs throughout *Fearless Jones*. In fact, COMMUNITY is a central subject in all your books: heroes like Easy and Paris work to improve their community. Villains like *Fearless Jones*'s Zev Minor and William Grove exploit their community. And somewhere in between are these upwardly mobile blacks who've ceased to bond with their people. Paris Minton admires and feels connection to John Manly, the Israeli at work to reclaim the identity of his people. Paris actually compares Manly to Marcus Garvey (an early twentieth-century black nationalist leader). I noticed that praise for Garvey also occurred in *RL'S Dream*. Nowhere in your books have I come across mention of Martin Luther King or Malcolm. The question I'm getting at is this: Do you endorse racial, ethnic separation?

**WM:** Well, Socrates doesn't talk about popular political heroes and he's the only one who COULD mention MLK because of the book's contemporary setting. It's a little too early for '50s characters to be talking about him. You know MLK was doing his work in the '50s but most blacks didn't know that much about him. Another thing, Paris doesn't actually compare Manly to Garvey.

**GD-T:** No he doesn't, just mentions Garvey in the context of Manly's work.

**WM:** He does. He says he's upset with Manly. Manly represents a person like Paris but who has attained the dream of political autonomy. So Israel has this political autonomy that Garvey wanted but failed to get. So that's what it was about, like I don't want to hear my dreams come true in another man's life. So he was actually jealous of Manly. But no, it's not like he's seeking racial separation. What he's seeking is political parity, equality.

**GD-T:** The idea of community is such a dominant theme in your books. It's something I really responded to—and I think most readers do.

**WM:** Well, the idea of community. Paris liked his community, but he was a very different kind of person because a lot of people didn't like the community. The idea of community and racial separation are WAY different things. The problem with the question is that he's in the community so therefore does he believe in racial separation? Well, no. There is the black community and the purpose of writing about the black community is that this is something that's not written about. You talk about black people struggling against white people and you talk about black people struggling against slavery, you have the history of racism. And this is all true but this is kind of an external view of the black community. An internal view of the black community is the community itself. How much you love that community. You love the food, you love the way of talking, you love the history, you know all these things that nobody else knows. Who else knows that there were whole black communities with blacksmiths and carpenters and milkmen and butchers and everybody in the community was black and all had jobs and professions which later on disappeared. You could hire a carpenter but couldn't be a carpenter. That's what happened ultimately. That's what that's about. Not about trying to separate out or say this is better, but say it was better when I was able to do something. And here I'm trying to do something and people are burning down my store and beating me up and mistreating me and police come in and say who the hell are you to start a business in the way I remember it. And in the world I envision, everybody should be able to do it.

**GD-T:** In *Fearless Jones*, we enter a world in which if you're a black man, the deck is stacked, a world in which war is a permanent condition. If *Fearless Jones* had been set in modern day LA, in what ways would the story differ? Are cops nicer? Has the justice system grown more humane?

**WM:** No, but they might not do the same thing. The police might not have stopped in a black man's business to ask that question. Police have seen enough individual black businesses start up that they don't really have the time to stop and harass Paris.

**GD-T:** So that wouldn't happen today?

**WM:** Well, it might not happen today. In the Socrates stories, where I'm writing about today, you have a whole other series of issues, some of which have to do with race and racism. Some of which have to do with issues that have been foisted on the black community by a long history of racism. So in the end of *Walkin' the Dog*, you have a policeman who's beating people, raping people, killing people, and he represents the way the worst of the police look now to the black community.

**GD-T:** And he's still there?

**WM:** He's still there. He's an isolated incident, but he hasn't been taken care of. If this had happened in Beverly Hills, the guy would be out immediately. But the notion is that there's a certain amount of corruption and when Socrates wants to make noise about it, he's the person who gets in trouble. It's hard for me to say, I wrote *Fearless* for the time it was, '50s LA, though I think America is still a deeply racist nation. How has America changed? Well we've got more people of color and poor people on death row than we ever have. Too many people in prison, 17 million people going in and out of prison.

**GD-T:** Yet, in *Fearless Jones*, the justice system in part is treated with a kind of irony that makes it funny rather than enraging. I mean, Paris spends six weeks in the can because the law thinks someone paid him to set fire to his business for the insurance, but Paris has no insurance and the Public Defender assigned to him doesn't read up enough about the case to even know this.

**WM:** Therefore, Easy Rawlins is drama verging on tragedy, *Fearless Jones* is drama verging on comedy. I think a lot of people read *Fearless Jones* and really empathize with Paris and the kind of quixotic nature of the law. Some readers will say I felt removed but I've talked to a lot of readers who said God I really felt for poor Paris when this thing happened. Also, there's so much more of an internal dialogue going on—when Paris sees Fearless in jail and realizes that Fearless is more free in jail than he is outside it . . . notions of who you are on the inside which this book is very much about.

**GD-T:** Let's talk about *Fearless Jones*'s women. In *Fearless Jones*, you've got, it seems to me, two poles of women: the adorable dangerous femme fatale, Elana; the ugly (but good-hearted) Gella and Charlotte. When I think about it, men don't stay with women in any of your books. Marriage may be an escapist fantasy briefly indulged in but nothing sustains with a woman (not even in *RL's Dream* with Mavis and Soupspoon. He sees her after a separation of twenty years, and bye-bye, so what?). Marriage in *Fearless Jones*: the adulterer Morris, the bigamist Landry Lanning. Are you sour on marriage, or does the noir genre force you to make your heroes loners?

**WM:** Charlotte's not ugly. She's got a scar. Didn't you notice those big beautiful lips? Sol and Fanny did have a marriage that worked and in the Easy books, there's Odell and you know that Mouse and Etta are always going to be together, no matter how separate their lives, no matter what.

**GD-T:** Yeah, but how about the central characters?

**WM:** Socrates was working toward a relationship, certainly. In America half of marriages "work." In the black community, there are even more pressures that pull people apart—economic pressures, pressures imposed by the white community.

**GD-T:** At one point, *Fearless Jones* had the working title Messenger of the Divine. Why did you change the title? Who exactly is the MoftheD in this book?

**WM:** Fearless is the Messenger of the Divine. He always was the title. It was a confusing title, so I changed it. It's not really so different.

**GD-T:** Is there anything confusing about having Paris as the narrator and having the book be called *Fearless Jones*?

**WM:** I don't see why it would be confusing. You've got a book called *Moby Dick* and you have Ishmael narrating.

**GD-T:** Touché.

**WM:** The book is about the story, the book is always the story, so if you buy the story it's okay. If after reading it, you said I didn't know whether it was about Fearless or Paris, then that's a problem. It's about an adventure that Paris and Fearless had which is clear, so it's not problematic. They're friends and they can really only do good work together so who is more important, well. . . .

**GD-T:** But one grows, really learns. Fearless is perfect, beginning to end, but Paris learns about himself when he's about to murder Theodore Wally.

**WM:** Yeah, I guess. But did he learn something or did we? There he is with his gun thinking here I am in trouble. Most people would think, I have a gun in my hand. I'm fine. I'm not sure this is a new element in his life. Here he is, he's got a gun [and is thinking,] I really wish I didn't. (sigh) It's an interesting thing. I would argue that Fearless does learn things, though on his level. The things he learns we think are silly. Like he says, I didn't know women could use sex like a weapon. God, everybody knows that and certainly he gets into trouble that he can't get out of by himself. And so he needs Paris. But neither has the same level of character development that Easy Rawlins has. Neither one of them [Paris or Fearless] asks very deep internal questions. Terrible things happen in the book. But in the end Fearless has money: he buys himself a car and his mother and sister a house, and when Paris gets out of jail he gives him enough money to start another store. And it's a lot of money! But because neither Fearless nor Paris asks very deep internal questions, they can have a happy ending.

**GD-T:** I really like the movement from Easy-Mouse to Paris-Fearless. I think the character duos in the later books are more carefully defined and seem to have much more room to grow.

**WM:** I don't know about that, but thanks for saying that. I like them as characters. Fearless, Paris, and I like the kinds of intelligence that they have. I've been writing about Easy lately—a series of six short stories about Easy looking for Mouse.

**GD-T:** Everyone I know is convinced that Mouse died at the end of *A Little Yellow Dog.* Are you telling me he's still around?

**WM:** In these stories in which Easy is looking for Mouse, no one knows if he's dead or alive, but in the last story . . . you'll have to read them to find out.

**GD-T:** I read in an interview with you about *Fearless Jones* that Paris and Fearless are probably going to meet up with Easy and Mouse at some point, and that your books comprise a vast internal community in which all these hundreds of wonderful characters will eventually join in a single community.

**WM:** They could. That's for sure.

**GD-T:** I've heard somewhere that you're doing a screenplay for two female detectives. Is this so?

**WM:** Not exactly. Two women who rob an armored car company.

**GD-T:** Jennifer Beals is going to play one of the characters, I hear. Is the film in the making?

**WM:** Yes, it's written. We're looking for a director.

**GD-T:** How do you feel about the adaptations of your books to the screen?

**WM:** I like them. *Devil in a Blue Dress* is a wonderful movie. I loved *Always Outnumbered.* I don't compare books and movies. They're different. *Always Outnumbered* was very strong. It was doing things that had never been done before. It was about black people coping with racist America and I feel the same thing about *Devil in a Blue Dress.*

**GD-T:** Did you do the screenplays? In your books, I love your dialogue, the way you write people is so rich and so funny, and they talk so right. On the screen, it doesn't always register for me.

**WM:** I did not write the adaptation for *Devil,* but I did for *Always Outnumbered.*

**GD-T:** When do you write?

**WM:** I write in the morning when I wake up. Never more than three hours. Three hours a day 365 days a year adds up to a lot of stuff.

**GD-T:** You're productive; you've produced so much material of such high quality in such a short time. I think you're a real national treasure.

**WM:** Tell that to George W.

**GD-T:** Having read most of your books now and having met hundreds of your imagined characters, I am curious about which character is the one you like best or, to use Charles Dickens's words, which is your "best and favorite child"?

**WM:** Which character is Dickens talking about?

**GD-T:** David Copperfield.

**WM:** That's the only novel written about a writer writing that I really liked.

**GD-T:** I'm writing a biography of Dickens's wife. (further discussion about Dickens)

**WM:** Well, I don't think like that, my favorite character. I really like writing about a lot of different characters and they all mean a lot to me—Paris and Fearless, Socrates, Easy and Mouse—even Chance in *Blue Light*. I don't think of them as separate.

**GD-T:** This was fun. Thank you so much for talking to me. I look forward to reading more of your books, and I will read them carefully.

**WM:** I hope we'll talk again. Good luck with your biography.

# Walter Mosley Talks Technology, Race, and His Return Trip into Futureland

## Hugo Perez/2001

From www.scifi.com, 2 November 2001. By permission of the interviewer.

Walter Mosley was not met with open arms by publishers when he sent his first novel out in 1989. As he tells it, their response was, "Well, you have to understand. White people don't read about black people. Black women don't like black men. And black men don't read." Mosley thankfully did not listen to them, and *Devil in a Blue Dress* was published in 1990 to widespread mainstream acclaim and success. It launched the best-selling Easy Rawlins mystery series, proved that black men, when given something that speaks to them, do in fact read, and made the editors that passed on Mosley's work eat crow. Through the Rawlins mysteries, Mosley fulfilled his desire to use popular fiction to create a sense of history for blacks, "One of the things is, historically, we [blacks] haven't written a great deal of popular fiction about our lives, and about our movements, and it's something that needs to be done."

Mosley has made a career of defying expectations and escaping the labels that publishers have ascribed to him, working increasingly outside of the mystery genre, with forays into literary fiction with his novel *RL's Dream*, science fiction with the best-selling *Blue Light*, and nonfiction with his examination of race and class at the end of the twentieth century in *Workin' on the Chain Gang*. Mosley's forays into other genres have not kept him from creating two other detective series, the recently inaugurated Fearless Jones series and the Socrates Fortlow stories, which were adapted into *Always Outnumbered, Always Outgunned*, an original HBO film starring Laurence Fishburne. Although he is not a writer who allows himself to be defined solely by his race, Mosley has strongly supported black writers and publishers through supporting independent black presses and bookstores and by helping establish a degree program in publishing at City University of New York targeting urban youth.

Mosley's latest book, *Futureland,* is his second foray into science fiction, a series of nine interconnected stories which reflect on some of the prevailing social issues of our time as they might manifest themselves a few generations into the future. In Mosley's vision of the future, the world is controlled by corporations, and individual freedoms have been greatly limited through technology and the changing nature of labor. The world is divided into those who work for the system and those who don't—the unemployed undesirables and misfits who are relegated to the purgatory of Common Ground, a permanent welfare from which it is difficult to escape.

Out of this world spring characters such as Dr. Kismet, the billionaire industrialist behind the world-controlling Macrosoft empire; Ptolemy Bent, the smartest man in history, who monitors radio waves and discovers a form of intelligence which he at once believes is God; and Folio Johnson, the Electric Eye, the last private eye in New York who is permanently wired to the net through an implanted electronic eye. Through the stories in *Futureland,* Mosley continues to create a pop-culture mythology for blacks, even as he deals with the issue of race, most chillingly in the story "The Nig in Me," in which a biological weapon created to wipe out people of color from the Earth backfires on the white supremacists who intended to use it.

**Perez:** You are best known for writing in the mystery genre, but you have increasingly worked outside of that genre. What does science fiction allow you to do that you can't do in other genres?

**Mosley:** In science fiction you don't have to accept the world the way it is. You don't have to run around saying, "I'm constrained by these notions of society, by these notions of history, by these general notions of morality." All of these notions or any one of them can go out of the window, and I think that's for anybody. For black people in particular, the future is all we have because the past has been taken away from us and the present is defined in certain ways. You can't write today about our president, or our senator, or our multi-billionaire industrialist. Black people tend to get pushed into certain cubbyholes that at least white people in the culture don't, and so what you can do with science fiction is you can make a whole different world. You could say, for instance, that in the year 2060 there are only black people. You don't even have to say why. In that way, you can begin to create worlds which become interesting and also become yours in a certain way.

**Perez:** Where does the Electric Eye fall in the spectrum of hardboiled detectives? How do you think being connected to the datastream changes the role of the detective?

**Mosley:** In one way, it gives you a great deal of information. He could be the smartest person in the world, that is, if he understands the information he is getting, and if the information he is getting is true. Both of these things for a large part of the time aren't true for Folio. So in one way, having access to all of that information, all other things being equal he would be the greatest detective in the world. However, because he doesn't necessarily understand the information that he is getting, and because there are forces at work keeping him from getting everything that he needs, it isn't that different.

**Perez:** Do you think that technology and access to information will create a greater divide between the haves and the have-nots?

**Mosley:** I think all throughout history, the greater the power, the more centralized the use of that power. I don't think there is any time where somebody got greater technology, greater power, greater ability to bring people together, to make their lives better. The more power you get, the more it trickles up, as Ronald Reagan forgot to say. I think that the idea that technology is going to liberate us is false. All you have to is look at that fifty-year span between 1950 and the year 2000. The amount of technological advance in those years that should open up people's lives is immense. Washing machines. Dishwashing machines. Vacuum cleaners. Machines that will paint walls. Prefabricated houses. Quicker ways to make cars. Cheaper telephones. All of these things happened. Thousands of things happened. And so how do people live today? Now two people have to work in the family instead of one. It certainly didn't liberate us. It's made us work harder. People have less money. And it's not because they've become less intelligent or lazy. What's happened is that the whole system, the whole structure has made it more difficult for us to have enough to stay alive.

**Perez:** What do you think of the promise that many people felt that the Internet could have as a vehicle for social change?

**Mosley:** It would be wonderful if the Internet was a panacea, but it isn't, and it never was. It wasn't a panacea, because it doesn't matter how much information you put on the Net. It's how you organize it that matters. People being able to get what they need to know and to be certain of that knowledge. The problem is that the only way to do that costs a great, great deal of money, and people trying really hard to organize themselves in that information. And because the easiest place to organize it is the television set, and because television is working on a cable system, and that cable system is a perfect fit for the Internet, it means that all that information will be centralized and you'll have to pay for it. So you'll be lied to, and you'll have to pay to be lied to. And I always thought that that was going to be the way to do it. Now, will there be a rogue Internet or a phantom Internet like there is in *Futureland*? I hope so, but I'm not quite sure how that will work at this point.

**Perez:** Many of the stories in *Futureland* deal with the relationship between technology and spirituality. What do you see as the relationship between the two?

**Mosley:** Technology for me is a tool. A hammer is technology. A stick is technology. A piece of rope is technology. A rope tied into a knot is technology. It doesn't really matter how advanced these things get. With these tools, we're able to question more. With these tools we're further able to articulate questions about the universe, and also test our notions about the universe. I think technology has always been a part of spirituality and the notion of trying to find out who we are and what we are. Physics comes back to the philosopher's question, what is existence? What is my life? What does my life mean? I also think it's human nature, to seek meaning, to seek meaning beyond does this mean I can have food, does this mean I can have sex, does this mean I can reproduce? I think all of these notions of these mechanical kinds of things are pedestrian, and the things that become more interesting is how we organize our society around those mechanical things? What are our relationships? How do we organize labor? How do we define ourselves? What do we allow to happen to people in the name of progress?

**Perez:** You've published several stories as first-run e-books. What do you think the future of publishing is in relation to the Internet? What do you think is the future of the printed book?

**Mosley:** I'm not sure that the future of publishing is in the Internet. The Internet one day will be television, and I think it will be called something else. The Internet is a primitive form of what is to come. It's like Morse code. I think that certainly because of ecological needs, and certainly because of costs, digital and electronic publishing will gain more and more acceptance and usage with people all round the world. And they will displace a lot of paper publishing. And certainly one day in some future, it will replace all of it. I don't think that's going to happen any time soon. A printed book will survive. And also there are certain dangers to electronic books, especially if those books contain information. That information can be changed according to other people's desires, needs, wants which is completely scary. Another important aspect of paper books is that they last longer than digital at this moment. You could write it today, and five hundred years from now it would still be printed. If you've made something digital, it will disappear in much less time than that. So, printing, especially the things that are important, is necessary.

**Perez:** How is this going to affect the writer?

**Mosley:** I think the real question is how is this going to affect the book. The book is one of the few ways that can excite aggressive thinking within the mind of a person. You can do it through relationships. You can do it through personal exploration and experimentation. And you can do it through reading. These are the three different ways I know that people have aggressive thinking. I don't think radio does it. I don't think television does it. There are a lot of mediums that just don't cause you to think in a way that causes you to grow. Somebody writes a book on the Internet and they write a sentence that says a train whistle was blowing in the background, you can say, "Well, why do you say that? I'm on a computer, I can have a train whistle blowing in the background as I'm reading. Why do I need to read it? I can have James Earl Jones or Mickey Mantle or Muhammad Ali read it to me because I can get their voices on here." And so the book slowly becomes a multimedia experience which tends towards television. And therefore weakens the book, and I think that's a problem.

**Perez:** Are there any resources on the Internet that you think are useful for blacks?

**Mosley:** It still is true that the greatest resource is your mind and how your mind works. It's a lot less important about specific technologies. One needs to be able to gather information from technology, so you have to be able to exploit the Internet. Now whether that is you doing it or somebody you work with or some other people giving out that information, I don't know. You know what I'm saying. Because a lot of times, I find that the Internet is often like the rice paddies. It's labor-intensive. Not worth my time. When I need to do research I usually have somebody else do it, because I know it's going to take eight hours, and in eight hours I can do a whole lot of writing. You have to understand what's available in your world and you have to know how to use your mind in relation to those things. And this isn't just for black people, it's for everyone. The truth is that we're in the twenty-first century and race is not the most important thing in the twenty-first century.

**Perez:** You have been a very prolific writer in the last ten years. What drives you to write?

**Mosley:** I want to write our stories, our history. The only way you can see yourself is through the eyes of others, and that's the writer's major job, to create a story in which other people can see themselves, and recreate themselves.

# Walter Mosley: A Seat at the Table

## Charles N. Brown/2001

From *Locus* magazine, December 2001: 6–7, 75–76. Reprinted by permission.

Walter [Ellis] Mosley was born January 12, 1952, in Los Angeles, California, and grew up in South Central L.A. In 1972, he moved to the East Coast and attended college in Vermont and Massachusetts before graduating in 1977 from Johnson State College, Vermont, with a BA in political science. In 1982 he moved to New York City with Joy Kellman, whom he married in 1987.

Mosley held a variety of jobs, including potter and caterer, and didn't get interested in writing until he was in his early thirties, while working as a computer programmer for Mobil Oil in New York City. (He took a poetry workshop in college and "wrote poems that were really awful!" though it did teach him how to be economical with his prose.) When the writing bug bit, it took hold with a vengeance, and he wrote every spare minute after work and on weekends, then quit his job to attend a writing program at City College of New York from 1985 to 1989.

In 1989 he showed his manuscript for *Devil in a Blue Dress* to his instructor, who passed it on to an agent, who quickly sold it to W. W. Norton. Published in 1990, it was the first in the "Easy Rawlins" mystery series, which numbers six books to date, was nominated for an Edgar, won a Shamus Award for Best First Novel and the UK John Creasey Memorial Award for first-time crime novels, and was made into a movie in 1995. Also in the series—set in Los Angeles between the 1940s and 1960s—are: *A Red Death* (1991), *White Butterfly* (1992), *Black Betty* (1994), *A Little Yellow Dog* (1996), and series prequel *Gone Fishin'* (1997), which was actually the first book Mosley wrote.

In 1997 Mosley began a new modern-day detective series starring Socrates Fortlow in a collection of fourteen linked vignettes titled *Always Outnumbered, Always Outgunned*. The book's stories were reprinted separately in various magazines; one, "The Thief," won the 1996 O. Henry Award and was featured in *Prize Stories 1996: The O. Henry Awards*. The entire collection was awarded the Anisfield-Wolf Book Award (for works that increase the appreciation and understanding of race in America) and was made into an HBO film in 1998. A second Socrates Fortlow collection, *Walkin' The Dog*, appeared in 1999. *Fearless Jones*, which begins a new mystery series set in the 1950s, appeared in 2001; a second novel is due in 2002.

Often compared to Raymond Chandler and Chester Himes and labeled a mystery writer, Mosley considers himself a novelist whose work includes mysteries. He has published novels outside the genre, such as "Blues" novel *RL's Dream* (1995), based on blues guitarsman Robert (Leroy) Johnson, which won the 1996 Black Caucus of the American Library Association's Literary Award and was a finalist for the NAACP Award in Fiction. His first science fiction work, *Blue Light*, appeared in 1998. *Futureland*, a near-future collection of nine linked stories, was published in 2001. (Two stories from the collection were available earlier in the year as e-books.)

He also has published nonfiction; he edited the essay collection *Black Genius: African American Solutions to African American Problems* (1999) and published a critique of capitalism in *Workin' on the Chain Gang: Shaking off the Dead Hand of History* (2000). He was awarded the TransAfrica International Literary Prize in 1998.

In 1996, Mosley was named the first Artist-in-Residence at the Africana Studies Institute, New York University, a post he continues to hold. He also serves on the board of directors of the National Book Awards and The Poetry Society of America, and is a past president of the Mystery Writers of America. He is currently divorced and lives in New York City's West Village.

"Sometimes I get upset with science fiction because of its elitist nature, which is funny because only within the genre itself can it be seen as elitist. I like *Star Trek*, but with the Borg, this has gone beyond being a comment on our culture, because it's too far ahead. *I* want to see how we become them. In my story 'Angel Island,' we have the technology to control children at school, insane people, prisoners, and soldiers, so we have the technology to control *everyone*. It's just small interactive computers and chemicals, kind of like ants use. Not going so far in the future that it already exists, but where you're trying to develop it. And once you've created it, you don't need to put it on people anymore, because they accept that role automatically. 'I'll do what you tell me to do. I just don't want to know the truth. I don't want to be in trouble.'

"*Futureland* is partly a reaction. Watch the beginning of *Star Wars*, and you see all these blond, blue-eyed, white-skinned soldiers. You think, 'God, so *this* is what the future's like! The white people killed all the black people and Asian people and native peoples, and it's all Europeans in the future.' Of course they tried to fix it, but they never really did. Either you're white or you're an alien or you wear a mask (because you might be black under there, with that deep voice). This is the fantasy—it's less speculation about what's going to happen and more the future you would *like* to have. So I wrote a book in which there's a plot to kill all those people. If you can identify sequences on a genome and you can create a virus that turns on when it recognizes those, then you create a disease to kill those people. You can kill the Jews, you can kill black people, and you can kill all kinds of people. It doesn't *work* in this book, but that was my notion. Within that notion, I wanted to talk about a larger world and all kinds of interrelations between people, and how people understand each other—the things that interest me. I'm interested in what happens inside the mind. In this book, a couple of times, somebody's mind is in someone else's mind.

"The concept of 'God' is introduced in *Futureland*, but it's not worked out yet. Almost all the books I write are in a series. So that's like a future notion. I'm not sure, and neither is Ptolemy, what he's discovered. When he's a kid he thinks it's God in the stratosphere, because his grandmother told him it's God, but later on he's not so sure. Whatever it is, it's not in the stratosphere but in the computer he programmed. It may be him.

"I've signed a deal with HBO to do three movies of *Futureland*, starting off with 'The Electric Eye,' with Forrest Whittaker as the Eye. The great thing about being a writer is, my novels and short stories belong to me. I pick the people I want to work with. One of the terrible, and great, things about America is, if you're not white, you don't have a lot of work, so when I'm doing a movie, I get the best actors in the world. Like *Always Outnumbered*—Cicely Tyson, Natalie Cole, Laurence Fishburne. . . . And they all said yes to the second 'Socrates' movie we're going to do next year!

"Even though I love America, I call it the Dark Empire. Things are getting better for us because they're getting worse for other people. We have embargoes against Iraq, Iran, Cuba. We're making people suffer who are not our enemies. We've killed all those Guatemalans over a period of twenty-nine years that Clinton apologized for. We attacked Panama, took out their president, and brought him here. You imagine Darth Vader walking into Panama and killing all those little Panamanians. In that respect, things are getting worse. Ten thousand people a day die of AIDS in Africa—the worst of any holocaust in the twentieth century—and if you tell people, they say,

'Uh huh. It's because of the way they have sex in Africa.' I think, 'Are you for real?' But you can get more airtime on O.J. Simpson. We have all this power, all this technological ability to cover information around the world, and still we talk about nothing. It's like in Michael Moorcock's *An Alien Heat*. They have these little rings connected to batteries in which they have the power of hundreds of millions of stars. They're sitting around with incredible power, but what do they do? Have kind of odd sexual practices and make things out of sugar all the time. When I read it I thought it was great but I didn't know why. Now I realize—because it's true!

"I've always read science fiction. There are two choices when you're a boy: either you can read the Hardy Boys or you can read Tom Swift. I wasn't interested in the Hardy Boys. And criminal mystery wasn't so interesting to me. I didn't really care who did it or why, or anything like that. Adventure was much more prominent in Tom Swift or other things like pirates, *Treasure Island*. I just enjoyed them more—a world where things were more fantastic. Maybe, every once in a while, I would be amazed by some possibility, but the possibility was always to *do* something.

"The first so-called novel I ever read was *Winnie the Pooh*. I loved it. You can call it a kind of passive fantasy—it's just like the world. After that it was Danny Dunn and *Voyage to the Mushroom Planet*. Then Tom Swift. At ten, I *really* got serious about comic books. Marvel was *it*, and was *it* for a long time! Comic books play a really big part in young black children's lives. It's a way to get beyond the limits of the world. Especially Marvel's comics, because the heroes always have all these problems. And you have the concept of the hero/villain from another race, like the Submariner—he's a villain to America, but he's a hero to his own people. And even if you're his enemy, you can see those heroic notions. Not long after that, I branched out. I was reading Herman Hesse. *Journey to the East* is certainly a book of fantasy! (I also think it's the best book he wrote.)

"I didn't start out writing mysteries. I wrote a book called *Gone Fishin'*, a coming-of-age novel set in the Deep South. Nobody published it, because it was about black men and written by a black man. Everybody at that time thought black men didn't read and nobody was interested in reading about black men—except maybe about their relation to white men or about black women. . . . So then I wrote a mystery. I like the mysterious, and I was telling the same stories, with the same characters and that same migration from the Deep South. But I also wrote the 'Socrates' stories. I wrote *Workin' on the Chain Gang*, which is nonfiction. I wrote *RL's Dream*, a novel about the blues. All things that I'm interested in. Different things come out in different ways. *Blue Light* is kind of like speculative fiction. I was trying to create an alien intelligence there. Octavia Butler said the funniest thing to me. She said she read *Blue Light* and I asked, 'Did you like it?' She said, 'Yes, it's very good, but it's not science fiction.' 'It's not?' She goes, 'No.' 'Why not, Octavia?' 'No science.'

"Most people in my line of work don't think of me as a mystery writer. I write mysteries, but I'm also writing about the lives of a lot of people in America who haven't been written about before. A lot people in universities look at my work as literary—'He has a way of making language immediate, while still adhering to the old concepts of novel and story and character development,' etc. A lot of people *want* me to be a mystery writer. They get mad at me when I write *RL's Dream* or *Blue Light* or *Futureland.*

"The thing that separates *noir* fiction, crime fiction, mystery fiction, from all the rest is plot—straightforward, simple. At least every five pages (and that's stretching it), you have to adjust the plot. So what a person has in his pocket, if there happens to be a mirror on the wall, if it was 2:15 rather than 2:10—all these have become very important in a mystery, because you're looking at it in a forensic way. The reader becomes a kind of forensic student, and the writer somehow has to be an expert. In most other fiction, you don't have to worry about that. Can you imagine Marquez worrying about the plot in *A Hundred Years of Solitude*?

"There's another problem. People will look at a writer like Robert A. Heinlein and say, 'Well, I can have a career like that. I'll write these books and sell a lot of books and make movies,' and so on. But most people, when they specialize, burn up; after ten years, they're not writers anymore. If you write the same story long enough, people will say, 'I've read it already.' A writer who diversifies is more likely to survive as a writer. You might not get rich doing that, but you'll survive. All writing is open dialog with people. It's not like your writing is the last word on it—your writing is the *first* word on it! Look at Shakespeare. He couldn't possibly have meant all the things people *say* he meant, but that doesn't mean all of that isn't true. Shakespeare has become a much larger entity than one person could contain. A lot of people read my books, and they're much smarter than I am. They'll come up with stuff and I'll say, 'Wow, that's true! I didn't mean that, but maybe you're right.'

"Nobody would publish my first novel, *Gone Fishin'*. I finally published it with a black publisher, which I was happy about. When I wrote *Blue Light*, my regular publisher said, 'We're not going to do this.' They absolutely refused. I have to add, every other science fiction publisher refused it too, except for Warner Aspect. You get production line and specialization, so you put the left front tire on the Pinto. That's your job: left front tire, left front tire. People start to expect you to do the same thing all the time. But I don't write mysteries—I write books. You have writers with many interests who won't explore those other things because their publisher won't support it; they can't figure out how to market it. Any person who's writing the same kind of book all the time . . . that's not inventive. I love Roger Zelazny, and I like *Nine Princes in Amber*, but his other books are much more interesting. He had to concentrate on that series for money, and I'm sure the publishers put a lot of pressure on him. The first book was great, but the tenth book? *Please.*

"My writing's a lot about relationships and also about politics. But for adults, the question is: What is science? It can be about machines, but if you look at people like Lewis Mumford or even Marx, they talk about technology and technique—how my life is formed according to the way the technology works. A lot of *Futureland* is about how society is organized. On one hand, I'm interested in atomic signatures and that kind of stuff, and on the other hand, I'm interested in what happens to poor people and to people of color, and how their lives get organized as we advance; what things we leave behind and what we carry on, like our prejudices etc. I can have my adventures, and I can also talk about social relations—not so much about individual relations (a little bit in the first story, about the great love between this uncle and his nephew), but about how an individual decides to govern himself in society.

"The goal in *Futureland* was to give black people hegemony in the world. The smartest man in the world is this guy named Ptolemy. In the attempt of the racist world and the capitalist world to destroy the blacks, the people end up destroying themselves. Then, only in the last paragraph of the book, there's the notion that even though that happens, the idea of race and racism is all internal. So you have some slightly black people chasing a *really* black person—and the world recreates itself. You can worry about the past and you can worry about the future, but you also have to worry about what's deeply inside us. All through the book, you do have black people and white people who get along just perfectly, who work together as friends. There's love between these people. But a lot of people in my book don't understand that; they only understand race. Then you have those crazy ideas of blending, where one guy moves 50,000 Kenyans into Tokyo, or you have an African nation buying Luxemburg. What's going to happen here?

"You also have the idea of international socialism, which I was very happy about, having the Itzis instead of the Nazis. When you're really experiencing things, some of the little details get too involved in it. When you talk about the past or the future, you get to clear away some of the confusion.

"I'm not really certain what my motivations are. I've written two books on my character Socrates Fortlow, the black philosopher. So recently I've been reading the Pre-Socratics—Parmenides, Zeno, Democritus, and these other people, all of whom were kind of like the science fiction writers of their time. (They didn't think so—they were scientists—but at some point there's no real line between them.) So you had Zeno proving that nothing changes, or Democritus thinking about the atom. All that stuff is terribly interesting to me, and it always has been. What *is* 'something'? What is 'nothing'? How does it work?

"When I was a kid, I guess I never really believed science fiction was defining the world for me. I was reading Isaac Asimov and Ray Bradbury, Roger Zelazny, Barrington J. Bayley—especially Bayley's short fiction. There's a short story he wrote about a guy who goes to visit another guy who says, 'You see this little box here? I've figured out where God is, and if I press this button I'll kill him.' He presses the button, and the other guy realizes that a light goes out in his eyes. There's another story with a window close to the edge of the universe, and if you look out the window toward *outer* space, where we are, your soul gets sucked out and you die. What is that? Is that science fiction? But it's an idea. So I always read science fiction, fantasy, but at the same time I was worrying about character development. One of the great things about Philip K. Dick is that he *did* that—he really had personalities. When I read his books, I thought, 'Wow, these people are doing things for reasons!' In all kinds of fiction, people do things and you don't know why they're doing them. And watching movies, I wonder *why* some people fell in love.

"I came into science fiction reading people who I think really were trying to say something about who we were, how we were, where we were, because that's what it's all about. Science fiction isn't really about 'is this going to happen?,' but a lot of people think so. 'He predicted the radio! Can you imagine that? He must be a genius!' And then there are all the genre mixes. Even though I have a detective story in *Futureland*, I'm not trying to blend *noir* with science fiction. I was really trying to say, 'These are the issues.' So you have Ptolemy, this genius kid living on this river in Mississippi—it's the year 2050, but it could be today, it could be twenty years ago, because these are poor black people.

"I can't imagine I'm the only person who ever thought that you could make a racially charged virus. I don't mind *talking* about it, and I don't mind talking about a way to control people. It's not that I want to warn people; I just want to talk about it. As far as being black and writing science fiction. . . . If you want to write a novel set in 1830, either you're going to write about white people or you're going to write about slaves. If you write a novel in which there's a black woman senator in 1830, that's science fiction! We have to be the subjects of science fiction in order to imagine ourselves anywhere else. I want to make the future more realistic. You *could* write, 'By the year 2027, there were no more men in the world.' Nobody can question it because 2027 hasn't happened yet. But I didn't want to make a false utopia. I wanted to create a world in which I could see black people and their issues and what's going on in a much larger world. So you have people like Dr. Kismet telling Akwande, 'More black people know me and love me and follow me through my Infochurch than know who you are.'

"In good books of science fiction, there are so many ideas, you're excited. One of my favorites is *Hothouse* by Brian Aldiss. Everything is so far in the future, the people are tiny and they're green, and the plants have become incredibly powerful, motivating but not intelligent creatures. It's so wonderful, I just love it to death!

"Ian Forrester said there are some people who just want instant gratification, but people like him want to talk about big lofty things. In the middle ground, there are people who are interested in the story. You say something interesting to them, so they wonder what's going to happen next, and they keep turning the pages. And of course that's the most important thing about writing—an interesting story is where everything comes together.

"*Blue Light* and *Futureland* are the only two books I wanted to read again after I'd written them. I like my books, but I've worked on them so hard, I don't want to read them anymore. But the notion of speculation brings me back to them. There's a place to shoot off into the future.

"Science starts as philosophy. With the Pre-Socratics and their kind of early physics, you have a place where there's something and a place where there's nothing, and there's really no reconciling it. 'I can imagine there being something, but I can't imagine it coming out of nothing'—those really elemental questions. Certain people are not interested in them, certain people are afraid of them, but other people want to know, How do I do this? How do I deal with time? Who am I? What am I? What is life? What is the soul? And science fiction is the easiest way to address those things. Also, I think it's the most intelligent writing.

"I've been doing the approach I use in *Futureland* for some time. The

'Socrates' stories are a series of stories, but they make a novel. A novel is one story, a long one. It can be satisfying in a certain way, but it's not possible for it to reach in a whole bunch of different areas, because it would become diffuse and would no longer be a novel. But when you do a group of related short stories—what Ursula Le Guin calls a 'story suite'—you create the arc in another way. It's really fun to do.

"Reviewers didn't understand what *Blue Light* was about. I'm not going to sell as many of *Blue Light* as I am of the next 'Easy Rawlins' novel, but that doesn't mean I can't write both of them. A lot of people love 'Easy Rawlins' but want to read about Socrates; others love *RL* and say, 'When are you going to write about jazz?' Of course, more people read crime fiction than almost anything, so my largest audience, black or white, is going to be there.

"When I go back and look at *Futureland*, I don't think, 'Well, this is a mystery writer moving over and trying to do this.' 'The Electric Eye' seems like it's part of my mystery connection, but it's the only part of the book that is. There's all kinds of different stories going on in there, all kinds of different worlds. There's one about intergender boxing—I don't know if it's a very good story, but I really loved writing it!

"A lot of fantasy, or at least a lot of the fantasy I like, talks to the child in us. This hopeful magical reality is not linked to your life in a future way, as somewhere you could get to, but in a kind of historical way. There are giants (who may be your parents), there are dragons who you can be friendly with, and there's Evil—absolute, complete, unequivocal, total Evil. It's more primal, so it has a different set of goals for the reader and for the writer. In *Creatures of Light and Darkness*, or even *Lord of Light*, Zelazny tries to do both—fantasy's looking backward and science fiction's looking forward. I reread both those books recently and just loved them, but I could have read another four hundred pages in both of them.

"Some people who read science fiction don't consider themselves outsiders, but I think a majority do. Anybody who thinks, anybody who questions the reality that sits in front of them, is an outsider. And if you're reading science fiction, you're most likely questioning things. For example, I talk to people and say, 'AIDS has no predecessor.' They look at me and ask, 'What do you mean?' There's no disease that kills everybody, and there's no disease we can't follow back through history. People idiotically bring up the Black Plague. Bubonic plague killed forty percent, maybe sixty, but it left everybody else. I say, 'Listen, Thucydides had the plague.' (They say 'Who?') 'He had it, he wrote about it—the Father of History. But far as I can tell, AIDS started in 1956. Don't you *wonder* about that?' People look at me, and all of sudden I'm *outside*. I feel really nervous. They say, 'Oh, you're one of those conspiracy theorists.' I just think the disease started about fifty years ago, and it happened to start when we were doing experimentation, trying to figure out something about polio. I don't think anybody did it on purpose, but I do think I've never really heard about another disease that kills everybody. If you're willing to say anything like that, think anything like that . . . you're an outsider if you question anything that most people agree with.

"In his early fiction, Samuel R. Delany got away with all kinds of sexual things you couldn't say today—you'd say, 'Well, that's in the future.' He learned, and he said, 'I'm gonna start talking about it *now*,' and all of sudden they stopped selling his books. I ran into him once, and he said, 'I had to get a job.' He's teaching now. He has like a high school education, but they hired him as a professor with full tenure, in Comparative Literature—for good reason.

"I'm hungry to see international science fiction. I'd love to see French, any kind of African science fiction. Ishmael Reed is doing a lot of translation and publishing on the Web. I love electronic books. I think all books where the copyrights are open should be put in electronic form and made available to everyone, especially young people. Dostoyevsky, Chekhov. . . . If you spend a lot of time on the road and you like carrying books around with you—how many books can you carry around?

"Speculative fiction, science fiction, is trying to open up your notion of the world. You have a very locked-in notion of your everyday life: the apple falls down, people age, you need food to eat, the wind blows, there's day and night—all these things happen, and it's very normal and regular. Some people feel unbelievably oppressed by that regularity, and also the regularity of everyday work. Reading is a way to get away from that, and always has been. For me, science fiction is a way of opening the world, where you can see things in different ways, imagine things in a different way. Things don't have to be as they are."

*Walter Mosley*

# Taking a Stand with Walter Mosley

## Libero Della Piana/2003

From politicalaffairs.net. The interview may be found at http://www.politicalaffairs.net/article/articleview/41/ (accessed 2010). Reprinted by permission of the interviewer.

Editor's note: Most well-known for his mystery fiction, Walter Mosley is also the author of numerous social commentary books, including most recently *What Next*. He has also published science fiction such as *Futureland* and *Blue Light*. This interview was conducted by Libero Della Piana.

**PA:** The mystery writer and commentator Gary Phillips wrote an article in *Colorlines* magazine in which he says that who gets killed in America, and why and who pays are themes central to the lives of people of color and the disenfranchised. He says no literary form is more conducive to delving into this than the mystery/crime novel. What do you think?

**WM:** I have to come at it like this: about half my books have been mysteries. Any fiction about living in a real world, not even a real world that exists, but just a real fictional world, has to be political. If indeed you don't talk about the politics of that real world, then you can't talk about the characters. For instance, if you have a woman detective in 1925 in New York, and you didn't explain all the barriers of sexism she would encounter investigating her case, it wouldn't be a fiction true to itself. If you were to write about a free Black man riding around with impunity in the South before 1860, it just wouldn't be real. Or, for instance, if you write a book like *The Scarlet Letter* in which there are no Black people and very few Native Americans, it's not real. It's what it is: it shows what the white world wanted to think about itself, but it doesn't talk about the real world at the time.

One of the problems we have in the mystery writing field, when I'm wearing that hat, is that people don't take it seriously. I don't think mysteries are any more political or more capable of addressing issues than any other literature. However, because people don't pay attention to it, you kind of have to make noise.

Crime fiction addresses crime and punishment in the United States. It talks about who gets arrested and found guilty. I recently wrote a mystery in which a Black serial killer is working in the Black community and no one knows it. You can't have that somewhere else. However in that community, "They're just a bunch of dead Black women." You know? "Because those are violent people down there."

**PA:** You've also written science fiction: another genre that is ignored but also has the potential to reveal political realities.

**WM:** That is the other part of fiction: to elate the readers, because they can see their world or the world they want to exist. If you are a radical lesbian feminist separatist, and write regular fiction, you really kind of have to, unless the fiction just turns its back on reality, deal a lot with males and male politics. But, if you write science fiction you can say, "Here in the year 2198 there were only women on the planet Earth." You can do what you want to do, which is kind of interesting. It brings up all kinds of other problems, because once you have that, what do you have to struggle against?

**PA:** It allows you to put tension in different places, draw different things to the surface. But you're still dealing with reality.

**WM:** Well, there's a reality. Once you get rid of all the men in the world, how do women relate to each other? Are there any pressures, conflicts, and problems? And are there ways in which you have to legislate people's lives? You thought before this male-dominated world was the problem—and maybe indeed it was.

**PA:** Your new book *What Next* is a memoir toward world peace. In it you draw lessons from your father's life.

**WM:** My father looked at the world much the way anyone who studies the Socratic method would. He questioned it, trying to be as objective as he possibly could, and wasn't able to. In doing this he discovered things which were amazing to him. For instance, my father didn't think he was an American. So when he went to Europe and they said it was a war between the United States and Germany, he wasn't worrying. He said, "Fine. I'm not an American. I don't have to worry about somebody coming after me." But indeed they did.

It was just the way he would think about the world, or the Watts riots or the relations between Blacks and whites. He needed to pay attention to those who are suffering in the world, not just himself.

These things were lessons to me on how I need to look, when I look at Black America. I understand Black America doesn't agree with George Bush and his war on terrorism, and isn't so befuddled and amazed that people around the world would hate us. That allowed me to look at the world differently than America presents itself to itself.

**PA:** You call on Black America, on individual Blacks, to play a particular role in the call for world peace. As people with a double consciousness, as Americans, and as Blacks. . . .

**WM:** Or as people who are afflicted by a double consciousness. I think we actually have a single consciousness. It's interesting. I think most white Americans have a double consciousness they're not aware of. And here we are, we're sitting here like, "Oh yeah; we know, we understand this. Yeah. You want this because that's what you want, but meanwhile you're killing people over there in Bolivia." That's not double, it's really very clear.

This is not a gentle book on Black Americans. It's addressed to African America. We are, Black Americans, the wealthiest, most powerful, most influential group of Black people in the world. But still Rwanda languishes, Sudan languishes, Liberia languishes. Uganda. Chad. There's this long line of people suffering from disease, war, and debt forced upon them by capitalistic thinking. We have $650 billion in spending money in America. We should be able to alter the course of American foreign policy.

**PA:** In *What Next* you address the oppressed and the struggling masses of people in the West, the U.S. in particular and the Middle East, and you say the real enemy is not each other, but global capitalism.

**WM:** Right. It's always hardest to see your own period in time, because you want to romanticize your history as it unfolds. You find people who talk about "those ignorant people back in Kush, three thousand years ago." And you say, "Wait a second man, those people were much more sophisticated than you are, much more. They knew how to live in peace for centuries. And when a war happened they knew how to squash it, and live in harmony with their neighbors." But it's hard because you see your life, and you think it's good. No matter how bad it is, you think it's good.

The problem with the latter half of the twentieth century, what typifies and embodies it, is the struggle between Communism and capitalism. The U.S. and our European allies were on the side of capitalism. Because we were, the common everyday person thought that capitalism was somehow the firmament for democracy. In believing capitalism and democracy are inextricably intertwined, we made a big mistake. Because in truth capitalism hates everything that believes in human rights, individuality, and freedoms.

**PA:** And anything that gets in the way of profit.

**WM:** Anything that gets in the way of competition for profit. I mean it's very specific. It's not just profit; it's the competition for profit. The only way you can compete is through wages, either direct or indirect. And so the people that capitalists like are dictators. That's what they love the best. They like people who don't support the rights of individuals, because those people are the ones that are going to give the best kind of competition between the corporations. It's very hard in America to talk about that because we have this history of fighting Communism. People say, "If you don't like capitalism, you're a Communist." I say, well, no. I don't like capitalism, it's the same reason you didn't like Communism. It's because it wants to take away my rights—even more so, as a matter of fact. This is something that's very hard to discuss, because people are living the romance of their own era.

**PA:** Do you think that that reality is more exposed now that the Soviet Union is gone, now that the U.S. is the only superpower? Has the romance of living in our own era begun to peel away?

**WM:** The truth was under the building and the building has collapsed, but the rubble still lies on top of the truth. As we clear away the detritus of the past, we'll see it, but who knows how long that's going to take. This is one of the reasons I wrote, *Workin' on the Chain Gang*, which is arguing that we have to learn how to control capitalism. Capitalism doesn't mind being controlled. If you tell somebody, "You have to pay $5 an hour to somebody, but everybody else does too, you don't have to worry about that," then capitalism says, "OK, fine. Those are the rules of competition." But as soon as somebody else can undercut them with $4 an hour, they will kill you to be able to do the same thing. That's important, and that's what the everyday person has to know. We all have to know that, because if we don't, then we all suffer.

**PA:** Do you think that the mood in the U.S. and in Black America in particular has changed since 9/11? Are there are more or less opportunities for folks to stand up for peace?

**WM:** You can always stand up and demand to be heard, no matter where you are. Always. That's not an issue. You could do it in Nazi Germany. There are lots of cases of where people said, "No." Some of them actually even survived. Is the environment conducive to it? Yeah, I think it is still. I think it is still.

**PA:** Are there some positive examples you've seen that give you some hope for Black America playing a role. . . .

**WM:** Wait a minute: I think we have it in Black America. I just came from Atlanta where there was a national Black book club convention. These Black book clubs are very well organized, and very connected and very grassroots, mostly women, but there are some men. That's the first example and it's an easy step to make. I mean it's a really easy step to make. Whether or not people are going to make it is another issue.

I didn't write this book to give answers: I wrote to say hey, we've got a big problem here, and we need to be talking about it. We have a war going on. We have a war on innocent people and young children. And we have a lie that permeates our nation. A lie saying that we can actually win a war against terrorism by killing people. It's an insane notion. It's like the last gasp of the white male domination of America.

# Walter Mosley: Fearless and Easy

## Craig McDonald/2004

From *Art in the Blood: Crime Novelists Discuss the Craft*. Rockville, MD: Point Blank Press, 2006. © 2006 Craig McDonald. Reprinted by permission of the interviewer.

When Walter Mosley's *Devil in a Blue Dress* debuted in 1990, he was purported to be one of two black writers working in the crime fiction genre. His series of Easy Rawlins novels—popular with critics, readers, and a former U.S. President—kick-started Mosley's sales and launched a wave of crime fiction novels penned by black authors.

Hard on the heels of his "presidential endorsement," Mosley shifted gears and set off in several new directions, publishing a mainstream novel, two highly praised volumes of linked short stories about ex-convict Socrates Fortlow, a nonfiction essay on race relations at the dawn of the new millennium, and two volumes of speculative fiction.

Mosley returned to his crime fiction roots with the release of *Fearless Jones*, the first installment of a new series of crime novels. Mosley also resurrected Easy Rawlins in 2002 with the release of *Bad Boy Brawly Brown*, the first new Rawlins novel in six years.

A follow-up collection of new Easy Rawlins short stories, titled *Six Easy Pieces*, was released in the U.S. in 2003.

Walter Mosley was interviewed on June 26, 2002, and again in July 2004. During the summer of 2004, Mosley was touring to support the release of *Little Scarlet*, a new Easy Rawlins novel set in the aftermath of the August 1965 Watts riots.

**CM:** Why did you return to Easy Rawlins, following a six-year hiatus?
**WM:** What can I say? It's a very difficult thing to answer. I didn't mean to stay away this long . . . all these years. Three years I would have liked, or four, but I had other things to do. I wrote a Socrates Fortlow novel, a nonfiction book, two science fiction books, and the *Fearless Jones* mystery. I don't see myself as being trapped within a genre or way of writing. So, for me, well,

I've been working. I've had six or seven books since the last Easy Rawlins book. Rawlins is one of the many things I do.

**CM:** If we have a man of letters right now, you certainly qualify: fiction, crime fiction, science fiction, essays, and monographs. You won a Grammy Award for your liner notes to a Richard Pryor album. Why have you been successful stepping out of the series character cycle when so many others who have been identified with an ongoing character and who have tried to write a novel or to go outside of that character's saga have not?

**WM:** It is a very difficult thing to do. But you know, sometimes it is difficult for different reasons. Sometimes their heart is in writing that series, so writing another book is very difficult and their heart isn't there and you feel that. Whatever I write, I am really in. The thing people say is, "You're a mystery writer" and I say, "Well, no, I'm a genre writer, but my genre is black male heroes." If I am writing about black male heroes, I am interested, so it is easy for me to switch types of books. The other thing is that a lot of people don't want to switch out of the genre they are in until it stops making money. Also, you're going to make less money if you write a collection of short stories, or a political essay.

**CM:** A mercenary move on their part?

**WM:** Right. You can be one of the really big writers and you're used to getting millions per book. Then you write some other type of book and they say, "Well, we can only give you $25,000 for this one." And the writer says, "Oh, can't you sell this book as much as the other books? It's me writing it, after all." But people don't read the books because it is you, they read them because they want to read the books. That problem doesn't bother me either, because I see myself as a writer.

**CM:** President Bill Clinton famously mentioned you as one of his favorite writers.

**WM:** It was 1994.

**CM:** And it wasn't long after that that there was your novel *RL's Dream* and the Socrates Fortlow books and the nonfiction. Is there a linkage there between the Clinton endorsement and your move away from the Easy Rawlins series?

**WM:** No linkage. I was working on the stuff, anyway. I had been writing *RL's Dream* for a while.

**CM:** *Bad Boy Brawly Brown* finds Rawlins in 1963. He's forty-four. He's feeling his age. Do you have any sense in the long-range how far you're going to take Rawlins?

**WM:** I'd like him to be eighty, ultimately. That'd bring him up to the year 2000.

**CM:** *Fearless Jones*—a new mystery series. Why did you choose to position that series in what is essentially Rawlins' territory—Los Angeles in the 1950s? Is there something you feel you can approach with the pairing of Paris Minton and Fearless Jones that you can't touch with Rawlins and Mouse?

**WM:** Absolutely. The Easy Rawlins mysteries are dramas verging on tragedy. The Fearless Jones mysteries are dramas verging on comedy. You have a whole different kind of world-view from Paris than you have from Easy. Easy Rawlins is a kind of existentialist. Easy saves your life and he realizes, well, it's just that many more years of suffering for you. Paris and Fearless get to the end of the book and they say, "Hey man, we rich!" They're not really rich—they've got $5,000 or something, but they think they're rich. They feel rich. And Paris has got his bookstore. He loves his bookstore. Things are hard and terrible things happen, but in the end, they are left kind of happy.

**CM:** *Fearless Jones* does provide an upbeat ending, compared to the new Rawlins book.

**WM:** Oh yeah. At the end of *Bad Boy Brawly Brown*, John says, "Boy, if I never have to call you again, it will be too soon."

**CM:** You've said that you had written three or four books about black male heroes before you realized that you wrote books about black male heroes. Does that self-consciousness manifest itself in your current books about black male heroes?

**WM:** It doesn't really. It's like if you have had three or four relationships, and at the end of the fourth relationship, you realized you really like strong-willed women. It kind of helps you the next time—it doesn't change anything, you just realize it: "Oh, hey, I like that." It's not an issue that I'm trying to fit into that.

**CM:** Whether it be Easy Rawlins, Paris Minton, or Socrates Fortlow, they all essentially seem to be banging up against the same racial barriers, even though they may be separated by forty or fifty years. They seem at equal probability of being rousted by the cops, for instance, for no good reason. Do you really feel that so little has changed?

**WM:** Racial issues in America intersect with class issues. There still is racism in America, and in the rest of the world in general. There is still the possibility of any black male being rousted because of profiling, or whatever. But it is most common among poor black people. If you are a poor black person, and you look like a poor black person, and the policemen believe you're a poor black person, they will abuse your rights a little bit more than if you have the telephone number of a good lawyer in your pocket.

**CM:** The LAPD has its well-deserved reputation.

**WM:** It's true everywhere. Chicago. Detroit. New York. I was talking to a policeman who was being very friendly to me who said to me, "Well, you know, I don't profile. It's just that most of your criminals are either brown or black." He just says it to me. Even if most of the people he arrested for crimes were "brown or black," that doesn't mean that most people who are "brown or black" are criminals. But that's where he carries it to, because that is what he believes.

**CM:** And not hearing himself, at all.

**WM:** And thinking that he is representing me. No, you're not representing me.

**CM:** Real estate and homeownership are a recurring theme in your fiction. Socrates Fortlow must fight a court battle to remain in his modest shack in Watts. Much is made of Easy Rawlins' homeownership and aspirations as a landlord. *RL's Dream* begins with Soupspoon Wise being set out while terminally ill. And Paris Minton loses his bookstore/home in the opening pages of *Fearless Jones.* Why do you keep returning to this theme?

**WM:** Wasn't this the dream in the 1950s—and all the way back—at least I want to own my own home? Now it's apartments, condominiums and everyone is into the stock market and blah blah blah. In the 1950s, if you wanted to have your money mean something, and retain its value, you put it into property. Today, if you want to be rich, you go into real estate. Easy is not very good at it, but Jewel, she is good at it.

**CM:** In *Workin' on the Chain Gang,* you advocate a disconnect or, at least an experimentation with a disconnect from popular media for at least twelve weeks. Did you do that yourself?

**WM:** I have done it, yeah.

**CM:** More than once?

**WM:** I haven't done it in a while. But I have my option of not doing it. In America, you have people who work more than any other people in the industrialized world. Their whole life is spent working for the company store. Then they come home to what's going on at home, the kids, the dinner. The this and the that. Television and the media pull them out of all that in a way, but you really have to find your own center. That means not looking at the television, or listening to the radio. Not going to the football game, but instead paying attention to what is going on in your family. It will change your whole life if you just do it for twelve weeks. A lot of people called me up or stopped me and said that they did that and they felt some effect. I'm very happy about that.

**CM:** I wouldn't normally ask a novelist about current issues. I've met other writers who just abhor these sorts of questions, but you're in a unique position to comment about this. September 11, 2001: You make your home in New York City. . . .

**WM:** I've finished writing a book called *What Next* which is a response to September 11 and the so-called "War on Terrorism," connecting it to my father's own experiences with America and realizing who he was in America and World War II. First, I talk about my father and his lessons and stories about that and how they impact me in looking at September 11. Then I go on to discuss the issues about what black America thinks and how we need to respond to the world situation. Black people are in a unique position to understand it more than most Americans.

**CM:** There was a good deal of comment, almost immediately afterword, that somehow those events were a reason to put racial issues and other social issues on the backburner: "We're all Americans now."

**WM:** America—especially white America—always wants to put racial issues on the backburner. Any reason you've got to put racial issues on the backburner makes them happy. But the truth is, most black Americans can say, "Yeah, there are problems in the rest of the world and the rest of the world is being targeted and overwhelmed." Really, on the last four airplanes I've been on in the past week, three times I've been pulled out and searched. And other black people have been pulled out and searched. Every once and a while, they do a white person, too. But there is a kind of a notion that it's not being "put on the backburner," I'm just not supposed to talk about it.

**CM:** Because that would be "unpatriotic?"

**WM:** The only patriotism today is working for peace. Because we have these crazy people who are running our government who tell us there is no defense from an "asymmetrical attack," meaning an act of terrorism. We have no defense from that, but, we should be declaring "war." You mean, I'm defenseless, but I'm declaring war? It's such an interesting notion. I believe that America should defend itself. I believe that we should be fighting— aggressively fighting—terrorism around the world. I believe that. But that's only a stopgap method. The real issue is we should have peace. The issue of peace is much more based on economics than it is on religion. So that is what I'm writing about.

**CM:** Did you go to "Ground Zero?"

**WM:** I overlook Ground Zero from my apartment. I watched the airplanes crash into the building. I watched the buildings fall. I watched the dusty masses making their pilgrimage away from it. I go down there because it is my city. I don't go down there particularly to see it. For me, it's not really a shrine or anything like that. But it's there. It's part of life. I wrote a story about it that was published in *Playboy* called "Pinky."

**CM:** I understand you go through numerous drafts, maybe a couple of dozen or more. I could see where at some point you could lose your bearings doing that.

**WM:** When you lose your bearings, you read it out loud into a tape recorder and then you're brought back into it.

**CM:** Do you write longhand or on a computer?

**WM:** The first draft is on a computer. But, then, longhand.

**CM:** *Gone Fishin'*, published by Black Classic Press in '97, that was your first novel. Did you go back and rework that for its later publication?

**WM:** I did. And, you know, it's funny: I didn't take any sentence out, but I reworked almost every sentence. It's a completely different novel that is exactly the same.

**CM:** Publishing *Gone Fishin'* with them was an experiment on your part.

**WM:** It wasn't an experiment.

**CM:** It was touted that way.

**WM:** Yeah . . . maybe it was an experiment for other people. For me, the truth is that you *have* to go to a black press. If you're a black writer in America, when you have a book, whatever that book is worth in the market, that is the control you have over it before you sell it. If you give it to a mainstream press, you're not really funneling it back into the black community. If you give it to the black community, then everybody working for it, everything coming from it, is going to be based on that. I think it is important for black writers to do that. Not many of them do it, and I wish more would. Not because the money would really make that much of a difference, but it would be a possibility opened up for other people to think, "Hey, we can invest in ourselves, work with ourselves, develop our own kind of business in the context of America." I don't think that people should solely do that, but at least partially do it. Otherwise, no matter how successful you are, you're not bringing anybody else along. Your success enriches the people who you write about who are oppressing you. (Laughing) So it's kind of like, hmm: How interesting.

**CM:** Workin' on the chain gang?

**WM:** Right, exactly. That is working on the chain gang.

**CM:** My understanding is that your first literary training is in poetry. I think I read somewhere that you discount your own skills as a poet, but you credit that with shaping your prose.

**WM:** When I wanted to become a writer, the one thing I did was to take poetry classes with a poet named Bill Matthews who is gone now. Everything you learn about poetry you can apply to fiction and it makes your fiction better; it makes it stronger. There are too many writers who are lax with their words.

**CM:** Just words supporting a plot.

**WM:** Exactly. If the reader is after the story, they don't mind. But if you're after *writing*. . . . So, you want to see writing: even if you read something, even like the translation of *A Hundred Years of Solitude*, it's just beautiful, every sentence. It's kind of wonderful. The reason people love Shakespeare is that the sentences are beautiful and of course there was a lot of poetry involved in it.

**CM:** Do you read a great deal in the crime fiction genre now?

**WM:** I tend away from it, these days, because I'm so worried about using somebody else's plot in my own story. Plots are insidious. They crawl into your mind and you begin to think they are yours.

**CM:** Who do you read for pleasure now?

**WM:** You know, I read so many things. I might reread the old fantasy/science fiction of Michael Moorcock. I've been reading *To the Finland Station*, by Edmund Wilson. I've been reading *Our Mutual Friend*, by Dickens. I'm kind of all over the place with that stuff.

**CM:** *Little Scarlet* is keyed to the Watts riots. I heard your central memory of the Watts riots is linked to the disruption of your performance in a play at age thirteen.

**WM:** The story is this: I was in a group called the Afro-American Traveling Actors Association and we did Civil Rights plays. On the main night, the height of the riot, we were down on Santa Barbara—now Martin Luther King—to do the play. Surprise, surprise: nobody came. Everybody was either rioting, fighting rioting, or hiding from rioting, but nobody was coming to the play. So, we drove back through the streets of Watts and South Central and saw all of this chaos . . . all kinds of things. I saw the riots, saw the ferocity and the violence and the fear and the burning, all that stuff, firsthand. But the thing that really got to me was when I was home, my father was in a room and he was drinking, almost crying, very unhappy. I asked him, I said, "Dad, what's wrong?" He said, "It's these riots." I said, "Are you afraid?" He said, "No, I'm not afraid. I want to go out there rioting. I want to go out there shooting. I want to burn down places. I want to throw rocks. I see these people, and they have the same rage that I feel."

So, I said, "Are you going to do it?" And he goes, "No, I'm not going to do it, because it's wrong to hurt people you don't know. It's wrong to burn down property. But it doesn't mean I don't want to do it." That had a big impact on me.

**CM:** You've constructed his world, and Easy's community, over several books and short stories. Did you approach this seismic shift in that world with some sense of exhilaration, or with some other emotion(s) knowing you were really turning a corner with what I take will be the direction of the series?

**WM:** I'm . . . not . . . sure. . . . I'm not sure about either part. There are a lot of different places for Easy to go. This is a very important one. But not the only one. The next one (*Cinnamon Kiss*) which is going to be a year later, is very personal. All through the 1950s and 1960s, there is this notion of the genius detective. The detective who sits in a room someplace, kind of like Sherlock Holmes, who can figure out all of the problems, but they have certain quirks to their personality.

**CM:** Like Nero Wolfe?

**WM:** Him and others. Wolfe is prominent among them—these guys who are really smart. I have created a character like that, a white character like that, for the next book, who hires Easy as one of his flunkies, basically, to do something. Easy has to do it because there is an illness in the family that he needs money for. And there are some major personal shifts for Easy in this book. The racial stuff happens, of course, because you can't be black in America and not have it happen, but there are other things going on.

**CM:** You were master of ceremonies for the National Book Awards in November 2003.

**WM:** I was indeed.

**CM:** There was of course the award to Stephen King and the ensuing controversy tied to that recognition. You've consistently made many comments about the need to move beyond the narrow confines of genre tags . . . and you did so again in your speech at that event. Any sense of fallout, or of shifts in the publishing world in the intervening months?

**WM:** It's a continual uphill battle. I was on the governing board of the National Book Awards when we gave Ray Bradbury the lifetime achievement award. It was amazing how many people hadn't read *Fahrenheit 451*. And you're saying, "Well, if you're going to talk about important American books, you can talk about *Catcher in the Rye*—the consummate coming of age novel. You can talk about *Invisible Man*. There's a lot of books you can talk about. But *Fahrenheit 451* is up there in the top ten. It has to be. It's really a book telling you something. I don't think we've even learned everything it's telling us, yet. I've actually been thinking about it lately . . . thinking there are things in that book that we could actually utilize today to help our struggles with literacy in America. But ultimately, it was pretty easy to give Bradbury the award.

I think it was more difficult with Stephen King because he's so popular or perceived as being so popular, even right now. There's always a problem, because, you know, popular literature is always the literature that survives.

**CM:** It's the literature that's often shunned by the intelligentsia in its own time, but it does endure, for the most part.

**WM:** And it's everybody from Homer to Shakespeare to Mark Twain to Charles Dickens. People will say, "Well, what about Tennyson?" I say, "Who reads Tennyson?" I mean, honestly? If you don't read it, it can't do anything for you.

**CM:** It's dead, essentially.

**WM:** Yeah. It might be great, and it is great, by the by. But it's the act of reading, really, much more than what you read, that alters you as the individual. It's the act of reading, of critical thinking. So, therefore, the book that makes you read is really a potent thing. That's part of what we were saying (with King). It's difficult. It's difficult to say, because you know, literary writers in America are actually marginalized by popular writing and they know it. And I have to say, I'm also a literary writer—that's obvious with *The Man in My Basement*. All you have to do is look at any bestseller list in America and you're not going to find a lot of literary writing on it.

**CM:** Is there more Socrates Fortlow to come?

**WM:** There is a novel, called, I think I'm going to call it, *The Junkman.*

**CM:** Kind of an oddball final question. I read somewhere that in 1959, at age seven, you appeared on national television on Art Linkletter's *Kids Say the Darndest Things!*

**WM:** Oh yeah. Where'd you come across that?

**CM:** Research. Do you remember the "darndest thing" you said?

**WM:** I came from a Baptist school called Victory Baptist Day School. What they asked for the show, is they asked us to tell Bible tales. I told about Noah and the Ark—you know, about how God took all of the married animals and saved them, two of each one. Art Linkletter asked me, "What did you learn from that?" And I said, "Always be married, and you won't be left behind."

# Interview with Walter Mosley

## Paula L. Woods/2004

Recorded at the Left Coast Crime 14 Conference (February 19–22, 2004) by Tree Farm Communicatons (www.treefarmtapes.com). © Paula L. Woods. Printed by permission.

**Audience:** (applause)

**Walter Mosley:** Wow!

**Paula Woods:** Welcome. Thank you so much for coming out. Thank you so much for this tribute, which will be one of many for our guest of honor. I think it's probably useless for me to introduce Walter Mosley, but I will try. Hopefully you read my appreciation of him, and those of you who have, know that he is probably one of the more prolific writers you will see at Left Coast Crime this weekend. He has written eight Easy Rawlins novels and a prequel, short stories as well as a second series—as if one was not enough—featuring Fearless Jones and Paris Minton, and two collections of stories about Socrates Fortlow. And, if that were not enough, he also has written two science fiction novels, a blues novel, *RL's Dream*, as well as his latest novel, *The Man in My Basement*. And, if *that* weren't enough, he has also written three books of social and political critique and commentary. And if that weren't enough . . . (audience laughter). And there is much more.

Walter is one of those people who made me a mystery writer. It was meeting Walter in 1993 at the American Book Sellers Association and seeing this black man and thinking, "Wow. I haven't seen a black mystery writer since I couldn't remember when." Walter was probably the first I'd ever met. And, I certainly hadn't heard of one since—and I'm trying to think of Gravedigger Jones and—Chester Himes.

**Mosley:** You're right.

**Woods:** So that sent me on a journey that eventually landed me here, writing books of my own. But, certainly, Walter's has been one of those influential series, and everything he's written has really enlightened me every step of the way. I'm sure a lot of you feel that way too.

Let me start with a couple of questions for you. I read the *New York Times*

"Q&A"—I don't know how many of you read that a few weeks ago—and I love the question about genre fiction (laughs): "Is genre fiction really on the margins, and how does it feel to be out there on the margins?" I'd like you to talk a little bit about how you see mystery fiction, how you see genre fiction, and where you think it fits in.

**Mosley:** Who's the guy who was running for president, who only won in Massachusetts? What was his name? I forgot his name. (audience laughter)

**Woods:** [Michael] Dukakis?

**Mosley:** Was it Dukakis? Let's say it was Dukakis. I was in New York one day, and it was time for elections, and New Yorkers were very happy. I said, "Why?" And they said, "Well, you know, because Dukakis is going to be president, and we'll all be happy." And I went, "Are you crazy? (audience laughter) Dukakis is not going to be president." This woman said, "Everybody I know is voting for Dukakis. (audience laughter) Everybody I've met is voting for him; everybody I've talked to." And I went, "Wow! You live in Manhattan, right?" (audience laughter) She went, "Yeah." I said, "He's not even going to take New York." (audience laughter) And I live in Manhattan. I never go to Queens, and if I had I would have known more about Dukakis at that time. (audience laughter)

But the literary world marginalizes, in its own kind of small way, genre fiction. Anybody who's a publisher, owns a bookstore, owns a distribution unit, anybody who works in Hollywood and adapts books into movies knows that the genres, especially the mystery genre and science fiction, are the biggest things. They're gigantic. People like Harold Bloom are actually marginalized by the genre. And so the idea that I'd be marginalized by somebody like Harold Bloom is ludicrous. I mean, (audience laughter) it's insulting. But it's also ludicrous because it's just not true.

**Woods:** Kind of like who's zoomin' who?

**Mosley:** Yeah, right. (laughs) It's so funny. I'm supposed to do a reading [at the conference]. I'm going to read a little talk because the problem about the marginalization of mystery writers is themselves, as a rule. We often belittle and marginalize ourselves and our work, even though we're doing the most important literary work in America today. (audience laughter) You know, it's funny. I knew you'd laugh, but I think it's true. I'll explain it when I give my talk. I have this whole thing all worked out.

We do really important work, and always have done really important work. But because people like Harold Bloom and the *New York Times* and other people feel like making our work smaller—you know, "the crime round-up" and that kind of stuff—we start falling into it and doing things that are really unpardonable, like referring to readers as fans. I think it's unpardonable. It doesn't matter if readers refer to themselves as fans. So, "I'm a fan of this person." Okay, fine. But for a writer to think it about a reader is really an unpardonable sin.

**Woods:** It [marginalization] reminds me of the *New York Times* because anytime I pick up the *New York Times* best sellers list, easily half of the books on that list, on the fiction side, at any given time are crime and science fiction.

**Mosley:** Right. Exactly. It's true. Those are the books that sell and make money. (laughs) The ones that are on the top of the list aren't necessarily the best ones either. (audience laughter) But the other issue is that it's not simply the one individual selling the most books. As a group, it's like we're a wave. We're like a whole river of thought and ideas, speaking to each other, and speaking to such a large group of people who wouldn't be spoken to otherwise. I mean, how else could I write about an angry black man living in Watts and have white readers? I mean, really.

**Woods:** Right.

**Mosley:** Honestly. In America?

**Woods:** Actually, that was my next comment and question. I've heard so many people come to your signings and say, "You know, I have an understanding of black men that I never had before, reading about Easy. Or reading about Fearless, or any of your books." I'm wondering, from your standpoint, because you talk a lot about black men and black male heroes, maybe you could talk a little bit about what writing those men means to you.

**Mosley:** I don't quite understand the question.

**Woods:** Well, Easy Rawlins, Fearless Jones, Paris Minton, Socrates Fortlow. In your books, you—probably more than anyone else that I know—have created a portrait of black men in America.

**Mosley:** I wrote a book called *What Next* last February. So, it was a year ago that it came out. It was a criticism of America's so-called war on terrorism. But half of it is also a memoir about my father.

In the beginning of the book, I start off with this thing. When I was a kid I asked my father—when I realized what World War II was, when I realized my father went to World War II—I said, "Dad, were you afraid to go to the war?" He said, "No." And I said, "Why not?" He said, "Well, I thought it was war between America and Germany." I said, "Well, it was." You know, because I had just seen John Wayne in a movie. I *knew*! (audience laughter) He said, "I know it was, Walter, but when I went there I didn't. I knew that America was fighting Germany, but I didn't know that I was an American.

I thought I was a Negro. Where I came from there were white people, who were Americans. They were the finest. There was the American person and the black person. That's what they would say. It was the kind of language that was used."

And so when he went there, he thought that if the Germans came up with their guns and their tanks and said, "Hey! Uh, where are the Americans?" (audience laughter) my father would say, "Dey over dere. (audience laughter) You just leave me with the French women and the wine. (audience laughter) And you go there and fight with Americans." You know he thought he was an appendage. But then, of course, the Germans started shooting at him at one point, and he said that's how he learned he was an American. He, literally, said, "Hey, I'm an American." The French called them Americans; the Germans called them Americans. So my father and his ilk have always been my heroes.

It's such an odd experience in America because black men are so rarely heroes. Most heroes, they're kind of like The Rock [Dwayne Johnson]; you can't quite tell. "He's black, no?" Or Michael Jackson. (audience laughter) "He's black?" (audience laughter)

**Woods:** Up until you, I would think about Hawk in the [Robert B. Parker] Spencer series. Hawk was there to do the dirty work.

**Mosley:** I like the Spencer series.

**Woods:** Well, I do too.

**Mosley:** Don't get me wrong, but Hawk is a stereotype. He's kind of a custom-made stereotype. It's not like Stepin Fetchit or something, but he's this custom-made stereotype. I remember when I first read him, and he was drinking Dom Perignon from the neck, driving this Porsche. I said, "Man, that's cool."

**Woods:** Puffy [Sean Combs] read that too. (audience laughter)

**Mosley:** I know. But the thing is to create real characters. Not anybody can do it. Anybody who reads, for instance, Susan Straight—she doesn't write in the genre—she's a white woman who's been married to a black man for many years. She has black children. She lives in a black neighborhood. She's raised black kids. She writes very convincingly about [black] characters. When I was editor this last year of *Best [American] Short Stories 2003*, she was one of the people that I awarded a place in the collection because she wrote so convincingly about this stuff. It doesn't matter who you are writing these things. The question for me becomes how realistic is the character in the pool of all the rest of your characters.

**Woods:** Right. I think it really is remarkable what you've done because, as

I think of all of those characters, we love them even with their flaws. To be able to create characters who, with flaws and all, are still our heroes really is a testament to creating totally rounded, totally authentic people.

**Mosley:** It's so funny. I don't go to schools. Teachers always want me there, but as soon as I start talking they want me to leave because (audience laughter) they ask questions. You know how teachers and librarians ask you questions? They'll say, "Well, in order to be a writer you have to read a great deal, don't you?" (audience laughter) You know, that's a question. And I say, "Well, *no.*" (audience laughter) And they say, "Well, you know students, we have to leave now." (audience laughter)

**Woods:** One of the things I love about your characters is they're always reading.

**Mosley:** Well, many of them read. Fearless Jones doesn't read. Mouse doesn't read. But Easy and Paris read. Socrates doesn't read all that much. He reads a little bit. He's starting to, you know. As I was thinking about those flawed characters, the ideal flawed character in the Western history of literature is Achilles. He has that Achilles heel, but there's much more. The Achilles heel is just a reflection throughout his whole character of all the things he does wrong in order to finally do something right at the very end of the poem, or the novel, or whatever. And I'm thinking, Homer was illiterate. I try to say that to teachers, and they like to kind of pretend, "Well, not in my mind he's not."

**Woods:** Right.

**Mosley:** He's illiterate, but not in my mind.

**Woods:** I love it. David Ulin said something about you in the *Atlantic Monthly*. I don't know if you remember the quote: "The Easy Rawlins novels compose a sprawling novel of manners about twentieth-century African-American Los Angeles that owes as much to authors like Dickens and Zola as it does to the aesthetics of noir."

**Mosley:** Uh huh.

**Woods:** (laughs) Sounds good! (audience laughter)

**Mosley:** That's true. That's true. He forgot to mention Shakespeare and Thackeray. (audience laughter)

**Woods:** There you go—Shakespeare. But I think it's important. We were talking about this earlier when we were talking about *The Man in My Basement*. The notion of the man in the basement is not just about [Ralph] Ellison's man in the basement; we're talking about Dostoevsky's [character] in the basement. So, I am wondering when you think about what you write, and the landscape, and what you draw upon in your writing, who comes to mind? Who, who are the touchstones for you?

**Mosley:** First, of course, is my father, who taught me so much. My father, when he was a kid, lived in Louisiana and he was very poor. He didn't have anything. I mean he was an orphan. My father (laughs) really had it hard. I think about my father's life, and I think, "Man, it would be better to live in Baghdad" because at least everybody around you is kind of like you. He used to go and steal books from this place, and it would be like little Westerns. And he would read the Westerns. He wrote a Western once and he sent it in, and they never responded. But a couple of years later he was reading one of these dime novel things and there was his story, pretty much the same. It was changed; they made it better.

**Woods:** With his name on it?

**Mosley:** No. No. His name wasn't on it. My father realized then he couldn't be a writer. He stopped writing, and he never wrote again. My father was a very good writer. It was interesting. I had him write something much later, and I was really astounded by how beautiful he did on a first draft of something. That was the first thing. My father was a storyteller; he loved telling stories. He loved listening to my stories.

Then, after my father, it's so hard to tell because so many people write not because of the greatest writers. I mean, I've read Zola; I love him. I read Marquez and think he's incredible. And I'm in Steinbeck country and I like Steinbeck, too. I read Brian Aldiss who wrote a science fiction novel called *Hothouse*. I thought it was just incredible. I love Richard Wright; but I like the *Long Dream*, the book that nobody ever talks about.

**Woods:** Yes, I've read that.

**Mosley:** The first book I ever read was *Winnie the Pooh*. I still love it. Bump, bump, bump, you know. (audience laughter) If you read a book that touches your heart, if language touches your heart, that is what makes you a writer. It doesn't have to be great language that touches your heart. But, in order to become a writer, you have to put your feeling into it in, in a way that's unimpeded by anything. By language, by thought, by all these other things. And then, later on, you make it work. So, even though I've read a lot of great writers and loved them, and loved them for the quality of writing, I'm not sure that that's what made me a writer. That's what makes me a reader. I want to read those books. But I want to write the books where my heart has been touched. Yeah.

**Woods:** For a long time, I think, readers have been on a journey with you and Easy. One of the questions that someone who caught me in the hall asked me today is, "Find out what's going on with Easy." Okay? I think some of us felt like you, maybe, jilted us for awhile with Easy, and went away, and did other stuff. Then, Easy came back.

**Mosley:** Well, Easy never left. I mean, for a while people thought Mouse was dead. They still ask me. I know people who don't read my books. They say, "Hey! What happened to Mouse?" I said, "Man, you haven't been readin' my books. You haven't caught up yet." (audience laughter)

**Woods:** That's right. How many of you [audience members] think Mouse is dead?

**Mosley:** You see, she [audience member] thinks Mouse is dead!

**Woods:** They're too afraid to raise their hands now. (laughs)

**Mosley:** That's okay because I write a lot of books, and they cost a lot of money. I understand. But I've always been writing. You see I'm not just an Easy Rawlins writer. That's for sure. And I'm not just a mystery writer. That's for sure. I have to write different kinds of things, and it takes awhile because most people don't want to publish you all that much, say once a year. And it should be the same character, and it should be the same story. And you should hit these points because this is why people are reading your books. It's so interesting because many people in here are writers; many people in here are readers. One of the truisms about writing which nobody ever talks about is that a writer's career, as a rule, for ninety-some percent of writers, is ten years. Ten years. You start, and hopefully you start doing well. But if you think about those writers who were doing well ten years ago, you wonder where they are today. They're almost all gone. They're pretty much gone. One of the reasons, there are many reasons, is because readers say, "Well, I've read that story. I'm tired of reading that. I've read this person. They're not bringing me anything new." Another one of the reasons is that publishers put so much pressure on, especially on genre writers, to keep doing the same thing.

**Woods:** A book a year.

**Mosley:** "Do that, do this, I wanted this. I want to do a story about this character." Readers get tired of it, and the writer gets tired of it too. The stories start to descend in strength. You think about writers who do that. Some of them have managed to stay around. And, some of them haven't. I just like doing a lot of different kinds of things. I'm really interested in writing and writing different characters. I'm trying to write a novel right now about a deconstructionist historian, which I think is really a kind of wonderful notion: a deconstructionist historian. You know it's way away from what people know about me. I'm going to have all kinds of trouble with my publisher. But, it doesn't matter because I. . . .

**Woods:** Well, not if he [the character] kills somebody.

**Mosley:** Well, he does kill somebody, (audience laughter) but there's no way you're going to get around it being kind of an experimental novel.

One thing I did, a long time ago, I went to a black publisher, Black Classic Press, a guy named Paul Coates, whom Paula knows. I published a book with Paul. Then, I published another book with Paul. I did this because I understand that if you belong to an ethnic group, it's important to support that group in various ways, one of which is economic. I mean, if you feel connected. I did it hoping that other black writers would do it, though they didn't. But I hoped that they would. The thing that I got out of it is that Paul will always publish my books. So, I thought, if I ever say, "Paul, I'm writing a crazy book," he'd say, "Well, will anybody publish it?" I'd say, "No." He'd say, "Well, I'll do it, Walter. Don't worry. We'll take care of it. Don't worry." I'd say, "Well, it's not going to sell." And Paul would say, "That doesn't matter."

**Woods:** The two books published by Coates were *Gone Fishin'*—I don't know how many of you remember the Easy Rawlins prequel—and the other was *What Next*. *Gone Fishin'* was one of those books that you couldn't get published in the beginning, right?

**Mosley:** Oh, no. They wouldn't publish it. There was a rule in 1987 or '88. It says, "White people don't read about black people. Black women don't like black men, and black men don't read. (audience laughter) You've written a book about two black men in the Deep South. It's written nicely, but what's the market?" It's a very interesting notion. But I did okay anyway. The book sold 60,000 copies. That was nice.

**Woods:** And *What Next* was another huge success for a small publisher. A huge success.

I don't know how many of the people in the audience know about your nonfiction books. What is your message in those books? You talked about *What Next* a little bit, but maybe you could talk about them collectively. What's the message you're getting out? What does it do for you to write those and then come back to the fiction?"

**Mosley:** Well, you have ideas. Certainly, one expresses his ideas in fiction, but one of the pressures of fiction is not to take a side. You just represent the characters in whatever way you're going to do that, and let the audience, the readers, make up their mind about what the characters mean and what they think. And they think different things. But sometimes you really want to say something that you really think, and it's not appropriate for a writer to do that through a character. I just don't think so. I can't do it. So, my characters are always very complex, and people come up . . . who was it? Orrin Hatch was talking to me about how much he liked my books once, you know. (audience laughter) Alright, Orrin. Okay. (audience laughter) He was like, "Could you send me a couple of galleys?" "Sure, I'll send you a galley." (audience laughter)

**Woods:** But he wasn't talking about *What Next.* (laughs)

**Mosley:** No, he wasn't talking about *What Next.*

Now, you see that's a different thing. I can explain my nonfiction by [an example]. I want to write a book now. The title is *The Non-Socialist, Non-Communist, Marxian POV.* That's what I want to write. That's my new book I want to write because, I think you know, I'm not very interested in communism or socialism, really not much. They don't seem to work any more than the ghetto works. But one of the things that I'm very interested in is how Marx talks about capitalism because I'm very worried about capitalism. I think that people need to be able to say the word "capitalism" critically, without being blamed for being a communist or a socialist. I do things like that. I want to talk about those kinds of things, so people understand. I want to talk about if America made a stance against terrorism, no matter who did it, no matter why, anywhere in the world, I would back it. I say, "Anybody who's ever been involved in terrorism, including us, we catch. If those terrorists need to be executed, fine. I don't care. Execute all of them." But it has to be us along with everybody else. I just wanted to say that, not because I'm an apologist for Osama Bin Laden or anything like that, but just because I want there to be peace in the world. In order for there to be peace, we have to be fair in the way that we deal out our power, our extraordinary power.

**Woods:** One of the things about *What Next* that I thought was interesting was that the subtitle was a message to African-Americans or it was addressed to African-Americans; and yet, as I read it—and I reviewed it for the *LA Times*—one of the things that I thought reading the book was "Well, yes, that's true, but it's also meant for other people, other people who question or want to find a way to question without feeling like they're unpatriotic." I think there was a much bigger audience for that book.

**Mosley:** I think it was a much larger audience, but I just wanted to say that I was talking to black people because it is so rare that black people look beyond our own particular victimology in America, and it's really important that we do, for many reasons: one, for the rest of the world, also for us. You can't just always look at yourself as a victim. You'll never be able to see above the surface of the water. You have to rise like Thelonious Monk, above the

surface of the water. I think that in black artistic culture, the jazz people between the thirties and the sixties were the people who rose up to a level that
was incredible. That was a worldwide level. America doesn't know it, but the
rest of the world knows it. Japan knows it. Europe knows it. America doesn't
know it yet. They say, "I don't listen to that jazz. It's not good."

**Woods:** Do you still have a jazz novel in you?

**Mosley:** I'm going to write a novel about jazz.

**Woods:** I know you've been saying for years that you were.

**Mosley:** I always do what I say. It just takes me a long time. To write about
jazz is very difficult. The thing is that all mystery novels are about something
else. All good ones are about something else. If they're just about the mystery they're okay, but they're forgettable. So, somebody killed somebody and
blah, blah, blah. Okay, fine. You might read it for that reason, but if you look
at Hammett, or Chandler, or [James M.] Cain, these guys are existentialists.
They're really talking about the rot at the core of America and what's going
on. They're talking about something which is much beyond. As a matter of
fact, the crime doesn't even matter very much. When you talk about that
other thing, it's hard. The subject itself becomes very difficult. Jazz is one of
the most difficult things to write about. I keep trying to think about it, and
it's very hard to come at it. So, I haven't been able to do it.

**Woods:** But, you successfully did it with the blues in *RL's Dream*.

**Mosley:** I did. I think I did. I sent the book to Julia Roberts.

**Woods:** Did you?

**Mosley:** Maybe we'll make a movie. (audience laughter) That'll be fun. Julia
Roberts and Morgan Freeman.

**Woods:** Who's she going to be though? (laughs)

**Mosley:** Kiki. She's going to be Kiki, the white girl.

**Woods:** Oh, Kiki. Yes. That's right.

**Mosley:** Really, we all know how you sell movies. (audience laughter)
You can be a student and say, "Oh, I don't want her."

**Woods:** (laughs)

**Mosley:** All these people, they're so like, "You know, in my movie I want
. . . ." Yeah. You want someone who can sell your movie!

**Woods:** You have not been afraid of Hollywood. I've talked to so many writers who say, "I'm afraid what they'll do to my books. I'm afraid what will
happen to my work. I'm afraid I'll lose control of my characters." You don't
seem to have that kind of fear.

**Mosley:** Well, you know that thing that [James M.] Cain said about it when
that guy asked, "What do you think about what Hollywood's done to your

books?" He said, "My book's right here on the shelf. Hollywood hasn't touched it as far as I know."

**Woods:** Yeah. Yeah. (audience laughter) Elmore Leonard says the same thing.

**Mosley:** It's funny. I've always had good experiences in Hollywood. Up until very, very recently I haven't at all thought of myself as a filmmaker. So, I let people do what they're going to do, and I do what I do. And if I don't like what people are saying, I don't go into business with them. One of the problems that a lot of people have is that they want everything. You know, you can't have everything. I mean, the guy gives you 250,000 dollars—well be happy. (audience laughter) I met a guy in a hotel once. It was early in the morning and he'd just been with this prostitute, and he was talking about how much she loved him. I was just like looking at him. "You really needed everything! You gave her the money. You got what you wanted. And now you want more. (audience laughter) You know, she didn't love you." I didn't say that. (audience laughter) But I thought it. Very loudly.

**Woods:** Well, now, let's bring it back to your books and film, okay? (laughs) (audience laughter) We've got to leave them in that room, okay? (laughs) You've had, two books. . . .

**Mosley:** Two books made into films, *Devil in a Blue Dress* and also *Always Outnumbered, Always Outgunned*. Both of them I just loved. It was great. I had a lot to do with the second one. I wrote the screenplay and was executive producer. And on *Devil*, Carl Franklin did an incredible job. They're going to show it tomorrow [at the conference] or, maybe, Saturday night.

**Woods:** Tomorrow night.

**Mosley:** Tomorrow night? Oh, great. That's a really good film. That's been a wonderful experience for me. I often hear, especially at mystery conventions, writers talk about how much they hate Hollywood and how awful those people are. But it's just a business. I was thinking, you got a book, right? You're going to make it into a movie, and I come up to you and I say, "Here's thirty million dollars. Now, you can make that movie. But I need sixty million dollars back." That's big pressure. All of a sudden you say, "Well, I want Denzel to be kissin' on Julia Roberts." But they say, "Well you know, you gonna lose Alabama and Mississippi." (audience laughter) Let's say he wants to kiss her.

**Woods:** Maybe he could just shake her hand. (laughs) (audience laughter)

**Mosley:** "Oh! Hi, Miss Julia." (audience laughter) The thing is that there's this reality. Now, of course, I would still want to make them do what I wanted them to do, but I wouldn't want the thirty million dollars. I'd say other people worry about that. It's a hard business, and I appreciate that. And that's what I tell people. They say, "Well, Walter, we're going to do this and this." And I said, "I don't like that. But I appreciate your problem, so let's not do business." That's what you do. But there's a lot of hunger. There's a lot of hunger among people in Hollywood, also among mystery writers who want things, and who have a vision of the world, and who know the way things should be. I try my best not to fall into that trap. It's sometimes very hard not to.

**Woods:** You've also done original writing for television, right? Pilots, that kind of thing.

**Mosley:** I have a pilot right now. I was supposed to do an Easy Rawlins series for USA Television. I've written the pilot. Everybody likes it. Everybody wants to do it. So, you figure it's about a 12 percent chance (audience laughter) of getting the pilot done. But that's the way it is. That's the business. I'm not criticizing that. That's the way it is. I'm going to have a meeting with them on Monday. We're going to talk, but it's very hard. I did a pilot. We shot it with Danny Glover, spent five million dollars. Then, we brought it back to CBS, and they went, "Eh, nah." And that was it. I was stunned. All this money. All this time. Danny Glover. And at the end, "Nah." But you understand, over the years, 120 million dollars is going to be spent. You want to lose five million, [or] you want to lose 120 million? Well, obviously, I'll lose five. If you don't have confidence in it, you shouldn't be behind it.

**Woods:** Are there any of your books that you think couldn't be made into film or that you think that you would never let be made?

**Mosley:** Oh, no. Listen, I'd let anybody make it into a film because then they pay me money, and I have more money, and I'd have more time. (audience laughter) I would have to agree with what they were going to do.

*Blue Light* would be very difficult. Anybody in this room who's read it probably doesn't like it. But I like it. (audience laughter) It's a crazy book, and it's all about the soul. That's a hard thing to [film], you know. It would be like Mel Gibson and *The Passion*. (audience laughter)

**Woods:** Let's not go there. Talk to me a little bit about *The Man in My Basement*.

**Mosley:** After we do this we're going to let you [audience members] ask questions. *Man in My Basement*, for me, it was an important book to write because one, it was a novel of ideas. I've always loved Gide and Camus and Malraux and all these people who wrote novels of ideas. When I was going to college, I studied them; and I loved those books. I wanted to do that. Also, I wanted to talk about these semi-opposing fields of innocence and evil. Not good and evil but innocence and evil, and how they work out in our world. I also wanted to talk a little differently about black people because on the far end of Long Island there are a lot of black people who descended from black people who were never slaves. They live out there. They have a whole different way of seeing the world and thinking about the world, even though it's mostly unconscious.

You have one guy, Charles Blakey, who's never done anything. He's a slacker; he's kind of a loser. He's a black guy who owns his house and is about to lose it. Then, you have this evil guy [Anniston Bennet] who's done many, many evil things, including selling an infant to a man who thought that his St. Bernard dog or his German Shepherd dog could raise a child. But the first day that he gave the infant to the dog, the dog kills the child. The main character, Charles Blakey, says to this man who's self-imprisoned in his basement in a cell, "Well, that was an evil thing you did." He [Bennet] said, "Well, yeah, it's an evil thing I did, but the mother of that child had eleven other children. I gave her fifty thousand dollars. I saved her whole family. What the hell have you ever done?" And it's a good question. Blakey says, "I don't know." To be able to talk about that question is important—because I don't have an answer to it either. We listen to it every night on television. People running for president say, "Well, I did this, I did that." "Well, I was justified." "Weapons of mass destruction." With all this kind of stuff you're listening to, it's hard to make up your mind. "Well, what's going on?" And I wanted to showcase this problem between two people, using what I do, black male heroes, but without having the regular baggage that usually a lot of my characters come with. It was lots of fun to write.

And I loved the criticism, especially people who don't like it. I really like the people who don't like my book. The people that do like it, I like that too; but the people that don't like it . . . . It's really kind of wonderful because they say, "Well, you know, you didn't really do. . . ." But I wasn't trying to do those things. Anyway, it's very short. You can read it. It's very short—if you're worried—and it would take you one day to read it. (audience laughter) I had one black reviewer who said about my book, "Well, you know, he didn't use the zingy dialect that he usually uses."

**Woods:** Oh, no. He didn't.

**Mosley:** I was like, "My God."

**Woods:** (laughs) No "dese, dems, and dose"?

**Mosley:** But it was somebody black. If somebody white said that, I could say, "Well, God—that's racist." I guess I could say it about somebody's who's black too. It was a funny thing; it was a great deal of fun to write. If you write

a mystery—and there are writers right here, and there are people who read—
if you write a mystery novel, a crime novel, you are not ever going to get
nominated for a Pulitzer Prize. (audience laughter) You forget it! You could
be Dashiell Hammett, you could be Raymond Chandler, it does not matter.
You're not going to be nominated because they are not going to let you into
their field. You already make too much money. (audience laughter)

You already have the top five spaces on—if you're [James] Patterson, you
got the top six places on the list. (audience laughter) They're not going to let
you come into their area to be talked about. They don't want to review. They
don't want to talk about you. That's not the only reason I wrote it [*The Man
in My Basement*]. You know, I can write these books [non-mystery] too. But
it was also to follow that dream of mine to write a novel of ideas.

**Woods:** Okay. Before we open it up to questions, you want to tell everybody
what's happening with Easy next?

**Mosley:** Oh yeah, I'm at a mystery convention. You're supposed to sell your
books. (audience laughter) I forgot. I love it. My new book is called *Little
Scarlet*. I'm very worried about it. I mean, I've written it, and I really think
it's certainly as good an Easy Rawlins novel as I've ever written, if not, I really think, the best I've written. It's about that other thing. It happens the
five days right after the Watts riots of 1965. Those five days. A black woman
has been murdered in her house in the middle of Watts during the riots, and
[her aunt], who the police have put in a hospital and given drugs, believes
that a white man has killed her niece. And the police are very worried because they don't want the riots to come up again. You know, it's not good for
the economy. (audience laughter) And so, they get Easy to go and research
the crime. To investigate the crime.

**Woods:** On behalf of the LAPD?

**Mosley:** On behalf of the LAPD. And if anybody knows the LAPD in 1965,
that's an amazing thing. (audience laughter) That was Chief Parker, and, my
God! I just want to tell you—this fact is in the book, it's really true—the
second day after the riots, Martin Luther King came to LA to have meetings with black leaders and white leaders to see what could be done. After
one day, he left saying, "There is no answer to this problem because there's
nobody in power in Los Angeles who's willing to deal with it." He never
said anything like that. He gave up in twenty-four hours. He said, "Man, I'm
gonna go back to where it's easy, in Selma." (audience laughter)

**Woods:** (laughs) In Birmingham!

**Mosley:** Jackson! (audience laughter) "You know, at least the white people
there, you know, care sumpin." It was an amazing thing. All of America,

the whole consciousness of America, changed in those five days. And that's what the book is about. It was really fun to write.

**Woods:** Where were you during the Watts riots?

**Mosley:** I lived in West LA.

**Woods:** What black people call West LA?

**Mosley:** Near Fairfax and Pico. I was an actor, and I was in the Afro-American Traveling Actors Association. We were doing plays. The main night of the riots, we were down to do the play. Nobody came. Nobody came to see us. But, we were down there to do the play. It was an integrated cast. So, when we were driving out in the station wagon with these white people, the white people are on the floor and the black people are looking out. (audience laughter) The police are driving by with shotguns. People are jumping out of windows, and alarms going off. It was wild. Things were burning.

**Woods:** My dad had a business on 108th and Compton Avenue.

**Mosley:** Did he have "Soul Brother" on the front?

**Woods:** Oh, yeah. Oh, yeah.

**Mosley:** Big sign: "Soul Brother."

**Woods:** "Soul Brother." You had to stand there to prove you were a soul brother. And the Chinese man down the street, who owned a grocery store, he had a little sign that said, "Me soul brother too." (audience laughter)

**Mosley:** "Oh, that's Chin. He's a good guy. Don't mess with him."

**Woods:** (laughs) Let's open it up for questions. Yes, ma'am.

**Audience member:** This isn't really a question; it's a comment. I just love Easy Rawlins, and one of the things I love about him is that you've written him to be honest to himself. I mean in terms of morals and what he does do and what he doesn't do. You have good characters and bad characters, but Easy bends the rules when he doesn't agree with them, or just breaks them. And he seems very comfortable with that. I guess I'm saying something that I don't see often in mystery books, and certainly we all do it. Yet to see it so bluntly there, I just find that extremely attractive; and it makes me think about myself and how I live life. There's just something that really struck me with Easy Rawlins, more than probably any other protagonist.

**Woods:** Let me just repeat it for the, for the tape. She was saying how much she admires Easy Rawlins for his honesty, and being honest with himself even when he bends the rules.

**Mosley:** Thank you. (audience laughter) Thank you for that. Yes sir.

**Audience member:** Can you say why you brought Mouse back?

**Mosley:** I will! (audience laughter) Well, you know, I never really thought he was dead. (audience laughter) But I needed Easy to be alone a little bit because it was a little too regularized—him and Mouse. I wanted Easy to be on his own, try to deal with things on his own. And also to feel that loss. Because there's a loss when you lose your good friend.

My father, when he was about sixty-something, he met this guy and they became really good friends. The guy lived in Texas, and the guy and his wife would come up and visit my mother and father, and they would do things together; and they had all kinds of fun. His name was Murphy. Then, one day, the guy died. Really, I've never seen my father affected by anything. My father has seen a lot of death. One night my father and I sat down, and he told me everybody he had seen die up until that time. It took two hours. He's seen so many people die that it was amazing. My father was not afraid to tell me illegal situations either. So, I had all these secrets I couldn't tell. I go, "My father was there." He told me all these things, but it never affected him. Then, all of a sudden, this guy dies, and it really put a pall over my father's life. And I wanted to do that with Easy. Then bring [Mouse] back, to see how that turn worked.

**Woods:** It's interesting because there's a lot in those books about his grief. It's really interesting how Mouse comes back, and it's as if he was never away.

**Mosley:** Well, he's a mythic character. Also, Mouse is so scary. Mouse is back five minutes, and all of a sudden Easy's worried for his own life, again: "This time I wished you'd stayed dead." (audience laughter)

**Woods:** The other thing I was going to say I liked about the end of *Six Easy Pieces* is that Easy has his little office. It's almost like, "Wow! There's a new chapter." You really get the sense that there is a new chapter coming up for Easy.

**Mosley:** I wanted to give him an office, and it takes a long time [to develop a character]. Over a period of time, I'm doing this with Socrates Fortlow. With Socrates Fortlow it's clearer because he's becoming a philosopher. So I'm spending time showing what are the bases of his becoming that philosopher. But with Easy, he's becoming something too. It's not something so wonderful. He's becoming a private detective. It's nice to see a change over a period of time. It also keeps me interested, and it keeps the story going along. Because if you keep telling the same story again and again, it gets pretty weak.

**Woods:** Yes sir.

**Audience member:** I love the *Six Easy Pieces* collection. I wonder if you were considering writing any more short stories. One of the things I liked was that they're short stories, but yet they're lengthy. They're telling a long story in the short stories. I just wondered what you thought of that, and if you're planning any more of the short story genre.

**Woods:** Are you planning any more Easy short stories?

**Mosley:** He didn't ask that.

**Woods:** Oh, he asked, "Any more short stories?"

**Mosley:** Evan Hunter, Ed McBain, was contracted to do a series of ten no-vellas from ten different writers. That book is going to be about this fat. I think Tor is the publisher. I wrote one for him [Hunter]. It's not a novel, but it's very long. It's called "Archibald Lawless Anarchist at Large" because I've always wanted to write about an anarchist. (audience laughter) An anarchist detective whose god is Bakunin. I just think there's nothing like that.

Then, Otto Penzler's got a collection that's coming out in 2005, and I wrote about a black private detective [Leonid McGill] in New York City, contemporary. But he's really a bad guy. He's got a couple of saving graces about him but not many. The only thing that makes him good is that the people around him are a little bit more evil than he is. (audience laughter) But that's about it. In this first story, he's been hired by a thief who's gang has robbed these people who put money in ATM machines. But the police have a pretty strong suspicion that this [thief] did it. And so, [McGill's] been hired by this guy to put the blame on somebody else. And he does. Then he gets into trouble in the middle of that. How he gets out of trouble is what's doing in the story.

I like writing short stories. I don't feel I'm very good at it, but I really like doing it. And I like writing the longer variety that you can really sink your teeth into and have a "novely" kind of feel to them.

**Woods:** Do you think either one of those could be a series?

**Mosley:** Both of them could be a series. Actually, I have a character that I like more than Mouse in the second one. [McGill] has a wife, a Swedish wife, and they have four kids, only one of which is his. But she pretends like they're all his. (audience laughter) One of them that's not his is a kid named Twill; he's sixteen and he's a career criminal already. But he's really lovable. (audience laughter) And he kind of takes care of his father. They go to a funeral at the end, and the son's wearing a thousand-dollar Armani suit, the sixteen-year-old son. And the father looks at him and he says, "I wonder where he got that suit? But I'm not going to ask." (audience laughter) I really like that guy.

And I'd love to write a series about either of them. Archibald Lawless also would be great to do a series about. It's very hard in America to have any kind of sophisticated view of politics. Because people say, "Anarchist? What do you mean? Do you blow up things?" I said, "No, man. Don't you know what an anarchist is?" "*No.*" (audience laughter)

**Woods:** (To audience member) Ma'am. In back.

**Audience member:** It's obvious that your father had great influence on your writing. Did your mother or other members of your family have an impact on your writing? And a follow up: which of your books would you say I should start with?

**Mosley:** My father, I think, has had the biggest impact on me. That's really true. My mother has had a much quieter impact. For instance, I love comic books. I've always loved comic books. I mean I haven't changed since the time I was twelve-years-old. That's honestly true. I love all the things I loved when I was twelve—the same music, the same comic books. But my father would get really mad at me, and my mother would say, "Roy, it's okay. We're reading books. We have books around us. Books are going to be an important part of his life." So, she kept my father from killing me. (audience laughter) And she gave me good excuses to keep on being who I was.

As for starting to read my books, because I'm at a crime convention, it's pretty easy to say *Devil in a Blue Dress*; or maybe if you didn't want to start with that one, *Black Betty*. If you wanted to read some other kind of work of mine, either *RL's Dream* or the new book that I've just written, *The Man in My Basement*, would show another way that I write.

**Woods:** (To audience member) Sir, in the back.

**Audience member:** Yes. I wonder if you feel a little more optimistic about genre fiction given that Stephen King just won a National Book Award. Does it make you feel like we have a chance or no?

**Mosley:** (laughs) You know, I'm an insider with the National Book Awards because for seven years I was on the board of directors. I was actually the host of the National Awards the night that he won, and I gave it to him. That should actually make me feel more positive, but, indeed, it doesn't. It's as if a Chihuahua was ordering around a St. Bernard, and then one day the Chihuahua let the St. Bernard eat some steak. And then, somebody said to the St. Bernard, "Well, now that the Chihuahua has let you eat some steak, do you feel more positive about your life?" (audience laughter) You know what I mean. I don't really have to say anymore do I? (audience laughter)

We need, for instance, to demand the book industry come up with an award for popular fiction. Because, really, the National Book Award is for important, intellectual literature. I think this is an important thing. We need to talk about that; we need to keep it. We need to keep the quality of it going because that night that Stephen gave that speech he said, "Well, you know, other people should be winning these awards," and he mentioned all these names. Many of those people really shouldn't win the lifetime achievement for the National Book Award. They really shouldn't. And they probably wouldn't win if they were nominated for the individual awards. It's kind of amazing to me that the book industry hasn't come up with major popular fiction awards, like the People's Choice Awards that they have. Why don't they have that?

**Woods:** Let's tell Dick Clark. (audience laughter)

**Mosley:** You need somebody who is forward thinking about it. There are mystery awards, but a lot of that is political. A lot of this stuff is political. We should have a much broader thing for whatever good writing is considered inside our genre. We should demand it. We shouldn't be talking to the Chihuahua. (audience laughter) You know, it's ridiculous.

**Woods:** There was another question. Yes, ma'am.

**Audience member:** I'm going to get back to Easy Rawlins. When you started him as a character did you have a plan for how he was going to develop, or did he sort of spring out or your head fully developed?

**Mosley:** The first book I wrote was *Gone Fishin'*, long ago; it wasn't in the crime genre. Mouse is in it, so it had to be a crime novel! (audience laughter) Nobody published it. Nobody wanted to publish it. Nobody would touch it. My publisher, when I brought it to them after they did *Devil in a Blue Dress*, just said "No." Then, they said, "Well, maybe if we published the first three together, this could be an introduction." And then, they said—when I said I was going to go to Paul Coates's Black Classic Press—"Well, maybe if you would promise to change it into a mystery, we would publish it." But, when I wrote that book, I had wanted to write about that migration of black folk from the western south into Los Angeles, and about all the aspirations, all the hopes, all the successes, and then all the losses, and all of that changing, the generations. I wanted to do that, and that's what I am doing. How the books unfold though, this is over time. I'm just having fun with it. When I'm writing, if I'm on page eighty-eight, I don't know what's going to happen on page eighty-nine. It's the same thing book after book. They come out. The next Easy Rawlins is going to be called *Cinnamon Kiss*.

**Woods:** Love that title.

**Mosley:** It's going to be way inside the genre. It's going to have one of those old time, genius detectives, who sits in the background and pulls strings. It's going to be dealing with Easy, and unhappily for him, Mouse. (audience laughter) It's going to be a lot of fun, but it's going to be very different. There's the story, but then there'll be a larger context.

**Woods:** We just got the announcement that—bang, we're dead, we're out of here. (audience laughter) Is there one last question that anyone would like to ask?

**Audience member:** This is a little more personal. You moved from LA to New York. What prompted it? I think your writing has changed since you moved to New York. Can you talk a little bit about that?

**Mosley:** No, it hasn't changed since I moved to New York because I didn't start writing until I lived in New York. It hasn't. I left Los Angeles in 1973, and I went to Vermont. I lived in Vermont on and off for seven years. I moved to Massachusetts; I was there for three, and now I've been in Manhattan for twenty-one.

If I could get around as easily in LA as I get around in New York, without a car, I'd do it. But I can't. I really hate driving. I like it that if I want a stick of gum, I don't have to get in the car, (laughs) and that's kind of it. Also, the possibilities in New York. In my head, I thought there were going to be possibilities, and it happened. I went to City College in Harlem, graduate school, for writing. Bernard Malamud had taught there. Edna O'Brien was teaching there when I got there. Grace Paley taught there. If you go to LACC [Los Angeles Community College] (audience laughter), believe me, they're not there. Edna O'Brien? She's got to be in Hollywood someplace, and you have to not be able to get to her. That's the way it exists. The class structure of Los Angeles was so definite, whereas in New York, it really isn't. There was a possibility for me that I don't think I would have had in LA.

**Woods:** Let's give a standing ovation to our guest of honor, Walter Mosley. (audience applause)

# Walter Mosley, Uneasy Street

## Christopher P. Farley/2004

The online interview may be found at http://www.powells.com/authors/mosley
.html(accessed 2010). By permission of the interviewer and Powells.com.

On August 11, 1965, a routine traffic stop in a residential section of South Central Los Angeles known as Watts sparked the largest riots in American history. Over the next six days, thirty-four people were killed, more than a thousand were injured, and over two hundred million dollars worth of property had been stolen, destroyed, or burned to the ground.

Why did this happen? What fueled the volcanic rage that was unleashed in Watts just one year after the landmark 1964 Civil Rights Act? And what were the lasting effects of the Watts riots on rapidly evolving race relations in America? These questions lie at the heart of Walter Mosley's exceptional new novel starring amateur sleuth Easy Rawlins.

In nine previous mysteries, Mosley has thrown his hero one messy problem after another. As Easy has embraced the dubious relationships and moral compromises necessary to navigate the labyrinth of South Central Los Angeles, he has become for readers a sort of tour guide through the racially charged underbelly of urban America. Streetwise, cynical, world-weary, and possessed of the wisdom born of hard-won experience, Easy long ago added his name to the shortlist of great hardboiled heroes. But in *Little Scarlet*, Easy digs deeper into the conundrums of his world than ever before.

As riots in Watts are winding down, the police discover the corpse of Nola Payne, a young black woman known on the street as Little Scarlet. Afraid that any attempt to investigate the murder will only reignite the violence, the police turn to Easy for help. Easy agrees to find Nola's killer, though on his own terms. In doing so, he not only exposes the roots of black rage, he also strikes a new and decidedly *un*easy alliance with white power.

*Little Scarlet* is potent allegory, incisive social commentary, not to mention a gripping read. It is also Walter Mosley's best novel to date.

**Farley:** You grew up in LA, correct?

**Walter Mosley:** Yes.

**Farley:** I'm curious what memories you have of the Watts riots?

**Mosley:** I was thirteen-years-old during the Watts riots. I have two memories: one which you'd think would have affected me writing this book but which didn't, and another which you would not have expected.

The first is that I was a member of an acting group called the Afro-American Traveling Actors Association, and at the height of the riots we went down to perform our play. But nobody was going to plays because they were either rioting or fighting rioting or hiding from rioting. So we drove back to West Los Angeles right through the riots. I saw all the fighting and police and people lying unconscious or, you know, dead on the street, and all that kind of stuff.

But that had less of an impact on me than the night I came into a room and found my father drinking and sobbing. And I said, "What's wrong." And he said, "It's the riots." "Are you afraid," I said. And he goes, "No, I want to go out there and riot. I want to fight. I want to burn. I want to shoot at these people." And I was very afraid, and I said, "Are you going to?" And he went, "No, I'm not, because it's wrong to hurt people you don't know, who may not deserve it, and it's wrong to burn down your own property. But I want to," he said. And that had a really big impact on me.

**Farley:** After the '92 riots in LA following the Rodney King verdict, Dan Quayle said: "When I have been asked during these last weeks who caused the riots and the killing in LA, my answer has been direct and simple: Who is to blame for the riots? The rioters are to blame. Who is to blame for the killings? The killers are to blame." Doesn't that accurately sum up an attitude that was prevalent after the Watts riots, as well? And if so, how would you respond to that attitude?

**Mosley:** Well, you know, listen, he's not wrong, in so far as it goes. If you shoot somebody and kill them, and somebody asked, *Who killed that guy?*, I'd have to say, *Well, you killed him.*

**Farley:** But the unstated message in Quayle's comment is: *And we therefore aren't obliged to think any more about it.*

**Mosley:** Exactly. And that's the problem. For instance, after 9/11 some people asked, *Why do people around the world hate Americans?* and then answered *Because they hate freedom!* I don't think so. There are reasons people hate Americans, and these reasons have to be addressed. One of the problems that people from Dan Quayle's ilk have is that if you ask these questions, they believe you are trying to exonerate whatever actions somebody took.

Now, of course, my father answered that question *No*. He didn't riot because he couldn't exonerate himself for doing it. And I wouldn't either. If you murder somebody . . . if you get on top of a building and aim a rifle at somebody and shoot it and kill them, that's murder. And I won't stand in the way of you standing trial for murder.

But the Watts riots are a metaphor for all of the rage that existed in all of the hearts of almost every African American. And that's what you have to deal with. And that's how America responded. You know, people sitting in Atlanta, Georgia, going, "You mean all those black people I see every day really hate me, to the level where they could understand taking out a gun and shooting at me?" To understand that that's the problem.

**Farley:** That sense of seething rage, even bitterness, comes through loud and clear in the book. Easy's anger is palpable. But some of the other characters are more defined by self-loathing than rage, especially Howard. I'm curious how you see the relationship between those two feelings. Are they related? Or is one a reaction to the other?

**Mosley:** Not only are they related, I think they're the same thing. You're born with a love for yourself, but you *learn* to despise yourself: because people in school think you're stupid, or because whenever the police see you they think that you're a criminal to the degree where you finally believe that you're a criminal. It's like that Chris Rock line where he says the police stopped him one day in his own car and before they were finished he believed he'd stolen his own car. In school you're treated as ignorant and told that you're ignorant and people get angry at you if you show any intelligence. You can't get good jobs. You can't hope for a future for yourself or for your children.

Even while all that's going on, you still know it's not true. Somewhere in your heart you know it's not true. On one level you're thinking it's true, and you're thinking, "Oh, I'm just another nigger," basically. And on the other hand you're feeling: "That is not true; I'm better than this and I deserve better than this." That paves the way for rage. And rage shows itself in many different ways. In the mother who kicks her son out of the house. And the son who hates all black women who love white men. All kinds of things happen there. And as Easy points out in the book, at one point the anger and the rage are so great you just go out on a hot summer day and start burning everything down. And that rage is partially exposed by people destroying their own community, which of course is self-loathing. So, you know, yeah, they are the same thing. But it's a very complex thing.

**Farley:** You also seem to be suggesting in the book that the Watts riots were a turning point for the black community. Throughout the novel, Easy notes ways that he's more courageous than he was before the riots. He carries himself with a little more pride, or even defiance. But there is also that scene with the sentry. . . .

**Mosley:** Yeah, he kind of chose sides.

**Farley:** Right. You write:

> The sentry took his job seriously. Who was the enemy? Black people. Even though he was colored himself it was his job to bar our entry and he intended to keep us out. Even though I didn't know it at the time, that was the beginning of the breakup of our community. It was the first time you could see that there was another side to be on. If you identified with white people, you had a place where you were welcomed in.

I was wondering if you could elaborate on that. One, in what way has the community broken up? And two, what does it mean to choose sides?

**Mosley:** Well, the powers that be, which are represented more by money than by race, needed to recruit people in the black community to do their work for them. Now, Easy is one of the people they recruit, because he's looking for the murderer of Nola Payne. He's looking to help the police solve this crime, so they can keep black people from expressing their rage.

**Farley:** And he knows he's being used.

**Mosley:** Yes, he knows he's being used, but he's being rather canny about it, so he's not allowing them to take him over. This sentry, on the other hand, is protecting property against other black people. He really was angry at Easy for daring to want to go into the place where he works. And, at least at that moment in time, this guy is protecting the system that is working against him. He is in essence the weapon of this establishment against Easy and people like Easy.

**Farley:** It makes me think of the handful of prominent blacks in the country who are perceived by some members of the black community as taking sides against blacks. I think of Harry Belafonte's comment about Colin Powell. What did he call him?

**Mosley:** He called him a house nigger, or a house slave, I don't remember which one he said.

**Farley:** And Clarence Thomas, of course, is widely criticized in the black community.

**Mosley:** Yeah, well, you know Clarence and Condoleeza and Colin are like that sentry, yeah.

**Farley:** You think that's fair?

**Mosley:** Well, I don't know if it's fair, and a lot of people would probably disagree with me, but that's what I think.

**Farley:** Of course, it is also significant that our current president, a very conservative Republican, chose a black woman as one of his closest advisers.

**Mosley:** Which is going to make a big difference for black people in the future. Not today, but in the future. In a way, he may be working against himself by doing that.

**Farley:** How so?

**Mosley:** Because he'll open the door. Now you can have black women as powerful as Condoleeza Rice in high government.

**Farley:** Do you really think that George Bush would care to keep that door closed?

**Mosley:** George Bush himself? I don't know the answer to that question. And I don't care. I think he sees black America in general as having antipathy toward him, and therefore doesn't consider black America his constituency. And he's right about that. But whether he's trying to keep people down. . . . I think that there's a system in America where black people are kept out of the vote, kept out of the mainstream in America. There's a great deal of racism against poor black people, not necessarily so-called middle-class or upper-class black people, but certainly against poor black people in America. There are great barriers erected against black Americans.

**Farley:** And often the people who aren't behind the barriers don't see them and so don't believe they exist.

**Mosley:** Especially some younger people, saying, you know, *I worked hard. I made it. How come he can't do it?*

**Farley:** Which brings to mind Bill Cosby, who recently stirred up a hornets' nest by criticizing poor blacks.

**Mosley:** Yeah, but Bill's comments are made out of love. They may be inappropriate at times, they may be critical to the level that they are not helpful, at times, but he's not saying them because of a dislike or an antipathy towards black people. He's saying it because of love. And I think most black people know that. You know, I'm critical of the way he's made some of his criticism. But I can't say that Bill doesn't like black people. Bill *loves* black people. And he has all of these great hopes and aspirations, and he feels in a way cheated by certain things that have happened. I think that the reasons these things have happened go far beyond the people he's criticizing. However, I'm not going to say he didn't have the right to say what he said.

**Farley:** The Watts riots were in 1965. Then there were riots in '92 after the

Rodney King verdict. I'm curious whether you have any insight into why LA seems to be such a flash point for racial anger.

**Mosley:** Well, the Rodney King trial happened in LA, so that's why.

**Farley:** But that wouldn't have been such a big deal if there hadn't already been a reservoir of anger there.

**Mosley:** But also, the riots in '92 weren't strictly race riots. Yes, there was the Rodney King decision, but there were all kinds of people rioting: white people, Chicanos, Asians. And the Watts riots were just black people, and they were just in Watts. The '92 riots happened all over the city, and all kinds of people were involved. You couldn't really say it was a black race riot. You couldn't even call it a race riot because white people were doing it, too. And in the sixties you have Harlem, you have Detroit which was a monster riot, you have Tampa (maybe Tampa was in the seventies, but it happened), there were a few places. So it's not just LA. But the LA riots were the big riots, the most impactful. And why is that? I don't know. But, you know, most big cities experienced riots in the sixties. And when Martin Luther King was killed, there were riots everywhere.

**Farley:** Yes, well I think anyone could see why there were riots after that.

**Mosley:** You can see why there are riots any time. Four hundred years of oppression, you know, and people still want to mistreat you. Your kids are still being arrested and thrown into jail when white kids are not being arrested and thrown into jail for doing the exact same thing. When you know for a fact that every night black men are arrested and beaten. And I'll say, for no reason because there is no reason. Once you're arrested, you shouldn't be beaten. That's not the police's job. But it happens to black people. And they have had no recourse for hundreds of years. It happened before the riots, during the riots, and after the riots.

So what are you going to do? A guy says, "I remember last week a cop grabbed me and took me down to the prison. And they beat me within an inch of my life. So why can't I riot?" And that becomes the answer. "So why can't I go out and fight and burn. Why can't I do that? Didn't they do that to me?" And, really, there's no answer. Because everybody would agree. Take some white guy living in Orange County. If the police systematically took his children and the children of other people in his neighborhood and took them down to the police station and just beat them mercilessly, and then framed them for crimes they didn't commit, kept them from their rights, kept them from all this stuff, they would be out there fighting. Anyone would be out there fighting. It's not a black thing. It's just not happening to these other people, so they don't do it.

**Farley:** I'd like to change the subject and ask you a few questions about writing. When you write a novel, what do you hope to accomplish? What effect do you hope to have on your reader?

**Mosley:** Well, the simple answer is that when you write a novel, what you want to do is tell the story well. That is ultimately what writing a novel is about. You want to tell a story well.

**Farley:** And you are definitely a reader's writer.

**Mosley:** How could one not be a reader's writer?

**Farley:** Well, I could name a few novels. . . .

**Mosley:** But people read those novels!

**Farley:** In another interview you said something to the effect that if you write in an obtuse style, if what you write is very hard for people to understand, then you are not doing your job as a writer.

**Mosley:** That's what I think, though! There are a lot of people who don't think that. Take *Finnegan's Wake*. Some people like *Finnegan's Wake*, like reading it. I find it really painful and very hard to read and I go, "Oh my God, does it really need to be this complex?" I think Joyce would say, "Yes, it did." And so he's answered my question. But I find it hard to get there. I believe that writing should be a clear pane of glass. There's a story on the other side of the glass and you shouldn't be distracted by the lens.

**Farley:** Do you have a specific emotional reaction you are trying to evoke in a reader?

**Mosley:** I would say yes, but yes with every sentence, with every paragraph, with every section and chapter. In one chapter it might be a kind of scintillating, physical sexuality. The next might be a very emotional, even philosophical chapter that might cause you to question yourself or someone else or someone's actions. Something might be very complex, where it's very puzzle-like and you have to work it out. But that would be due to the whole book. What I want you to get out of it in the end I don't know, because people get different things out of books. If you tell me when you read *Little Scarlet* I said something to you, I might tell you that I didn't mean that. But that's what *you* got. And if you've read it, *Little Scarlet* belongs to you just as much as it belongs to me. You know what I'm saying? I'm not trying to tell you what you should think. I don't believe in writers as teachers. I think what writers do, if they're successful, is open dialogue. So we can think and wonder and go different places with it.

**Farley:** How in general do you come up with plot and character? Do you have any systematic way that you work out your plots? Or do you just discover the story as you go?

**Mosley:** I discover it as I go along, as a rule. Even if I were to outline it, I discover it as I go along.

**Farley:** How does that work when you're writing a mystery, which is very plot driven?

**Mosley:** Well, writing is rewriting. You write the first draft and it doesn't work. But then you discover those things that you wanted to happen and you go back through it and you keep rewriting it until it does. One thing is that a novel has to be too big to be held in your head. And so you have to allow yourself to make mistakes. If you don't make mistakes, you're not writing. There are some people who do write books that are so simple that they don't really need to do any experimenting. But I don't call those novels. You know, it's writing, it's fiction, but it's kind of weak.

**Farley:** And how has the experience of writing a novel changed for you over the years? Has it gotten any easier? Or does it stay the same?

**Mosley:** It's not really a lot different. It's always the same level of difficulty. I'm a better writer now. And that's not necessarily to say that I'm writing better books, but I'm a better writer. But the better you become, the more challenges you find. For every barrier you go over, you find another problem. *You* get better, but it's the same level of difficulty.

**Farley:** I read the *Best American Short Stories* [2003] you edited and I was curious what that experience was like for you, how you got involved. Did they just call you up?

**Mosley:** Yes, they just called me up and asked if I wanted to do it. I was shocked, actually, that they wanted me.

**Farley:** And how was that as an experience?

**Mosley:** Well, it was hard work going through all those stories. You're fed stories by a few people who go through everything. There's no way you're going to go through everything, so a lot of people bring you stories. And I really believe that a good story and good writing don't always happen in the same work. You can have very good writing, which might have been a good story at some point. But seeing that we've already heard it about twenty times, with the same quality of writing, it's kind of meaningless. You know, "Well, I've read that story." And you can have a wonderful story that the writing is lacking in. You know what I mean?

So, for instance, if you're going to write a coming-of-age story, it better be really interesting, because we've heard this story. We have Salinger already. We've heard about the young white guy, or the young black guy, or whoever the young Chinese woman coming of age, you know, with the father who wanted to do this and the mother that wanted to do that. You better show me something really new.

And also I argued with them because, listen, this is the best stories in America. It is not the "Best American Literary Stories." It is not the "Best

American Iowa Writers Stories," or "*New Yorker* Stories." You know, it's the *Best American [Short]Stories.* Maybe the best story is a crime story. For instance, Doctorow's story in that collection is a crime story. I don't think he thinks so, but that's a crime story.

There are all kinds of possibilities for stories, and if I can't see every different kind, how would I know which ones are the best? And I'm not sure, but I think it's the first time that *Best American Short Stories* kind of went off and allowed a couple of genre stories to be considered as some of the best. I might be wrong, but I think that's true. I didn't let them show me who the writers were or what the magazines were that they came from, and, on the whole, I was able not to know that. So there's a wide swath of fiction in that collection. I think the magazine best represented was a small magazine called *Tin House* with three stories.

**Farley:** They're from Portland.

**Mosley:** Is that where it is?

**Farley:** Yes, the tin house the magazine is named for is just down the street from us here.

**Mosley:** But as a rule these collections don't pay that much attention to the smaller magazines. And I'm not even sure why. So I felt I was doing something different, or beginning to do something different. I know that there are the *Best Mystery Stories* and the *Best Science Fiction Stories* and the *Best Essays* and stuff like that. But the best stories means the best stories, no matter who wrote them, and no matter what genre they were written in. I know this one has done extraordinarily well. A lot of people bought this collection, and I'm very proud of it. I'm really looking forward to seeing what they do next year.

# Walter Mosley Interview

## Connie Martinson/2005

Interview transcript from the Connie Martinson Talks Books Collection at the Claremont Colleges Digital Library (http://ccdl.libraries.claremont.edu/home.php). Published by permission of the Drucker Institute, Claremont Graduate University. The video recording of the interview may be found at http://ccdl.libraries.claremont.edu/cdm4/item_viewer .php?CISOROOT=/cmt&CISOPTR=44&CISOBOX=1&REC=16 (accessed 2010).

**Connie Martinson:** Hello. Welcome to *Connie Martinson Talks Books*. Well, he's back. Who? Easy Rawlins. And he's in a new book called *Cinnamon Kiss*, written by my guest, Walter Mosley. It's published by Little, Brown and Company. Welcome, Walter.

**Walter Mosley:** Thank you very much.

**Martinson:** It's such a short time between this book, *Cinnamon Kiss*, and *Little Scarlet*, and yet in reading it, it seems like years away.

**Mosley:** Emotionally it's a very different book. It's set in a very different way than *Little Scarlet*.

**Martinson:** Let's tell our friends: at the beginning Easy is very concerned because his daughter, Feather, has an undisclosed, unknown blood disease. There is a doctor in Switzerland who may have the answer, but it's going to cost 35–50,000 dollars. And the year that this takes place is?

**Mosley:** 1966.

**Martinson:** That means even more money than it would today.

**Mosley:** Easy would have had that money because he owned some properties, an apartment building and a house or two in Watts, South Central; but because the riots had just happened, property values had gone through the floor. He owes more on the mortgages than the places are worth.

**Martinson:** He has two offers; one is legal and one is slightly illegal, from our darling friend Mouse. (laughs)

**Mosley:** Yeah. Easy says, "I need 35,000 dollars." He asks everybody he knows, "How can I get it?" Mouse is the only one with an answer: "Well, listen. I know an armored car we could rob. Let's get together. I'll just call

**165**

some people up. We'll set it up. We can rob it, no problem." It turns out Easy doesn't do that. He should have.

**Martinson:** He should have because he goes with a man named Saul Lynx to San Francisco; and I love the scene. It just lends itself to the era when they made movies that were called "noir films." He goes to San Francisco and there, almost as if he is Robert Mitchum in an old movie, goes to the big estate, the big mansion of a man named Robert E. Lee. Robert E. Lee never talks to anybody, but he is *the* private eye or private investigator for the big corporate money. And he has an assistant named Maya.

**Mosley:** Yes. There's all this great lineage. You have people like Sherlock Holmes, Nero Wolfe, and Maigret. You have these great detectives in different areas that have been the mainstay for the genre. Of course, Easy's never been involved in that world. Easy's a guy. He knows some other guys. He's kind of down and dirty. I wanted to bring in one of those great detectives and kind of debunk them in a way—not completely but in a way—when they face somebody like Easy Rawlins. It was a lot of fun for me.

**Martinson:** Robert E. Lee turns out to be not just a little man, but a very little man. I kept thinking of the old Swifty Lazar who, when you met him, had very little hands. He was a very little man. That's what I see Robert E. Lee being.

**Mosley:** In some ways, he's a little man. I think if I were to write a detective series about Robert E. Lee that would have been a great deal of fun. He would have been small; and he would have had this extraordinary ego; and he would have hid behind this big, amazon, beautiful woman. He would have been a great detective in a certain way. But put him in relationship to Easy, and a whole other kind of personality evolves. Then, you have somebody like Mouse who sees him. Mouse says, "The first time I saw him, if I wanted to kill him, I'd have to shoot him in the head."

**Martinson:** (laughs) Yes. Then, of course, what is it about getting bonds and papers that a man named Alex has stolen, or not stolen. That we don't know. He has the assistant, Philomena, who is Cinnamon Kiss.

**Mosley:** People hire Easy because he's black and because there's no way into the black world. You need somebody who's going to come and represent your interest. Everybody trusts Easy. Easy says, "I will do what you need me to do. I'm an honest man. I'm gonna do what you need me to do." And, so he's going to find this woman, Cinnamon Kiss, Philomena Cargill.

**Martinson:** That brings him back to LA. He really has, in this book, very convoluted nightmares. It is as if the past keeps coming back and the threat of death is in his nightmares.

**Mosley:** I think that one of the things that I was doing in the dream life of Easy, in this book, is showing that he's having a very hard time of it. His girl-friend may or may not be having an affair with an African prince.

**Martinson:** That's Bonnie for those who are the faithful followers of Easy Rawlins.

**Mosley:** At the same time that she may or may not be having this affair, whatever she's doing, she is the only person who has the inroads to save his daughter's life. He has lost almost everything. His daughter has this terrible disease. Everything is really, really on Easy.

**Martinson:** Even age.

**Mosley:** Yeah. He's getting older and the world is changing. So his dream life becomes—well, some may call it rich. They're demonic in a way, the dreams that he has. What he's trying to do, the things that he has to consider. The fact that he would consider robbing an armored car with Mouse, really al-most completely shatters Easy because he's been trying so hard to have that middle-class life.

**Martinson:** Talk a little bit more about Mouse.

**Mosley:** Yes. I think it's hard to talk about Mouse in this book without also talking about Jackson Blue. You have these two people who have been in Easy's life since the first book. Mouse, the killer and later the professional criminal.

**Martinson:** But a great friend.

**Mosley:** Well, he's a good friend. Then, you have Jackson, the genius who is cowardly and no matter how smart he is, he's willing to throw that away in order to rob ten bucks out of your wallet. Easy's relationship with them, in this book, changes drastically. He understands that both of these men have gone past him in the world. They deal in a world like powerful white men deal in the world. Jackson works for this French president of this com-pany that insures insurance companies. Mouse is dealing with a nationwide syndicate in which he robs, and steals, and makes all this kind of high level dealing. It's a very interesting book. Of course, Mouse, at the same time, is going through his own psychological problems because of his relationship with EttaMae. We see how closely Etta controls his life.

**Martinson:** Also, in Jackson Blue's life, I love that Jewel is in real estate.

**Mosley:** And brilliant in real estate. One of the things that I love to talk about is that race, and racism to a great degree, is psychological. It's not all psychological, but to a great degree it's psychological. So, you have Easy who wants to be a real estate mogul, but his history doesn't allow him to do it, doesn't allow him to understand how the world works. Here you have this much younger woman, Jewel, a young black woman, who understands real estate as if it were second nature because she isn't limited by the bugaboos and the weight of racial injustice that lies on Easy's brain.

**Martinson:** She is one more generation away from, say, having a grandfather who had been a slave. She now might say, "Oh. I had a great-grandfather who. . . ."

**Mosley:** And "I don't remember him, but I can live in *this* world." She's more advanced than Easy in these things. It's funny because a lot of times I'll talk to people about my books, and—it's funny because people read books in funny ways and I don't have anything against it because we all do—they'll say, "Well, don't you have any strong women characters who are really doing things in the world?" Well, who is Jewel? Who is EttaMae? At the same time, I have these very sexy people like Cinnamon; and they take up a lot of space in people's minds.

**Martinson:** But Cinnamon is also saying, "Look, I work for him, but he took me places where nobody else would have taken me. He took me to his family. He took me as if he were color blind."

**Mosley:** So she lives also in a different world than Easy. Everybody's living in different worlds. People are starting to separate. After the Watts riots, people are going off on their own in the world, and Easy's noticing this. So he's a little bit more isolated.

**Martinson:** That was also the era when the Writers Guild started training to bring more young, black writers into the cinema world.

**Mosley:** Was it Budd Schulberg who started the Writers' Workshop in Watts? It's true. A lot of things began to change, and a lot of things didn't change. You have that world where things get better, and they get worse; and, of course, you have the hippie movement, which I really try to talk about in this book. That becomes my own memories. At this point in my life, I'm fourteen years old; and my experiences are beginning to show up in this book. Before that I'm writing about memories of people in my family, stories that they told me. Now that world is changing, people I actually know are in this book, or like people I know anyway.

**Martinson:** How about Easy's son?

**Mosley:** Jesus.

**Martinson:** And his girlfriend, Benita. And the fact that they're living together in his house. Again, the sixties was that period when the pill came in, and therefore the threat of pregnancy could be avoided. Just having sex. . . .

**Mosley:** You could have sex. People were having sex even before the pill, but it was a little easier to get to it with the pill.

**Martinson:** That's the woman's role in this. She's the one who's really changing. And Bonnie goes off to Switzerland with Feather.

**Mosley:** Also, she stays with her African prince there. That becomes the problem for Easy. It's really enjoyable. I write mysteries sometimes; sometimes I don't write mysteries. But very often I write them. I'm interested in the mystery, and I'm interested in what's happening, and I'm trying to say something to trick the reader so you don't know who the killer is. But the thing that's so important for me is that people become involved with the characters, that people care about them. They get angry at them. They say, "Well, why did he do that? Why did he do this?" I've been having a lot of fun with that because women are very angry at me with the decision that Easy makes about his relationship with Bonnie at the very end of the book.

**Martinson:** I'm going to let *you* give it away because I'm not—they're going to have to read it. (laughs)

**Mosley:** Well, I'm not going to give it away. But people just get upset about whatever that decision is. And I just love that people care about him enough to be mad at him.

**Martinson:** I thought he was going to end up with Cinnamon. She's strong; she knows who she is; she comes to him saying, "I need you." He comes in on that and says, "I had to remind myself that I was still single." I think that had to do with Georgette and a sexy girl there, but that still is a part that plays to him.

**Mosley:** There's a thing that Easy recognizes in this book. It's very small. When you're writing, there's a desire when you really want to make a point to underscore a little bit too much. I don't do that. I understate things. But there's a moment when Easy is with Cinnamon whom he just loves being with, physically but also intellectually. She really stimulates him. He asks her, "Do you love me?"

**Martinson:** And he said, "I've never asked anyone that before."

**Mosley:** Yeah. This is a big change. For the first time, Easy realizes that he needs love in his life, which is why he asks her the question. It may have less to do with her and more to do with his changing. When she looks at him, she says, "Sure." He knows that this is not going to work. What he's gotten from it is recognizing something. But it's hard for a black man—especially from that period of time—to recognize. "I don't need anything. I don't need anybody. You don't love me—fine. I'll go on—I'll find another woman." Now he knows he has to find somebody.

**Martinson:** Also, I must say, he has a great ability to cook. Whenever he is nervous or not happy, boom! He's at that stove cooking or eating.

**Mosley:** Hmm. When you are trying to achieve some kind of character development in a novel, there has to be the pedestrian notion of the character's life. It has to come out in certain ways. One of those things is having kids. Easy has adopted kids. Whether a woman's in his life or not in his life, he has these kids. They're not his blood, but he loves them more than anything. He puts his life on the line for Feather. Another thing is that he likes property, taking care of property, growing plants. He loves to cook. And he knows how to cook.

**Martinson:** How much of Easy do you take out of yourself now?

**Mosley:** That's hard to say. I don't think there's a whole lot. I like to cook, but I haven't adopted any children.

**Martinson:** Anybody who can put the flavors—the cumin, the mmm—into that dish, knows what he's writing about.

**Mosley:** I like to cook, and I see that as a kind of a male thing because my father cooked everyday in my house when I was a kid. Everyday. My mother never cooked. So that seems like a very masculine thing for me, a man sitting there cooking.

**Martinson:** Great chefs are always men. Or, have been until Alice Waters.

**Mosley:** That's true. Men often do that. There's the guy who says, "I'm a great chef" which means he does all those very special things and needs special tomatoes from Argentina. That is not Easy. Easy says, "I open the 'frigerator and I can make a meal out of anything that's in there. I'll figure somethin' out." That's why women are actually the great cooks; they work with what they have at hand.

**Martinson:** I'm thinking of the politics in Los Angeles that Easy's living with. It's just when Willy Brown is coming up in San Francisco. It's also when Tom Bradley is rising in the police force and is getting together a group of people who were disenchanted with Sam Yorty. Sixty-six is a changing time.

**Mosley:** It is. In this book, I'm paying more attention to it on the national level for politics and the social level, i.e., the hippies, for what's happening locally. But you're absolutely right. I'm so interested in what's going on in Vietnam. Us saying, "Well, we know that [Nyugen Cao] Ky is a dictator, but we support him anyway. We don't like the democratic revolution in South Vietnam." I'm interested in going more into that generation because of how the world was changing so rapidly, especially for somebody like Easy. Everyday I look at myself differently, and everybody looks at me differently. And I look at them differently. Things are changing so quickly that when Easy sees that the white woman with a little child he saves from running into the street, thanks him, even though she's from Texas, he can tell she is not noticing a difference between color because she's a hippie now. She's dropped all that stuff. Even the good things are difficult for Easy to deal with.

**Martinson:** In that section I asked you to read, we saw the history that he had come from. He talks in terms of what would happen if a black man sees a white man murdered or dead. The immediate public reaction would be, "He did it." I don't think today it's quite that blatant.

**Mosley:** It's interesting. What's happened is that the black community has been separated.

**Martinson:** Economically?

**Mosley:** Yes, and also socially. So, you have a lot of black people who are in the upper and the working class, or maybe in the middle class, or maybe even rich. Those people know that's not going to happen to them. But racism on another level has been institutionalized in the inner city. So, for instance, you're walking down the street with a guy, and he's a member of the Crips or some gang. The police stop him. They get your name, and they write you down, "gang affiliated," because you were walking down the street with somebody in a gang. Later on, maybe you commit a crime or you don't commit a crime, they were going to send you to prison for three years for this crime, but because you are on a list somewhere—"gang affiliated, gang related"—they can tack on some more time. You know what I mean? So, there's a kind of institutionalization of the same thing that was happening to Easy in the forties, the fifties, and the sixties. Now in the twenty-first century, it's another thing. Who can exist, what young man or woman can exist in the 'hood and not be gang related?

**Martinson:** That's like joining a fraternity.

**Mosley:** Worse. Joining a fraternity, it's just that you're ostracized, people don't like you. If you don't have somebody at your back, you can get killed. You can get beaten up, you can get robbed, you can be mistreated every day of your life, unless you have somebody to watch your back. So, you have to. It's not just that you want to. You have to hang out with these groups.

**Martinson:** On a sociological basis then, how do you get that group to start to be more constructive when, on a street deal, they can make more than what the straight guy can make in a month?

**Mosley:** I think that the amount of money that people make, especially when they're young, is not a big thing. For instance, somebody my age would think that more than somebody who is fifteen.

I think that the reason that people belong to angry and to violent gangs is because they have no other alternative. Another way to look at that is that there is no hope for a good life. So, we have to start offering hope to young people: the chance that you can live a good life, the chance that you can live in comfortable surroundings, the chance that you'll be able to eat. Because the thing is that with making money I could buy what I needed. "Well, what did you need?" "Well, the first thing that I needed was some food. And the next thing I needed was some nice clothes. And the next thing I needed was a place to live." Whatever it is, you can get that by working somewhere, or you can get that because the society believes in you.

**Martinson:** That's Jackson Blue. Jackson Blue is going to end up president of something.

**Mosley:** Oh, yeah. Jackson Blue's going to be a very successful guy. But he's a genius.

**Martinson:** Yes. But where did that innate genius come from?

**Mosley:** It's not so much where does it come from, it's what happened to it. All of these kids who live in poverty, below that line, in the United States, among them there are hundreds, thousands of geniuses, and that genius gets lost.

**Martinson:** Who helped you develop your genius, Walter?

**Mosley:** It's interesting. My father was a really brilliant guy. He was very, very, for him, successful. It's just like Easy talking about himself. My father was the same way. He got himself some property. He worked very hard. My mother, who's Jewish and from New York, infused some money from her own family into our experience. So, I was very lucky in that way. But a lot of people are not as lucky, coming from single-parent, maybe no-parent homes. I think that anybody who's offered the chance—they're offered love in their life and hope for their future—is going to think twice about doing something that's going to put that in jeopardy.

**Martinson:** Interesting listening to you. You do always put in Easy a decency and a positive [aspect], as a way of resolving things.

**Mosley:** Which is why people ask me sometimes why women are so attracted to Easy. And there's always a little doubt: "Why are all these women attracted to Easy?" I say, "Well, because Easy wants to help." When you meet Easy, you know he loves children. He wants to take care of children. If you need help, he's going to help you. He really is. He's never going to abandon you. He will put his life on the line for you. This is what people like, men and women.

**Martinson:** And, they're going to love *Cinnamon Kiss.*

**Mosley:** I hope so.

**Martinson:** Thank you, Walter. Will you autograph my book?

# Walter Mosley's Search for Context

## Maria Luisa Tucker/2006

From AlterNet.org. Posted March 24, 2006. Found at http://www.alternet.org/media/33828/ walter_mosley%27s_search_for_context/. (accessed 2010) © AlterNet.org. By permission.

Walter Mosley's latest monograph, *Life Out of Context*, is a cognitive journey that tackles the big questions many of us have furtively attempted to answer. How can we make a difference in a topsy-turvy world where average citizens seem so powerless? What can be done to help the masses of people suffering in poor nations? Is there an effective way for us to individually fight for global justice in a corporatized, corrupted world?

Mosley invites readers into his thought process as he attempts to answer these questions over a series of sleepless nights. He wonders how he, or anyone, can respond to the forces of globalization, exploitation, and racism. In taking on such a large task, he thankfully starts from a perspective that many can relate to. He is not part of a movement; his life, he writes, is "filled with contradictions and seemingly nonsensical juxtapositions," just like the rest of us. And that's exactly why Mosley's words resonate.

As the title suggests, Mosley searches for a political context, beginning within his own professional life and moving on to the tragedies of the African continent. Ruminating on the idea of context, Mosley writes: "I am living in a time that has no driving social framework for a greater good. There are many, many disparate notions about how to make a better world, but these are just so many voices singing a thousand songs in different keys, registers, and styles—a choir of bedlam."

He argues that it's irresponsible and dangerous to leave the fate of the world up to political leaders because they "are just as likely to mislead as they are to lead." He rightly points out that our political experts "are not interested in the truth. Their only goal is to prove a point of view."

As for Mosley, he focuses on asking questions, imagining change and prompting others to use what they have—their vote, their voices, their profession, their talents and ability to protest—to challenge the forces of economic globalism and exploitation. Among his suggestions are the formation of a Black Party and a House of Representatives comprised of elected officials representing identity groups—gay people, blacks, angry white men, the elderly, etc.—rather than geographical areas. In essence, he asks that we all re-envision ourselves and our own political context—and he begins with himself:

**MARIA LUISA TUCKER:** One of the first reactions to your essay is surprise that you have written something outside the context that most readers know you in, which is fiction. How have you responded to that?

**WALTER MOSLEY:** Well, I know that many people see me as a fiction writer (many others see me as only a writer of crime fiction). I tell people who say this with surprise (or disappointment) that I've written a good deal of nonfictional political work. There are essays here and there in various periodicals, the collections of essays that I edited, *Black Genius*, my political monographs—*What Next, Workin' on the Chain Gang*, and now *Life Out of Context*—and then there's the political aspect of almost all of my fiction.

**MLT:** What kind of responses have you gotten to your suggestion that black people create their own political party?

**WM:** To begin with I do not feel that African-Americans should form a political party but that we should form an interest group that hones in on the few issues that are most important to us on racial, economic, and moral grounds. Many people are excited to hear someone saying something that has been on their minds too—specifically that the two-party system is corrupt, undemocratic, and exclusionary to peoples of color. There are those who claim that my stance is divisive. I understand this response, but I believe that the division is older than this nation and that the only way to come together is to come to our political senses by defining what it is we believe and then concretizing those beliefs.

**MLT:** The idea of creating a separate black party is not new. The Black Panthers were a political party and now there are groups like the Malcolm X Grassroots Movement, which advocate the takeover of the South, and many hip-hop political organizations, which share the same demands you suggest in your essay (universal health care, revamping of the penal system, etc.). How is your idea of a black party different? Or is it different, perhaps, because it is more palatable coming from someone who is not considered a radical or a separatist?

**WM:** Again, I am not advocating a political party, per se. My notion of a black voting bloc or interest group is based on the notion that all Americans are the victims of a capitalist oligarchy that keeps us from moving forward in a practical and common-sense fashion. There should be a gay interest group, a real Republican interest group, maybe an angry young white man interest group; there should be political bastions based on age, labor affiliations, and one's status as an ex-convict. My desire is to gain enough seats in the House of Representatives so that neither the Democratic or the Republican interest corporations will have a majority in the House. That way, we the people can have a say in the system that supposedly represents us. If this is more palatable than some other idea—cool.

**MLT:** You present a picture of people desensitized to atrocity, which is often true. However, I think it's also true that some people respond to the atrocities of the world with huge amounts of grief. I know a lady, for example, who has worked to help poor left-behind children every day of her life but refuses to watch the news because she finds the images too upsetting. So my question is—do you think everyone needs to view him or herself within a global context that includes problems so large and numerous that it is impossible to understand or help in every situation?

**WM:** With faith and hope, nothing is impossible. Just look at the civil rights movement or the political (nonviolent) successes in South Africa. Should everyone look at the world on a global scale? The more the better I say. But don't get me wrong—people should do what they can. Any step toward the light is a step in the right direction.

**MLT:** How can people stay in tune to what's happening in the world without being overwhelmed with each day of war, AIDS, pollution, natural disasters, and the like?

**WM:** If I were to say that the pain we are experiencing in the world today was greater than our ability to deal with it, how could I imagine the history of the twentieth century? The millions dead from China to Russia to European Jews, Gypsies, and homosexuals. We can save Africa. We can reduce the prison rolls. We can save the world—again.

**MLT:** You put forth some ideas that you later retract. For instance, you propose putting up huge electronic billboards in major American cities that show images of starving children and other atrocities, and later you say that this idea is not feasible. Are there any ideas in *Life Out of Context* that, since its publication, you have changed your mind about?

**WM:** *Life Out of Context* is a monograph. That means it is there to cause dialogue. My mind is not in question here. What *is* in question are issues that must be considered and ways of thinking which are outside of the box that the corporate shills have put us in.

**MLT:** You ask individuals who live in America to take responsibility for global problems that are caused or exacerbated by American corporations and government. How are some ways that individuals can respond to global problems?

**WM:** The last chapter of my book talks about how political activism on a personal level has to do with your interests and ideals. One, like your friend, might decide that children suffering anywhere is what he or she wishes to concentrate on. They might start teaching in a prison or working for separate political voting groups. Taking action causes ripples in the system; it transforms not only the one taking action but the people around him or her. Doing anything positive on about the average of an hour and a half a day could begin the avalanche.

# A Conversation with Walter Mosley

## John Orr/2006

From Triviana.com found at http://triviana.com/books/mosleyqa.htm (accessed 2010).
Reprinted by permission of the interviewer.

We aren't yet halfway through 2006 and the talented Walter Mosley has already published four books—*The Wave* (science-fiction), *Life Out of Context* (political meditations), *Cinnamon Kiss* (an Easy Rawlins mystery), and his latest, *Fortunate Son*, which is literary fiction, a beautiful, involving, and touching parable about blacks and whites in America.

Don't blink, he has a Fearless Jones novel coming out in September. There are . . . [many] books by Walter Mosley—mysteries, literary fiction, science-fiction, fiction for young adults, collections of short stories and political essays—listed at Amazon.com.

And he is not publishing hackwork. He has been called "brilliant" by the *Washington Post* and other newspapers; the Associated Press has said about him "only Mosley has employed detective fiction as a vehicle for a thoughtful, textured examination of race relations in the United States. Only Mosley puts white readers, if just for a few hundred pages at a time, in a black man's shoes."

His prose is so well crafted he crowds the top of the pyramid with Toni Morrison, E. L. Doctorow, and John Steinbeck.

We spoke with him recently by phone about his latest novel, *Fortunate Son*, and other matters.

**Q.** Do you ever sleep?
**A.** You know, I only write about three or four hours a day, but I do it every day—and that seems to be enough. Balzac in the forty or fifty years of his writing, wrote 180 novels with a pen—a quill pen—I figure he wrote between three and four novels a year. I was married, not anymore, we didn't have children.
**Q.** What do you do the other twenty hours a day?

**A.** What do I do? I belong to political organizations, give talks, give readings, I talk to other writers about their writing. The kinds of things that people do. I enjoy New York, wonderful city.

**Q.** When I read *Fortunate Son*, I thought: Parable.

**A.** Well, listen, what else can you think? My publisher told me, I said, "Well you know, it's a parable." He said, "Don't say that!" (Laughs.) He said, "Don't say that, people won't want to read it!" I go, "What am I gonna say? It seems like a parable to me."

Though, not a parable in such a way where at the end of it you're going to say, "Well, this is right and that's wrong." It's the kind of parable where you'd say there's possibility and there's choice. And there's probability. There's possibility, probability, and choice. And that's the world you live in.

**Q.** According to Milton, that's what God gave us, choice. Correct me if I'm wrong about *Fortunate Son*: Black man and white man in the United States are bonded and even though sometimes the results of that bond in this culture lead to danger for both of them, they have to stick together to survive. Is that too simple? Am I misreading?

**A.** When you say "have to" you know, I wish that were true, that people had to. They don't have to. They can choose to, but they don't have to. There's a bond of love between the two brothers, Eric and Tommy, and that's what they want, they want that love, they want each other in their lives. They love each other. That could not be.

And so I wouldn't want to say that their relationship is inescapable; that would be a little too optimistic, actually.

But, I do think that a lot of it is the way we see the world. A lot of the work is the way in which we see the world. The world that we live in, what we see and what we don't see.

Tommy is this great example of somebody who really sees deeply into the world. He's an unbelievably unlucky person. He has really bad luck. But he's also incredibly fortunate because he's able to take actions into his life and to see things, and to see beauty in life, no matter how bad things go, he's able to see and understand beauty, and he's able to maintain a certain innocence; whereas his brother Eric, who is so lucky that it really, you know, it strains the imagination to believe in his luck—but then when you see it, you see, well, this is not helping him. This does not give him a better life, that fact that he's bigger, stronger, smarter, more beautiful, more talented, and luckier than everybody else doesn't give him a good life. And in a great way, which is why I called him Eric, which is that name that is embedded in our nation's name, the name we call ourselves, America, because even with all that, without that ability, without the beauty that Tommy brings to life, his [Eric's] life is nothing.

And that's certainly a direct criticism of the country. But, you know, hey, listen, you know, you can have everything, it doesn't mean anything.

Q. Again, parable. I've come to think there's no difference between the races, but in America, because of color of skin—and in other countries—people have been forced to be raised in different cultures. It's the cultural differences that make the difference.

A. Yeah, it's what people believe. If you believe it, in your mind and in your heart, there's a certain truth to it. Whether or not there's any kind of objective truth to it in the world in general, well, no. There's no kind of way you could think or accept that.

Except—if you're a poor kid raised in South Central—some of that area is nasty, it's really tough. It's a hard life to start out in, and you don't get the breaks if you're raised up in Sherman Oaks and get to go to a nicer public school, or you're raised up in Beverly Hills and have a lot of money, like Eric.

But you know there's another thing. Using that kind of equation doesn't cover all the bases, there's a few others to be covered. For instance, you're a poor white kid in Bellflower. You know, living in a tiny little house, or living in a trailer, let's say. Your father's gone, your mother's not treating you right, the school you're going to is filled with poor kids that are also not being treated well.

So you could say, well, the poor white kid and the poor black kid are the same. And the truth is there are lot of similarities and there are a lot of problems which either one of them might carry through their lives, but there are also racial overtones in this country.

Q. I agree.

A. It's important to remember, because you know—a lot of times black people will say, "Those white people, they're all rich." Well, no, they're not. A lot of them are poor. Go to Appalachia. There's some *poor* white people in Appalachia.

Q. If you're black or Asian or hispanic—my wife is Asian—and I'd never even thought about the issue of racism with Asians, but my wife says she is treated with racism every day, and now I realize, yeah, that happens all the time.

A. Well, America's a very racist country.

Q. If you're Asian, Latino, or black, you get the fact of your racial profile thrown in your face a lot of the time, I'm sure.

**A.** But, you know, Tommy in this situation, in this story, represents something other than that. Tommy doesn't pay too much attention to race. Eric is his brother, Eric's father is his father. He has friends who are black, he has friends who are white, he lives in a world where there's all kinds of people and he deals with people individually, which you have to do. And when Eric finally says to Tommy on the train, or in the plane (it was the train), "You wouldn't understand, you know, because these things happen to me, where everything happens for me—all I have to do is walk into the room and people can die." And Tommy says to him, yeah, but if it was important to you that the tide doesn't rise tomorrow, would it hold back?"

There's an understanding that Tommy has of being in the world, the greatness and the beauty and the excellence of being alive. And how small we are in relation to the rest of the world.

**Q.** Do you think Eric lacks that?

**A.** He doesn't understand it because his mind has been made small. I think he has an inkling of it, which is why he always wants to get back to Branwyn, and he always wants to get back to Tommy, because they showed him a larger world. But in his own world, he's the best—everything happens for him, nothing happens for anybody else, you know until he meets his girlfriend. There's nobody who can stand in his way. And so his world, kind of contradictorily, becomes smaller.

**Q.** Like the top of a pyramid.

**A.** But a really tiny pyramid. He doesn't see the whole world around him.

**Q.** Race is not an issue to either of the brothers, in the book.

**A.** But there's tons of racism in the book.

**Q.** Certainly. Tommy's father. There's an angry guy for you.

**A.** Yeah.

**Q.** A few years ago a reporter I knew, a black man, was telling me that he thought racism was worse in the United States today than it had ever been. He was in his middle twenties, maybe his late twenties, I think, at the time. I thought, oh, man, you don't know your history.

**A.** (Laughs)

**Q.** But, since I have you on the phone, tell me where you think we are in our history, regarding racism.

**A.** An interesting notion, really. If you look in South Carolina in 1805 and you see 60 percent of the population black and in chains, with a life expectancy of forty years old, you say, "Oh my God, I was wrong!" You know, if I thought what I was living in today was worse than then.

That's one way to look at it. I'm going to give you a few different ways to look at it.

If you look at, for instance, the 1970s and '80s, and the impetus for opening up race relations and making more things possible for more people, today, for instance, schools are more segregated than they were in the '70s and '80s—more separation inside of schools. A lot having to do with private schools, a lot having to do with income, a lot having to do with kind of unconscious, unexposed racism.

You can say, "Well, what does that mean?" Then you can say, "There are more black people making money, more black people and other races, doing better."

It's not an easy thing. We have a million black men in prison, two million black men on their way back to prison, three million young black men being groomed for prison.

This is like, an extraordinary situation—is it better or worse than it was thirty or forty years ago? I'm not quite sure about that. I know it was really bad right during Reconstruction—lots of black people were just put to prison and kept there, in order to work on the chain gangs, to kind of continue slavery.

However, the big problem with looking at it this way is to look at it in terms of America. Because we live in a global world. Our economy, our lives, our decisions, our money, not only influences our nation, it influences a whole nation . . . tens of thousands of black people die every week in Africa, from disease, from war, from famine, and from neglect.

Is that worse than it was? Absolutely. Is it because of racism? At least in part. Because I know, and everybody else knows, that if this was happening in Europe, we'd be doing something about it. When you have five thousand people a day—that's an upper number, but not an impossible one—dying of malaria, hey, there's no way we'd let that happen in France. Or Germany, or England or Italy. But it's fine to happen in Central Africa, so, the guy who made the statement, I'm not sure how informed he was, and what he was speaking about—

**Q.** He was talking about the way black people are treated in public in the United States.

**A.** Well, if you've got that all by itself, that alone, it would still be difficult to answer, depending on what black person you were and in what part of the country you are.

If you're a black kid living in South Central L.A. and you get arrested for shoplifting, and if—all other things being equal—you get a suspended sentence. But because your cousin across the street is a member of a gang and you were seen walking down the street with your cousin and the police said you were gang-related and you get fifteen years, well, for that kid, it was hard. When I was living in South Central, I didn't have it that hard.

It's still a difficult question to answer. I'm not trying to say, "Woe is me!" but I am trying to say, it's a very fluid situation, racism in America, and how it appears, and how people identify. A lot of people come up to me and say, "Well, listen, that kid had a choice," you know, "just like you did," they'll say, and what am I going to say? Well, you know what I usually say is, "Fuck you, you don't know what you're talking about, the kid didn't have any choice. He was born on that street and his cousin lived across the street and he went over to say hi. What kind of choice was that?"

**Q.** What was your life like as a kid?

**A.** My life was actually very simple as a kid. You know, listen, I lived in the '50s and '60s in South Central, among an immigrant black class from the Western South—from Louisiana, from Texas, some from Western Mississippi. And these people came to work! And there was lots of work! This was when America had hegemony over global politics. And so there was a lot of work. Everybody I knew worked, two, three jobs. Everybody owned their house, everybody had, like, you know, notions for the future.

There was still racism. Racism? That's why the Watts riots happened. There was more of a glass ceiling than there is today.

But you know, it's interesting. When you look at it you have to . . . in the end I don't think you can make simple statements, like it's better now, it's worse then. Certainly, if you look at the slave quarters in South Carolina in 1810, yeah, we're better than that. I'm not trying to say anything about that. But there are a lot of bad times and there are people who are suffering who have become invisible and who are vilified for their situation, not for their potential, characters, or personality.

And so it's a hard thing to deal with, a hard thing to answer. I think there's more opportunity today than there was, say twenty, thirty, forty years ago.

**Q.** Did you ever read *The Good War* by Studs Terkel?

**A.** I haven't read that book by Studs, although he's one of my favorite people in the world.

**Q.** He talks in that book about how, on American military bases during World War II, German prisoners of war had more rights and freedoms than did black American soldiers. You look at something like that—

**A.** The military's much better than it was then, for black people.

**Q.** I just read some things recently that you said about Condoleezza Rice and Colin Powell which were amusing.

**A.** You mean, *Life Out of Context*? Or maybe it was in *The Nation* magazine.

**Q.** I don't remember. From what I've seen about you, you're no fan of George W. Bush.

**A.** Well, listen, I don't like the Democrats, I don't like the Republicans. I don't like George Bush. But, I don't like to point to him as the one and only enemy, because if I did, then I'd bring in all these fucking Democrats who do the same goddamned thing to me, only they pretend to be my friend.

**Q.** (Laughs)

**A.** I'm no fan of Bush. Let's be clear. No. But you know, if you're a Republican or a Democrat, I'm not a fan.

**Q.** Look at what this country has done since Bush was elected, and elected in a very suspicious way, with Florida basically cheating that vote.

**A.** Not unlike John Kennedy in 1960.

**Q.** True, a long history—

**A.** A long history of stealing elections, yeah. (Laughs)

**Q.** So, here's one where the Republicans won, and in my view this has been the worst administration in American history, based on what they've done worldwide and what they've done to the economy, what they've done to the environment, the invasion of Iraq, the awarding of these huge contracts without bids to Bechtel, their friends, the whole thing just kind of pisses me off, and then he gets reelected, which means most of this country wanted this. They wanted this corruption and this terrible administration, otherwise they wouldn't have reelected him.

**A.** You can't assume everyone has your knowledge. I'm not disagreeing with you, but you can't assume that—

**Q.** My only point about this, Mr. Mosley, is that if the country is willing to accept all this other crapola, how can black Americans, African Americans, get this country to do something realistic about Africa, when they won't do anything realistic about anything else?

**A.** I would encourage you not to ask that question.

**Q.** (Laughs)

**A.** I would encourage you not to ask that question because what it is, it is an expression of hopelessness and cynicism. Once you embrace hopelessness and cynicism, you might as well kill yourself.

And really. I don't say that to people, but I feel like saying it. "OK, fine, listen, why don't you just go in a corner and shoot yourself?" And let the rest of us do the work.

That's the first thing I would say. But the second thing I would say is this. How? OK, I'll answer the question: Withdraw from the Democratic party. Form a black voting bloc based on eight or nine basic principles that a large portion of the black population would agree with—and might not only be through black people, by the way—might be, you know, universal health care, a living wage, all kinds of stuff. Do that, and begin to have an impact. Because the biggest problem that we have today is that most people have a choice between the Democrats and the Republicans.

There is virtually no difference between them, both of them are dominated by corporate America. Both of them represent an oligarchy and don't have anything to do with true democracy in America.

And so, one of the problems that people have is that, you know, they have elitist liberals on one side, and you know, criminal, so-called conservatives on the other. Well, I say, listen, both are the same thing. I'm going to vote for George Bush, or for John Kerry, who's going to do everything that Bush did, but he's not going to, you know, sound stupid doing it.

I already got a guy doing what Bush is doing, why would I get another guy who says he's going to do the same thing?

For me, it makes no sense. I was on a panel with one of the leaders of the Democratic party in New York, talking about electing Bush, and while he was saying, you know, they need the black people, I—in front of a thousand people in an audience—I said, well, excuse me, I'm happy to vote for you, but what can we do about all these black people we have in prison, and he turned to me and said, there's nothing we can do about them.

That was it for me and the Democrats. Really. The Republicans say that, but they don't want me to vote for them anyway. They don't ask me to vote, they don't invite me to the White House. Democrats do—but they don't plan to help me either.

So it's time—I think that gay Americans should withdraw, I think that real Republicans should withdraw from their party, I think that Asian Americans should do it, I certainly think that women should do it. I think that we should try to create a virtual parliament in the House of Representatives and to start to say something in that way.

But to say that we can't do anything—it's not true! And also, to accept it, then, one should stop talking about politics at that moment.

**Q.** I love what you're saying. You know that some of the questions I ask are to spur a response.

**A.** Oh, yeah! I'm not angry about it. I hope you talk about my book some, though. My publisher would be very mad about this conversation. This conversation is completely about my other book, *Life Out of Context*, a political book that I came out with in January.

**Q.** Which I haven't read. There are lots of good mystery writers out there, but as far as I know, you're the only one who's writing brilliantly about what it was like to be black in L.A. in the time of Easy Rawlins.

**A.** I'm just writing about my character.

**Q.** But it's a great thing, and you're educating people, educating people who might come, you know, somebody from Iowa maybe, is going to read your book and learn something worth learning.

**A.** That's the wonderful thing about mysteries, you can bring in people into different worlds.

**Q.** Regarding *Fortunate Son*, who's going to read this book? Are you preaching to the choir?

**A.** Anybody who likes literature, right?

**Q.** One of my editors wanted me to write about you because, she says, and I agree, that you are one of the most important writers working today. In that sense, I put you right up there with Toni Morrison and E. L. Doctorow.

**A.** Well, thank you very much, I appreciate that.

**Q.** And also in the terms of the beauty of your prose. You just knock me out, man. You're up there again, with Doctorow and Morrison, and John Steinbeck, who's one of my favorites who wrote about important things.

I have to ask you about Easy Rawlins. In *Cinnamon Kiss*, his girlfriend goes to Europe, saves his daughter's life, but he dumps her because he thinks—and by the way, he's had some fine sexual and emotional adventures while she's been gone—but he dumps her because he thinks she got too close in the heart to this other guy, in Europe.

**A.** Hmm-Hmm.

**Q.** To me, that was like clay feet in my hero, man.

**A.** (Laughs)

**Q.** That he was dumping this woman for some of the same things he'd done—the difference between them was mighty slight. What are you going to do with Easy Rawlins? And why'd you dump that woman? Freeing him up for something else?

**A.** No!

**Q.** Are you working on his emotional development?

**A.** *He's* working on his emotional development. And it's a very hard situation, you know. I don't know. When people ask me about it, I say, "Well, you know, put yourself in that situation. He didn't leave her for being with the guy, he didn't leave her for what was happening, he left her because she was uncertain which one she wanted to be with. And the woman he is with has to be with him completely." Now. . . .

**Q.** But he doesn't have to be with her completely?

**A.** He strayed from her once he understood that she was with this guy and she couldn't say she was going to be with him. It was over at that point.

**Q.** Is he insecure? Is our guy Easy who's so terrific. . . .

**A.** Is there a human being who isn't?

**Q.** He's your human being, not mine. Well, interesting. Something you're going to develop further?

**A.** Oh, absolutely.

**Q.** You have another Easy coming?

**A.** Not soon. I have another Fearless Jones coming out in September.

**Q.** Have an Easy Rawlins in mind after that point?

**A.** Yeah, won't be long, maybe a year after that.

# Hardboiled to Hardcore: Interview with Walter Mosley

## D. Scot Miller/2007

From PopMatters.com. Found at http://www.popmatters.com/pm/feature/hardboiled-to-hardcore-interview-with-walter-mosley (accessed 2010). Reprinted by permission of PopMatters.com.

Writer Walter Mosley calls his new book a sexistential noir. Seeing that *Killing Johnny Fry* mixes incest with loneliness, golden showers with ennui, and strap-ons with a longing for connection, the description fits like a latex glove.

"I think of this book as being in the tradition of Camus' *The Stranger*," Mosley tells *PopMatters*. "I'm talking about loneliness, the moment when existentialism and mid-life come into contact with each other, the aloneness of people in America, the deep melancholy of America, and the deep feelings of sexuality in all of our lives."

When the book was released on 2 January, readers who have followed his Easy Rawlins and Fearless Jones crime novels met a new kind of hero and, once again, a new side of Walter Mosley.

*Killing Johnny Fry* is the story of forty-five-year-old black translator Cordell Carmel who walks in on his longtime, non-live-in girlfriend Joelle being sodomized by Johnny Fry, a white man wearing a red condom. A disquieted and turned-on Cordell walks out without being seen and begins an erotic journey of self-discovery that takes him beyond himself and the world he thought he knew.

Like Meursault in Camus' book, Cordell has been numbed by the postmodern condition. "He's been living in this apartment with this weird paranoia," says Mosley. "He's a translator and not even an interesting translator. He's with this woman, but it's not like he loves her. There's a desperation he doesn't recognize. The pain locates him like a light in the dark and that's the thing that brings him through."

**187**

*Killing Johnny Fry* is in the noir tradition; only where there would be violence in a hardboiled novel, there is hardcore instead. After Cordell walks out on Joelle and Johnny Fry, his mind simmering over with thoughts of revenge, instead of going to the local pawnshop for a .38, he goes to the local porn shop for a DVD, *The Myth of Sisypha* (an homage to Camus). Instead of confronting his girlfriend and their mutual acquaintance, he keeps mum and uses the betrayal to stoke his passion and transform his life.

"All of these terrible things that we feel, that have happened to us, that we do and there's no way out of it," says Mosley. "Joelle has that experience. How she was so severely molested that she needed it in some way, and Cordell is even worse because he isn't connected to anything. He sees her on the weekend, they have sex once or twice, and she says, 'You can't come over on weekdays,' and he just accepts that. He accepts the life that he has and it's a completely interchangeable life. The truth is that most of us have to live that way. It's a hard thing to get out of in our own minds. We might not be able to get out of it at all in our own lives, in our own culture; but in our minds [we might be able] to see ourselves as something special, something different, someone who has an idea which is itself original."

Mosley is no stranger to re-invention. The once computer programmer turned best-selling, award-winning novelist and essayist has written over twenty-five books over the last fifteen years in genres ranging from science fiction to social commentary. "If you're a writer in America," says Mosley, "you write one book, about one guy, again and again and again, until people get tired of it and then you retire. I write a lot of different things and a lot of those things have become real. Like I've become a political activist through my writing. This book reflects a part of my life. I wanted to know more about my own sexuality, especially for men."

His subtle prolific rise has made him more than a crime novelist in the tradition of Dashiell Hammett and more an international man of letters, in the tradition of Chester Himes. And like his character, Mosley knows what it's like to be trapped in a world of expectations. As he speaks of Cordell, the lines blur between sex and writing, writer and written.

"Everything is based on capitalism and capitalism is based on specialization. And that's based on ending freedoms for individuals instead of making it possible. You have to struggle with that. As I'm writing the book, I realize that Cordell is not going back to work," a still astonished Mosley says. "I keep trying to fit it in, but he's just not going back. He never went again. This is a moment of realization. Something has to change."

During his week-long journey into the soul, Cordell rekindles passionate and public sex with pathological Joelle, sodomizes a young photographer, has strap-on and then phone-sex-three-way with his upstairs neighbor, Sasha Bennett, who is also having an incestuous affair with her brother, seduces young Monica Wells, a single mother he meets on the subway, meets Sisypha, the star of the porno he purchased and goes with her to the underground Sex Games, where he is fucked senseless and sodomized in an aria of depravity before his confrontation with Johnny Fry.

Whether or not readers will grasp the philosophical implications of Cordell rimming the photographer or lapping up a prostitute's mother's milk in a sex club is open for speculation, but it's clear that the author's motives are far more than writing a good one-handed novel.

"A lot of people who've read this book just see sex, sex, sex. I have to ask, what book are you reading? Even though all of the elements that are in my other books are there, maybe even more blatantly, the reviews say sex, sex, and sex. I'm writing this book to say this is the modern world. This lonely, melancholy, alienated, middle-aged man represents a great deal of America and a lot of where America is going."

In spite of being the drab and frumpish milquetoast initially drawn by Mosley, Cordell Carmel is a classic hero, while being one of the first of his kind.

"I write about black male heroes. Black men have been forced into silence by American culture. We don't exist. We don't fucking exist," Mosley said. "I realized as I was writing this book that there are very few first-person, black heterosexual sex books written, a man actually talking about how sex feels."

From Jim in *Huckleberry Finn* to Mister in *The Color Purple*, the heterosexual black male is more sidekick, prop, or foil than hero. In an age when black male sexuality is most often a secondary character as seen through the eyes and bodies of non-black males, Cordell Carmel is given the one element that is most denied heroes of his class, vulnerability.

"Here was Cordell with Joelle, a woman he didn't truly know, and then here comes Johnny Fry who just meets her at a party and gets all the way to the depths of her that day. Something that Cordell was incapable of reaching. And he feels bad about himself because of it."

"It was as if I was set adrift, but not yet dying, on a lone raft in the middle of tranquil and treacherous sea," Cordell says at the beginning of his journey, and it is from this feeling of inadequacy, raw and untainted with ego or bluster, which Cordell Carmel shines. As he encounters these people and situations, he approaches each with a greater lust for understanding and connection.

"When I went to Karen Rinaldi (Bloomsbury Publisher/Editor) with this book, she said, 'This character Cordell is really sweet.' And that's exactly what I wanted. I don't want readers to be all upset, or to think the sex is too much or it's all so intense. Cordell Carmel is sweet. He doesn't quite get it. He lost. He's confused. He's trying to make it and he needs people, especially women, to give him some kind of support in the world."

Cordell's heroic battle is with malaise, or Sartre's nausea, and the void created by postmodern existence. His antagonist, more than Johnny Fry or Joelle, is the machine that has allowed his disconnection from the world, and the world from him, to flourish.

"This book is not about love, it's about obsession and compulsion and the need to connect. Cordell is adrift and there's nothing he can do," Mosley says. "He can't find himself, he's trying to and this compulsion is helping him. With Sasha we have a person who can't remove herself from this relationship with her mother. She can't talk to her mother, but she fucks her brother as a way to connect. Sasha teaches Cordell about pain. I love their sex, but the primary scene is when she's squeezing his bandaged hand, she knows she's hurting him and she asks him, 'Why don't you ask me to stop?' There's a real connection there. You see the connection between them. He's unable to say stop. It's a form of understanding that he is a victim of life. He hasn't been aware of it. She intuits that. She takes his hand, at first it's a generous gesture, but then she squeezes to see how he reacts. The moment of connection becomes deeper."

As with all great heroes, his journey begins at the tip of his sword, but does not end there.

"Part of the problem with modern culture is that people don't want you to change," Mosley says, again blurring the lines. "They don't want you to wander out one day, forgetting to go to work and never going back. They need you to work everyday and in order for that to happen they need to regularize the world. So you have a television with all kinds of channels: sports, music, food, and you're supposed to look at that and go to sleep and go back to work. Your world is reinforced that way so you'll live that life. So when someone asks you about the world you'll say the world is like this and like that. Racism comes out of that. Sexism comes out of that. What I'm doing is trying to create a whole new world that exists underneath the world we're living in. In doing that, I'm saying there's all kinds of options for you. You don't have to stay where you are. You can be somewhere else. You can be someone else. That's especially true for black men, because we're actually nowhere. It's amazing what happens to us. It's amazing how we strain to maintain our dignity and end up like Colin Powell, the only one who knows what the fuck is going on, but is unable to tell it."

*Killing Johnny Fry* is Mosley's most daring book to date. At a time in his career where he could churn out box-office-ready mysteries, he writes a pornographic meditation on mid-life and rebellion. The only drawback is that the plot meanders at times, losing itself in its many turgid prods and thrusts. This can be explained by Mosley's writing technique, which he will be outlining in *This Year You Write Your Novel*, due out in April 2007, where he likens writing to steering a rudderless rowboat: "Writing a novel is not like you're riding on a highway to a destination, it's like a journey by boat. You have to continually check your course so you don't miss your destination. What matters to me as a writer writing a book is the destination."

At the end of *The Stranger*, Meursault realizes that life is worth living, and even though he's in a prison condemned to death, he will fight until the last minute to enjoy, and feel, and embrace life itself. *Killing Johnny Fry* ends with the same open-ended uncertainty of Cordell's fate, and the same ambiguous challenge to the reader.

"Our potential in this country as a people and as a nation is almost limitless and our vision is just a few degrees short of 360. We're the most locked-down and locked-up people in history with the most potential in history. That's the contradiction. The book is about that," Mosley says. "You can find out amazing things if you're willing to open your eyes and look out in the world. Cordell sees that getting sex is not all that difficult, a lot of people are willing, desiring it, but he changes his career and learns to trust. He becomes able to have new experiences and realizes that he can change his direction.

"That's the notion of mid-life. It feels like you're falling, but you're not. Find out who you are and take that path. Address your own pain. Like they ask at the doctor's office, 'What hurts?'"

# Walter Mosley

## Tavis Smiley/2007

From The Tavis Smiley Show, 24 October 2007. Broadcast and transcript found at http://
www.pbs.org/kcet/tavissmiley/archive/200710/20071024_mosley.html (accessed 2010). By
permission.

**Tavis:** Good news for Walter Mosley fans. His favorite detective, Easy Rawlins, is back. However, the bad news is it may be for the last time. The new book from the award-winning author is called *Blonde Faith* and is the tenth in the Easy Rawlins mystery series. Walter Mosley dedicates this latest novel to the late, great August Wilson.

Back in the spring, he was on this program with a work of nonfiction called *This Year You Write Your Novel*. Apparently, he took his own advice, because Easy is back as is Walter Mosley.

Walter, good to see you.

**Walter Mosley:** Great to see you, Tavis.

**Tavis:** You all right, my friend? You doing okay?

**Mosley:** I'm fine, great.

**Tavis:** I saw this wonderful piece recently in the *New York Times*, it was very clever, "In Memoriam, Easy Rawlins, Distinguished Investigator, Loving Father, Beloved Friend and Colleague." It appears that this may be it for Easy, and I don't want to give the book's ending away. You read this, you think it's the end. But it may not be the end.

**Mosley:** It may not be, but in my head, it is. In my head, I think this is it for Easy Rawlins. It's been ten books. I kind of, like, took an inventory recently in my mind and I realize that I have more books in my head than I have time in my life to write. And Easy Rawlins has been covered. He's been covered. I've done a lot of work on him. It's possible that I'll return to it, but I'm not thinking about doing it. Now I have all this other work to do.

**Tavis:** How do you make a decision, though, to either kill off or put on hold a character that represents the bread and butter? You're a fine writer, but people not often so easily walk away from the bread and butter stuff.

**Mosley:** I'm a writer. So many people in America are writers. Everybody in America is affected by capitalism. You put the left front tire on the Pinto, that's what you do for your whole life, you get your insurance, you get your retirement, all that stuff. But the truth is that I'm a writer, an artist; I want to do all kinds of different books, all kinds of different things.

I want to write about other detectives, I want to write about different eras, I want to talk about different aspects of Black male heroes. And as much as I could write more about Easy, it would be the same about Easy.

**Tavis:** You think so? There's so much. . . .

**Mosley:** A lot. Him and Mouse and Jackson Blue, and they've gotten to such a perfect place in their lives. Easy's at the peak of his powers, Mouse and Jackson are really—they're something else. Jesus is married, he has a child. Life is. . . .

**Tavis:** Life is good.

**Mosley:** It's understandable.

**Tavis:** Tell me more about the storyline for those who obviously are just rushing out now to pick up a copy of *Blonde Faith*. It takes place a couple years after the Watts riots here in L.A., of course.

**Mosley:** Yeah, it's a couple of years after the Watts riots; a guy that Easy has met only recently, Christmas Black, is in trouble. Mouse is being sought out by the police, the police were planning to kill him for a murder that he may or may not have committed. But really what's really going on with Easy is that in the last book he broke up with Bonnie and he realizes he was wrong. He's trying to figure out how to get back together with her, but he can't find it in his mind.

A couple of chapters in, she calls him and says, "I'm engaged. I'm getting married to this African prince." And so Easy's trying to deal with his inner demons while after these two guys, the two deadliest men in Los Angeles, in Southern California. And so that's the book, and in it you begin to understand how complex racism became after the riots.

After a real movement toward integration, racism became so complex and understanding it became so complex that as Easy moves through his day you begin to see, boy, this is more difficult than anybody can imagine. Easy says to a guy, "Listen, only three out of every ten people I meet are racist, but that's an awful lot, you run into a hundred people a day."

**Tavis:** Yeah. (Laughs) How do you decide, or how do you know, when you have gone close enough to the line without stepping over it with regard, Walter, to entertaining people and not preaching to people? Because you always attach to the storyline, you always wrestle with larger themes like racism; in this book, the Vietnam War. You never shy away from that, but how do you know when you are at the point of crossing that line between entertaining people and Walter Mosley's politics seeping in?

**Mosley:** Well, my politics don't seep in. Actually, honestly, I'm just telling the truth about Easy's life. Easy, in one part of this book, is going to go to a very nice restaurant. He's taking out this young woman he's met; he's trying to forget about Bonnie, he's trying to take her to this restaurant. Well, the guard when he goes into the restaurant tries to stop him.

The hostess at the front desk tries to stop him. The policemen on the street wonder what he's doing in the neighborhood. I'm not making this up. This is real. This is a real thing for Easy. And so if I went beyond it and started to philosophize about it or have him actually try to make something different, then I'd be going too far. It's like if I were to write about a woman in 1901 in America, and I forgot to say, "Well, she doesn't have rights over her body, rights over her children, rights over her income, and she can't vote." If I left all those things out of her life, it would be a fantasy I'm writing. You have to say these things. But then you get right back to your story. Well, what's the story about? Why is he going to the restaurant? What's going to happen with the woman? What's going on? The story continues to go.

**Tavis:** What's your sense, as the writer, as the creator of Easy, for what the through-line has been where his character is concerned, that attaches us to him? You keep referring to him as, and indeed he is, a flawed character; he's not human and divine like the rest of us, only human; has his good points and his bad points. What is it about this particular character, Easy Rawlins, that's kept us attached to him, that causes us to be endeared to him over ten books?

**Mosley:** Well, I think that in one way, it's an identification. You have, like, for instance, a lot of Black men and some Black women who read Easy and say, "This is a real character in my life that I've known." And other people say, "This is a real character in my life that I've known." And on the other hand, you get things like I remember I got a review on Amazon for *Cinnamon Kiss* when Easy at the end of that book broke up with Bonnie because she saved his daughter's life, but in doing so she rekindled this relationship with Joyuge Cham and so he breaks up with her. And a woman wrote. It was like a letter to me rather than a review on Amazon. She said, "That's it, I will never buy another one of your books because you had him do something which I just cannot accept."

And I thought, wow, that's great. (Laughter) She loves Easy, and she loves him so much that she's never going to read him again. I thought, God, that's a wonderful thing. But that identity, that his choice means something to her, and I think the real truth about that, it's about the writing itself. It's not about the characters, or race or masculinity or anything. It's about writing a character that you identify closely enough with that you get angry at.

**Tavis:** Over ten books, over ten appearances by Easy Rawlins. How much have you heard over the years from Easy fans, from fans of yours, about what they like, didn't like, or they thought the storyline ought to go? How much interaction?

**Mosley:** People don't usually tell me what they think I should be writing, which is good. Every once in a while, I'll write some science fiction stuff and they say, "You should never write that again," and that's okay. (Laugh) I say, "That's all right, that's all right; you think like that, that's okay." But no, no, no, people usually just want to talk about decisions Easy makes or Mouse makes or Jackson Blue makes, somebody like that, and where they're going with those ideas and thoughts.

I think that Easy has entered the consciousness—there are not very many people ever in American history who write about Black male heroes that you can put a name on. Not many at all. And it's because of the nature of the country. Black men have been vilified partially because people are afraid of them, and the other part because people feel so guilty about what's been done to Black masculinity.

And so it's hard, even among Black people, to create heroes that exist in other cultures, races, etc. And so in order to have a hero like Easy Rawlins, or Fearless Jones or Socrates Fortlow, people are very happy just to have that hero. So they don't want to really change it and say, "Man, good, you got it there? That's good."

**Tavis:** Leave it the way it is, yeah.

**Mosley:** Just leave it there, don't run away with it.

**Tavis:** I think I know what you meant by this, but just to make sure that I'm clear, to say nothing of the audience being clear, when you say Black male heroes that you can put a name on, what did you mean by the latter part?

**Mosley:** Well, Easy Rawlins. I like that Mouse, and people start quoting things Mouse says, and they start quoting things that Easy says, and the notion that there's a name. There's a name on a character; it's like Zorro or some other character who people say, "That's my hero. Batman, that's my hero."

**Tavis:** I raise that only because I think a lot of people perhaps don't think that Black heroes even exist, much less can have a name put on them.

**Mosley:** Yeah, no, I understand that, and of course they do exist. And certainly in my life, certainly in yours, there are all these Black men who are wonderful. It's not that there aren't other people who are wonderful. It's just that the Black men who are wonderful kind of fade into some kind of background and it's like they become caricatures that we could put—well, either it's the pimp or the preacher or the sidekick, not a man out there in the world, making a difference in the world.

**Tavis:** I can think of, and I don't want to start listing names, because we'd be here for the rest of the week doing this, but I could list a bunch of names of people, heroes, shall we say, who've had a movie, a sequel, another sequel, another sequel—we're up to, like, four or five of these things now, they all stink except for the first one, that's my own personal opinion. We got one good Easy pic[ture], *Devil in a Blue Dress*; ten books, though—why not more motion pictures?

**Mosley:** I don't know. I made this movie with Tri-Star and that was good. The movie kind of broke even. Unluckily, it came out the same weekend that O. J. Simpson was found not guilty, so there were no Black male heroes in America (laughter) that weekend.

**Tavis:** That weekend, yeah.

**Mosley:** And we were still the number two movie.

**Tavis:** Yeah, it was a great movie, though.

**Mosley:** And the movie broke even. And then afterwards with DVDs and VHS, they've made many, many, many millions. . . .

**Tavis:** So why not another one, then?

**Mosley:** It's beyond me. Like they never wanted to make another movie. I've written a script for HBO that Mos Def and Jeffrey Wright have said they want to star in, and I'm working with them. Hopefully, we're going to do something.

**Tavis:** It's an Easy treatment, or something different?

**Mosley:** Oh, it's Easy. It's *Little Scarlet*, which is one of the best. I actually think this book, *Blonde Faith*, is the best of all the Easys, but *Little Scarlet* was a very good book and about the Watts riots, etc. They want to do it; they want to do it for a price. We're trying to work that out, so we'll see what happens.

**Tavis:** What makes Walter Mosley the writer say that he thinks this one, *Blonde Faith*, is the best of the Easys?

**Mosley:** I think that it gets the deepest into Easy's heart. Easy is a good person, but he has a very dark heart. And inside of it, lots of things have gone wrong. All the things that have gone wrong for so many people, including Black people around the world, reside in Easy. Easy was at Dachau, Easy was in World War II, Easy lived in the Deep South when Jim Crow was the master.

Easy has changed his life, even though everything was set against him. And this book, I think, underscores all of that, and in a way that's clear and fluid, and his ideas about his friends have changed. Jackson Blue, friends.

**Tavis:** This is a dangerous question to close on with a guy like you, but since you mentioned earlier you want to do other stuff, should this be the last Easy Rawlins book, what else is in your head that you want to tackle?

**Mosley:** Well I can tell you that at least three books [are] coming out. In December, I have a book coming out called *Diablerie*, which is a very noir novel, kind of a Black anti-hero. Then I have the *Tempest Tales*, stories that I had written for Savoy and some more coming out from Black Classic Press in April, and then Basic Books is coming out with the new Socrates Fortlow collection called *The Right Mistake*. So right there I got. . . .

**Tavis:** At least the next three.

**Mosley:** Yeah, yeah.

**Tavis:** All right. And finally, somebody sent me an email the other day, and I've known you for years and I said I think I know this story, but I've never asked Walter this question on television. So Easy has his own idiosyncrasies. You love wearing that fedora, and people know it's part of your trademark. When and where did the fedora begin?

**Mosley:** It was about twenty years ago. I was in New York and I'd always worn a beret my whole life and then all of a sudden a beret just wasn't working anymore.

**Tavis:** So you went from Che Guevara to this?

**Mosley:** Yeah, right, well, (laughs) Che Guevara, that's kind of like going backwards. From Che Guevara to a gangster. And then I started writing and publishing, and the hat kind of followed me along with it.

**Tavis:** It works.

**Mosley:** But what did they email you? What did they say?

**Tavis:** No, they just wanted to know.

**Mosley:** Oh, they just wanted to know why. . . .

**Tavis:** Could you please ask Walter Mosley why the fedora?

**Mosley:** Hey.

# Interview: Walter Mosley

## Marcus Gilmer/2009

From The Chicagoist.com. April 2009. Found at http://chicagoist.com/2009/04/06/inter view_walter_mosley.php (accessed 2010). Reprinted by permission of the interviewer.

For fans of mystery novels, Walter Mosley needs no introduction. Mosley is best known for his Easy Rawlins mysteries such as *Devil in a Blue Dress* and *Six Easy Pieces*, but his literary prowess spans several genres. In under twenty years, Mosley has written thirty-three books in genres such as mystery, science fiction, young adult, several nonfiction books, and even erotica. The winner of awards such as a PEN America's Lifetime Achievement Award, an O. Henry Award, and even a Grammy (for his liner notes on a Richard Pryor boxset), Mosley has also been recognized for the way he addresses race in his writing, winning the Anisfield-Wolf Book Award.

But for all the genres he's covered, mystery has been where Mosley has made his name and now he brings us a new series based on a new character, Leonid McGill. In the new book, *The Long Fall*, Leonid McGill is a man trying to get back on the right path before it's too late. A private eye who plies his trade amongst a group of friends and an even bigger group of enemies, McGill—a hard-drinking ex-boxer—is trying to set things right for himself and his family, including his favorite son, Twill. As he tries to move from "crooked to slightly bent," McGill learns the hard way that transformation isn't always easy. When he turns information about a group of young men over to a client and those men start turning up dead, McGill searches for answers from the underworld to the mansions of New York City, all the while crossing paths with a wide range of characters who remind McGill of the past he's trying to run from.

It's another masterstroke of mystery from a writer who knows how to create suspense at its best. We caught up with Mosley ahead of his appearance this week in Chicago and talked about Obama, the importance of race, the importance of father-son relationships in the book, and how Mosley keeps up his prolific pace.

**Chicagoist:** Several times in the book, the main character references the Obama candidacy and talks about how certain other characters aren't judging him based on race, that the world has changed some in that regard. Do you share that perspective?

**Walter Mosley:** [Laughs] What perspective? In the opening scene of the book, the secretary is more worried about what kind of clothes you wear, what age you are, than she is worried about race. But when [McGill] goes to the bar in Albany, those people are very worried about race. When McGill goes to the office of The Most Important Man in New York, The Most Important Man in New York realizes only two African-Americans have ever been in his office.

When you ask, "Do I agree?" then yeah. The secretary doesn't care. The people in Albany do care and The Most Important Man in New York doesn't care, but many haven't gotten to the place where they have any impact on his life. What I'm trying to say in the book is that there are all kinds of different ways people respond to things.

**C:** It feels like in that first instance—when Leonid suggests the secretary isn't judging him based on race—there's a bit of cynicism in his voice.

**WM:** When you say cynicism, what do you mean?

**C:** That he says it with a grain of salt.

**WM:** No, no, it's absolutely true. This woman doesn't dislike him because he's black. She doesn't care. She's protecting Roger Brown, who is a black man. She calls Brown "mister" in an office of first names. What's important is that he [Leonid] has to be able to understand that at every moment. There was a time in America where everybody was racist to one degree or another, whether they knew it or not, and it might still be true today. But it's in such different ways and forms that Leonid has to really decipher what people were saying to him.

**C:** The story takes place while Obama is still a candidate.

**WM:** That's correct. I had no idea he was going to win.

**C:** Did his victory have any effect on you in terms of writing characters like Leonid?

**WM:** No.

**C:** For several of the characters in the book, it seems origin is just as important in identifying them as their race, the way Leonid describes them. Specifically, the women in his life: his wife Katrina and Aura, another woman with whom he's had a relationship. They're introduced by way of their heritage: Scandinavian, etc. Is this a reflection of that issue, that people don't view race in quite the same way they used to?

**WM:** Well, it's so complex. There's a moment in the book when there are three people. There's a blousy kind of red-faced white guy who's also big and hulking, there's a little guy who looks like he's carved from porcelain, and there's another guy who's white but his skin is dark. Leonid remarks that in old-time Europe, those would have been three different races. That's the way they would have looked at it.

In America, a lot of people ask me, "Do you feel like you have more in common with Obama because you're multiracial and he is, too?" [Ed's Note: Mosley's father is African-American and his mother is Jewish.] My response is that almost every black person in America is multiracial. We're all descended from the Scotch and the Irish and the English and the French and the Native Americans and the Ethiopians; there's all this mixed blood in America. There are very few people who are purely white in America. At one point, that didn't matter: you were colored or you weren't and that was a definition. That's no longer true and that's what Leonid is dealing with. Again, he's dealing with the complexity of race because it is an extraordinarily complex issue in America today. Not that it doesn't exist, not that it's less important, it's just very, very different.

**C:** Another aspect of the novel that was very potent was the underlying thread of the father-son relationship. There are at least three different father-son relationships that play a role in the novel. How early on did this theme develop? Was it there since the beginning?

**WM:** Oh, yeah, absolutely. I had written a short story called "Karma" in which Leonid and Twill [one of Leonid's sons] play important parts; it's where I came up with these characters. The relationship with Twill is extraordinarily interesting because in previous books I had written about black men who adopt children, bring them in, and it's kind of unconventional. In this book, Leonid's helping Twill—and his other kids, too—but he's helping Twill negotiate a difficult life but at the same time, Twill is helping him. Twill is as much there for him and it's kind of the way I see the modern world. That young people are extraordinarily important to the future of America and in many ways they know it and they're doing the work.

**C:** That's interesting because early in the book we learn that Twill is not Leonid's biological son.

**WM:** No, but that really doesn't matter.

**C:** But Leonid does seem to have a more open relationship with the two children who are not biologically his.

**WM:** Yeah, the one that's like him is too much like him. [Laughs] I mean he loves that son, he loves Dimitri [Leonid's biological son], but the problem is they're so much alike that they almost repel each other.

**C:** What was it like creating this new character, Leonid McGill? What was the best part of that for you?

**WM:** Some questions are hard to answer and that one's impossible to answer but I can answer another one. I really enjoy writing about Leonid McGill. I find him an extraordinary character, mainly because he's such a direct reflection of America today: a country that's been going in the wrong direction for so many years who's decided that they're going to try to do right by themselves and the rest of the world. And in Leonid's case, by himself and everyone else.

**C:** And like this country, finding it's more difficult than just one action.

**WM:** Yeah, well you know, it's like Obama deciding to close Guantanamo. It's not easy. It's like America saying, "Oh yeah, maybe we shouldn't have allowed the owners of the banks, insurance companies, investment companies, and the oil companies to have free reign over whatever they wanted to. Maybe they don't have our best interests at heart." It's a very interesting, very problematic thing. Internally, you know what you want to become but you are something else. That's Leonid McGill. He knows what he wants.

There's a scene in *Moby Dick* when Fleece is throwing stuff over the side and the sharks are coming after it and they're eating each other and he gives a sermon and says if you sharks would learn to control your appetite, you sharks would be angels. It's a wonderful scene and, in a way, Leonid McGill is one of those sharks and all of the sharks around him are eating each other.

**C:** Well, it's interesting you bring up the sharks that surround him. The book is filled with dozens of characters, some directly related to the plot and others that seem to pass through just to fill in the reader on the life Leonid has lived and his background, characters I assume we'll see in future novels.

**WM:** You absolutely will.

**C:** Like the gangster "Tony the Suit"?

**WM:** I'm not so sure about Tony. I think Tony sees his story end in this book. But the godfather of those gangsters who's trying to lead Leonid on what to do even though Leonid couldn't quite figure out what he meant, he'll be back. The man who gets him information that's described as looking like a moray eel, he'll be back. A lot of those characters will be back. Even the girl, Twill's friend, will be back.

**C:** Especially in a first book in a series like this one, do you worry at all about the reader's ability to keep up with all the characters or do you just trust they'll be able to?

**WM:** That's the way I write. You know, in a day in your life, you'll run into thirty to forty people. I read novels, and a character will only see two people all day long. Who lives that life? One's life is filled with people; we're social beings living in cities. There's the guy sitting in the lobby downstairs reading his newspaper, there's the guy you buy your food from, there's your boss, there's the person working for you, there's your girlfriend or your wife and your kids and your kids' friends—there are all these people. I don't understand how I can write a story without having the normal relations of life in it. So, yes, I hope the people can keep up with it, but this is my thirty-third book and they've kept up so far.

C: That's a fair point. And as someone who's written so many books across different genres, how does writing mystery differ from writing other genres?

WM: Well, it's hard to compare a literary novel to a mystery novel; they're both literary. But with a mystery novel, you have to address the plot every three or four pages. Every three or four pages we have to get back to: what's this story about? That's what a mystery is; you're solving the mystery therefore the plot is kind of ornate and very structured. In a literary novel, it's boy meets girl, boy loses girl, boy gets girl back again. That's enough plot for a literary novel. You can use a lot more space to get to know the characters and how these people feel: how they relate, what they do. They're different kinds of books and they both pose their own problems, but they're still books, they're still the same thing, really.

C: Who or what inspired you to begin writing mysteries?

WM: I had written a book called *Gone Fishin'* with Easy Rawlins that wasn't a mystery but nobody wanted to publish it. And then I started writing another book about Easy Rawlins, and I didn't know it was a mystery until I reached a certain point and realized it was a mystery. It was almost like a non-event.

C: As you mentioned, you've written thirty-three books in just under twenty years. What inspires you to keep such a pace?

WM: You know, it seems like a hectic, daunting pace, but the truth is I just write every day. Just every day. And I write for about three hours so it's not like I'm killing myself. And if you write every day, you write a whole lot and that's all there is to it. I know a lot of writers who take time off or do other things and for good reasons; that's not a criticism. But for myself, the most enjoyable [time] in my life is writing so I do it every day.

# PIP—*The Fall of Heaven*— Walter Mosley

## Rick Pender/2010

From the 24 January 2010 Walter Mosley interview provided courtesy of "Around Cincinnati," 91.7 WVXU, Cincinnati, OH. Found at http://www.wvxu.org/schedule/aroundcincinnati_archiveview.asp?ID=1/24/2010 (accessed 2010). By permission.

**WVXU:** It seems likely that you've read something by my guest this evening on "Around Cincinnati." Novelist Walter Mosley is one of America's most versatile and prolific writers. His output over the past two decades includes more than twenty-five works of fiction, and he can count among his fans movie stars and at least one past president of the United States. His best-known title, *Devil in a Blue Dress*, was made into a big hit movie starring Denzel Washington as his recurring solver of murders in East Los Angeles. The character's name is Easy Rawlins. But, to kick off 2010, Walter Mosley is traveling down a different path. He's written a play. His first. And it's receiving its world premiere at the Cincinnati Playhouse in the Park. *The Fall of Heaven* is on stage for the next several weeks. And, Walter Mosley, I'd like to welcome you to Cincinnati.

**Walter Mosley:** Well, thanks a lot. It's great to be here.

**WVXU:** Some of our listeners, I'm sure, are familiar with your work, and maybe a few read *The Tempest Tales* which is the book on which this play is based. It's about a colorful character named Tempest Landry. I wonder if you could tell us a little bit about him and his story.

**Mosley:** Well, you know, Tempest is a resident of Harlem. He's not a good guy. He's not a bad guy. He has a wife that he loves deeply and a girlfriend that loves him very much. He has some children here and there on the side. He doesn't steal, necessarily, but if he sees a dollar tip sitting on the table and nobody's looking, he might pick it up. If there's a key in a door, he might turn the lock. But, all in all, he's been a good man, and he's lived a pretty decent life trying to do the right things. One day, he's shot down by the police. It's a case of mistaken identity. And he's killed. He goes to heaven. Waiting in line, St. Peter comes up to him and says, "You've committed enough sins, we're gonna send you to hell." And Tempest, for the first time ever in the history of this process says, "I'm not goin'. Because, you haven't proven to me that I'm bad enough to deserve hell." It turns out, to everyone's surprise, that human free will means that you can actually say no to damnation. They don't know what to do. They're very upset. This could really upset the apple cart. So, what they do is they put him in a new body and send him back to earth with an angel. And the angel's job is to convince him of his sins. Once he accepts them, he goes immediately into hell. But this leads into a long and convoluted conversation in which both the angel and Tempest learn many things.

**WVXU:** That, then, is the story of the play.

**Mosley:** Hey!

**WVXU:** Where did the story come from?

**Mosley:** Who knows. Originally, you know, one of my favorite writers is Langston Hughes. So, Langston Hughes wrote a series of vignettes, the Simple stories, which he published in the *Chicago Defender*. These are very, very short: One thousand to fifteen hundred words, which *The Tempest Tales* are also. [The Simple stories are] about a reporter who goes to Harlem and interviews an everyman. And he goes again and again and has these talks. They aren't really stories. They're more vignettes. And they aren't connected in the way that my stories are. But that's where the original idea came from—to have the interlocutor and the everyman.

**WVXU:** What about Tempest's character? Is he just somebody you dreamed up? Or, where did that particular thought come from?

**Mosley:** Well, I think Tempest resides in the hearts of many young working-class men, regardless of race. Here you are, you're trying to have some confidence in yourself and belief in yourself. You have this young body which you kind of exalt in, in a certain kind of way. You try to do the right thing. But, often, you get pulled off to the side by certain attractions or desires.

**WVXU:** You published *Tempest Tales* about two years ago; and now, it's evolved or the content of it has evolved into a play. I'm wondering what moved you to write a play? Because this is the first time that you've done that, I believe.

**Mosley:** Yeah. This is the first time that I've gotten so far as to want to produce ever. I've written a couple of things that I've called plays, but they didn't really work. There's a mechanical answer and there's a spiritual answer, a heart answer. I love theater. Just love it. I was an actor when I was very young, and I was very bad, but I still loved it. I think, a bad actor loving acting is the best possible thing. I love the theater. I love the feeling of the theater. I love the darkness. I love the light. I love the audience. I love the suspension of disbelief. It's great. Another thing is that I write everyday for three hours. If you write everyday for three hours, you write a lot. One day, I went to my publisher, and the publisher said, "Walter, hold up." I said, "What?" "For the last three years, you've delivered three books every year. This is too much. You are beginning to compete with yourself. We want you to bring up less books." I go, "I can't stop writing everyday." And he said, "That's not our problem." And so, I said, "Well, maybe I could write other things. Let me see. You know, workin' on writing some screenplays." I said, "Well, I'll write a play." My producing partner, Diane Houslin, said, "Walter, you should write plays. You'd be really good at plays 'cause [of] your dialogue and stuff like that." Plus, she didn't know how much I loved theater. I went, "Yeah. You know, she's right." And so, I started writing plays. So, now I can maybe only write one and a half novels a year. And people won't get so mad at me at my publishing house.

**WVXU:** So, there are a lot of theaters in the United States. You're based in New York, I think, but here you are in Cincinnati, doing a production of your play. What brought you here?

**Mosley:** Well, you have a wonderful playhouse here. That's to begin with. One of the premiere regional theaters. You have Ed Stern, who is really a very wonderful, and interesting, and intuitive fellow. Those two reasons alone are enough for me to want to come to Cincinnati. Also, I like Cincinnati. And really, I hate saying that because people ask me why and I never really know. I just like being here. I like the town. Whenever I come to do talks—I did a big talk at the library here once, and book tours—I find it an interesting place. And Ohio's such an interesting state because the different cities, Cleveland, Columbus, Cincinnati. The only thing they have in common is they start with "C."

**WVXU:** The letter C. (Laughs) That's right.

**Mosley:** You know? And I find it very interesting. I found it very literary in many ways. Another reason to want to come to the Cincinnati Playhouse is that it's a very good, very strong playhouse. For whatever reason, over time, its main constituency has been a white constituency. I think that theater should be for everyone. So for me to bring a play in, I think that I can bring a new audience in and possibly have some impact there, which I think would be good for everybody concerned.

**WVXU:** The playhouse has helped with that task by hiring a very esteemed director, Marion McClinton, who has a history with August Wilson's plays and that sort of thing. That has to have been a good experience for you too, I would think.

**Mosley:** Oh! It's wild. I love working with Marion. He's a wonderful director.

A wild man there. The actors love him. And for the last few days, I've been sitting around watching him change scenes. You'll see a scene, and say, "Hey! That's pretty good." And Marion comes up and says, "Well, do this and do that and maybe we'll do this, and you stand here," and all of a sudden, "Hey! It's much, much better. This is wild." Things that I don't understand. I don't understand directing, so it's wonderful to see.

**WVXU:** Well, you raise an interesting point, as a novelist, you're God, you do whatever you want and those characters do what you want. In the theater, you are working in a much more collaborative environment. You've got actors who are interpreting lines, dialogue that you've written. You've got a director who is navigating them around the stage. How has it been, moving into this kind of experience?

**Mosley:** The difference between writing novels, which is a very solitary thing and plays, which is collaborative, I think you're there. Because, you know, if you write a screenplay, really, you're two levels below the food vendor. They get your screenplay and immediately they're hiring new writers to rewrite your screenplay. You don't own it anymore. It doesn't have anything to do with *you* anymore. It's the star's, it's the director's. In the theater it's different. The playwright, also, is God in the theater. Everybody loves them. They're important. You can't change their words unless they say yes. It's really very interesting. But the collaboration for me, it's easy for me to take a backseat and say, "The actors know their job—let them do their job. The director knows his job—let him do his job. The stage designers, the light designers, the clothes designers—all of those people—I'm not being at all critical in that way. I'm letting them do what they do, and while they're doing it, they're teaching me more and more about the theater.

**WVXU:** I want to ask you a question about your career as a writer. I know you did not start out in life to be a writer. In fact, I believe you were working in the world of computers and programming.

**Mosley:** Yeah. I was a computer programmer for sixteen years.

**WVXU:** Yeah. What moved you to change directions? Were you writing during that time?

**Mosley:** No. I was not writing.

**WVXU:** No?

**Mosley:** I was a consultant programmer. I was working at Mobile Oil on 42nd Street on the weekend. Because, when you're a consultant, your job has to get done or you're in trouble. So, I was in there and I was working, and I got tired of working and instead of writing code on the computer, I wrote a sentence: "On hot sticky days, in Southern Louisiana, the fire ants swarm."

And I said, "Ah! That sounds pretty good. That could be the first line of a novel. Maybe I could be a novelist." I said, (laughs) innocently. And I started writing then. And, I kept writing.

**WVXU:** And here you are.

**Mosley:** And here I am.

**WVXU:** Twenty-plus years later and doing this. Well, if those of you out there listening would like to see the latest writing adventure of Walter Mosley, you'll be able to do that in the next month or so at the Cincinnati Playhouse. His first play, *The Fall of Heaven*, is on stage at the Cincinnati Playhouse in the Park through February 20. If you go to wvxu.org, you'll find a link to learn more about the play and the Cincinnati Playhouse. Thanks for taking the time to come in and talk about your new show.

**Mosley:** Thanks a lot. It's been great.

**WVXU:** For "Around Cincinnati," I'm Rick Pender.

# Index